The U.A.R. in Africa

The U.A.R. in Africa

EGYPT'S POLICY UNDER NASSER

Tareq Y. Ismael

Northwestern University Press

Evanston · 1971

Tareq Y. Ismael is Associate Professor of
Political Science at the University of Calgary.
He is the author of *Governments and
Politics of the Contemporary Middle East.*

FOR MY MOTHER AND FATHER

Contents

Contents

Maps

Preface

It has often been observed that Africa's emergence into world politics dramatically influenced the international system. Yet more profound, though little noticed, have been the changes in the regional subsystem. The competition between the emerging African states to fill the power vacuum created by the departure of the colonial powers and to influence regional politics became a feature of the new subsystem. Foremost among those nations attempting to play an influential role in Africa was Egypt, the first African nation to free itself from foreign domination. Indeed, as Colonel Nasser clearly perceived, Egypt was inextricably linked to the rest of Africa and had an important role to play in the new order that was emerging on that great continent.

> We cannot under any circumstances, even if we wanted to, stand aloof from the terrible and terrifying battle now raging in the heart of that continent between five million whites and two hundred million Africans. We cannot stand aloof for one important and obvious reason—we ourselves are in Africa.

> Surely the people of Africa will continue to look to us—we who are the guardians of the continent's northeastern gate and constitute the link between Africa and the outside world.[1]

Although Nasser clearly foresaw that the nationalist sentiment raging throughout Africa would be irresistible and that Egypt would have an important role in directing that sentiment, not even he was able to foretell the swiftness with which the mass of the continent changed from colonies into independent states or the potency of the Pan-African movement that developed in the wake of that swift change. Thus, Egypt's African policy has evolved out of a continuous reassessment of Egypt's interests on the continent and a continuous readaptation to the very fluid African scene. An examination of this evolution of Egypt's African policy is the subject matter of this study.

Part I of this study is an examination of the evolution of Egypt's African policy and of the correlation between Egypt's African policy and its East-West relations. Part II is an examination of the substance of the U.A.R.'s present African policy and includes a study of that policy's principles, objectives, and instruments. Part III tests the theories established in Parts I and II by applying them to case studies of the Sudan and the Congo. These particular case studies were chosen because each represents a different facet of the U.A.R.'s policy: the Sudan represents the U.A.R.'s traditional and vital interests in Africa; the Congo represents the overextension of the U.A.R.'s African commitment.

How significant is the U.A.R.'s policy in Africa? Representing the most stable government in Africa after Ethiopia (not including the Union of South Africa) and containing the largest population after Nigeria, the U.A.R. plays an important role on the continent. The U.A.R. has participated in, and has to some extent influenced, the phenomena occurring on the Africa scene, especially between 1955 and 1961. During this period Egypt became the spokesman for African liberation and made the African voice clearly resound in international forums.

1. Gamal Abdel Nasser, *The Philosophy of the Revolution* (Cairo: National Publication House [1954]), p. 69.

I have attempted to maintain as high a degree of objectivity as possible by reducing to a minimum personal observation. Egyptian newspapers and publications by the U.A.R. Information Department have provided the main sources of information; these publications are generally considered to reflect U.A.R. government attitudes and policies. *Al-Ahram,* the oldest Egyptian newspaper; *Rose El-Youssief,* a well-known and highly regarded journal; the *Egyptian Political Science Review,* the only professional journal; *Nahdhat Ifriqiya,* the only journal devoted exclusively to Africa; and *Al-Jumhuriya,* the revolution's only daily newspaper, were emphasized because of the personal involvement in the government and friendship with Nasser of their respective editors—Muhammad Hassanein Heikal, Ihsan Abdul Quddus, Abdul Qadir Hatim, Muhammad Ishaq, and Anwar al-Sadat. The *Arab Observer* is a weekly government publication in English; it is devoted to news and political commentary. However, in utilizing Egyptian newspapers, I am aware of the tendency toward overdramatization. (Nasser himself complained about this to the Preparatory Committee of the National Congress.)[2] Because of this, it was often helpful to gain perspective by referring to the *New York Times,* the *Christian Science Monitor* and the *Times* (London).

Most of the Arabic material utilized in this study was obtained directly from the Middle East. The Library of Congress, however, supplied many of the back issues of *Al-Ahram* and *Rose El-Youssief.* Translations from Arabic are my own.

In the preparation of this work, I owe thanks to Miss Francis Huston, Associate Professor of English at Eastern Washington State College, who meticulously edited the manuscript, and, of course, my wife, who contributed to this manuscript in many subtle ways, not the least of which was her constant encouragement. I am indebted to Professor Benjamin Nimer of The George Washington University who guided this research in its initial stages as a doctoral dissertation. I also wish to express my thanks to President Emerson

2. U.A.R. Documentation Research Center, *Dairat al-ma'arif al-siyasiya al-'arabiya: nashrat al-wathaiq* [The Arab political encyclopedia: bulletin of documents], X (November, 1961), Section of the Preparatory Committee for the Popular Forces of the National Congress, 6–7.

Shuck of Eastern Washington State College who afforded institutional funds to help defray research and secretarial expenses. A portion of Chapter Five appeared, under the title "Religion and the U.A.R. African Policy," in the *Journal of Modern African Studies,* VI (May, 1968). It is reproduced here with the permission of the editor of the journal and its publisher, Cambridge University Press. Also, a summary of Chapter Seven appeared, under the title "The U.A.R. and the Sudan," in the *Middle East Journal,* XXIII (Winter, 1969), and is reproduced here with the permission of the *Middle East Journal.*

Tareq Y. Ismael

Part I

The Evolution of the Policy

Chapter One

Traditional Interests
in Africa

Egyptian political, cultural, and religious interaction with Central Africa has been the product both of history and geography. Expansion southward along the course of the Nile from the population centers of the Lower Nile Valley has been a natural and continuing process. Commercial activities dating from the predynastic period not only introduced the riches of Central Africa into Egypt but resulted also in Egyptian social, cultural, and eventually political, influence on the peoples of Nubia.[1]

Nubia, always an important focus of Egyptian attention, is geographically bound to Egypt by the Nile River and has been, historically, regarded as an extension of Egypt. It is the gateway into Central Africa, and by controlling Nubia, Egypt could control the caravan trade routes along which passed Abyssinian gold, and ostrich feathers, oils, ebony, ivory, resins, animal skins, captive wild

1. G. A. Reisner reports that "pre-dynastic graves contain now and again a Negro, while ivory and resins are abundant, and figures of the elephant, the giraffe, and the ostrich appear in the drawings." He concludes, therefore, that "the trade routes to the south had been open even in those days" ("Outline of the Ancient History of the Sudan: Part I, Early Trading Caravans [4000 to 2000 B.C.], *Sudan Notes and Records,* I [January, 1918], 6).

animals, and black slaves. Commerce led to war, and Egypt conquered Nubia between 3100 and 3000 B.C.

During the Sixth Dynasty (2625–2475 B.C.) Egypt sent many expeditions deep into Nubia and the little-known areas beyond. The explorer Harkhuf made four expeditions into Nubia and under Pepi II (2566–2476 B.C.) returned from one of them with a richly laden caravan and a pygmy from one of the tribes of inner Africa.[2]

The kingdom of Punt (west of Cape Guardafui in present-day Somali Republic) was raided many times during the reign of Mentuhotep III (2019–2007 B.C.) but had established close commercial relations with Egypt by the time of the Eighteenth Dynasty (1570–1365 B.C.). Queen Hatshepsut (1493–1480 B.C.) sent a mission to Punt,[3] and her son and coregent Thutmosis III (1479–1447 B.C.) required Punt to pay tribute to Egypt. However, Egypt's interest in Punt was not entirely commercial. The Egyptians believed that they had very old bonds with its people and that they were descendants of a common ancestor. In Egyptian drawings the men of Punt were pictured with the inverted beard traditionally worn by Egyptian gods, and in Egyptian literature Punt was described as the holy land, or land of god, because it was the source of incense used in religious ceremonies.

The Egyptianization of Nubia was progressing steadily at the time of the establishment of the Eighteenth Dynasty, and it continued during the empire period (1350–1150 B.C.). Two governors, appointed by Egypt, controlled the country from their respective centers of Wawat in the north and Kush in the south. With reference to this period, H. A. Macmichael writes that "trade was developed, the mines of the eastern desert were worked for emeralds and gold, taxes were collected, temples built, and the settlement of colonies increased."[4]

Kush—the Cush of the Bible, the Ethiopia of the classical writers

2. James Henry Breasted, *A History of the Ancient Egyptians* (New York: Charles Scribner's Sons [1908]), p. 126.

3. There is a very colorful account in Salim Hassan's *Misr al-qadima* [Ancient Egypt] of a mission which Queen Hatsheput sent to Punt under the leadership of the head of the treasury [Cairo: Matba'at Dar al-Kutub al-Misriya, 1948], IV, 327–35).

4. *The Anglo-Egyptian Sudan* (London: Faber & Faber, 1934), p. 22.

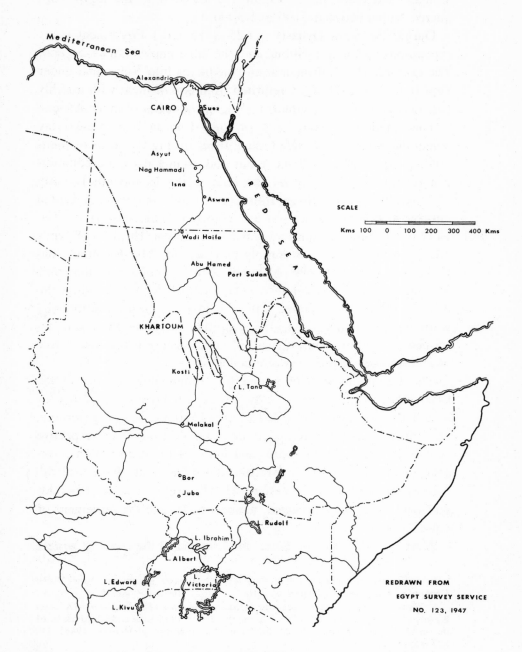

Southern Boundaries of Egypt in the Reign of Thutmosis III, 1479–1447 B.C.

5

—was considered so important that the king of Egypt himself led at least three military campaigns against it, and it was brought under complete Egyptian control by about 1879 B.C. Its importance to Egypt lay in its strategic geographic location. Although its actual boundaries shifted from one era to another, it generally approximated the area of the Nile Valley region lying south of Egypt up to the juncture of the Niles, including Abyssinia and the eastern region of the Red Sea. By controlling Kush, Egypt gained control over the gold mines of Wadi Alady and the Eastern Desert, had access to the gold of Abyssinia, and controlled the trade routes between Egypt and Central Africa. Egypt's occupation of Kush lasted for almost four centuries, to about 1600 B.C. Macmichael states that

> The Egyptians followed up their military and political occupation by filling the land with Egyptians — soldiers, officials, priests, merchants, and craftsmen. Southwards of Phile, temples were made, decorated, and maintained. . . . Each of these was a center of propaganda, a community of scribes learned in Egyptian medicine, law and religion, and of artisans trained in every ancient craft. . . . The viceroy himself with his personal staff probably shifted his quarters from el-Kab or Elephantine to Semneh or Napata as the season or the necessities of the administration made it seem advisable. . . . Most of the Egyptians were permanently domiciled in the country and had brought their families with them. The decimated tribes grew into a completely submissive population, were racially affected by intermarriage with the ruling class, and became more or less Egyptianized. The country as a whole was thoroughly Egyptianized, especially in religion.[5]

Kerma, one of the leading settlements of Kush, had developed by the Twelfth Dynasty (1970–1936 B.C.) into a distribution center for goods. Its trading network reached south to the Atbara River and as far west as Darfur and Lake Chad. Here also developed "a special local civilization, a curious modification of the culture of

5. *A History of the Arabs in the Sudan: And Some Accounts of the People Who Preceded Them and of the Tribes Inhabiting Darfur* (Cambridge: At the University Press, 1922), I, 19.

Egypt deeply affected by local forms, materials, and customs."[6] The factories at Kerma distributed their products throughout Ethiopia and as far as Middle Egypt. The Egyptian administration in Kerma grew so powerful from the profits of the local factories and from taxing traffic that passed along its trade routes that Kerma was able to survive even during the period of Egypt's disintegration which was climaxed by the Hyksos' conquest of Lower Egypt (ca. 1700 B.C.). Kerma's power was broken shortly thereafter, most likely as a result of being overrun by the native Ethiopian tribes who had realized the weakness of Egypt.

Kush rebelled against Egyptian rule and was independent from about 1700 to 1600 B.C. King Thutmosis I (1530–1520 B.C.) returned it to Egyptian rule. His forces besieged the area, occupied the region between the big bends of the Nile, and built a fort as far south as Abu Hamed. Thutmosis had, as he justifiably boasted, "penetrated valleys which the royal ancestors knew not."[7] Robert I. Rotberg suggests that "Egyptian soldiers may have even ventured beyond the Fifth and Sixth Cataracts to the site of modern Omdurman—where tropical Africa began." According to Carl Roebuck, during the Eighteenth Dynasty (1570–1365 B.C.), "Nubia and Kush became culturally and economically a part of Egypt."[8]

From the eleventh century B.C. Egypt was in a state of decline. About 945 B.C., during the period that northern Libyans gained control over Egypt, southern Libyan tribesmen achieved domination over Nubia and founded an independent monarchy with Napata as its capital. In approximately 300 B.C., Merowe, located in southern Ethiopia, became the capital of the Ethiopian monarchy. Ethiopia had long been completely Egyptianized, and the culture of the Ethiopian monarchs was merely a modification of Egyptian culture. Describing this phenomenon, Reisner states:

6. G. A. Reisner, "Outline of the Ancient History of the Sudan: Part II, The Egyptian Occupation of Ethiopia During the Middle Empire (2000 to 1600 B.C.)," *Sudan Notes and Records,* I (April, 1918), 78.

7. *A Political History of Tropical Africa* (New York: Harcourt, Brace & World, 1965), pp. 8–9.

8. *The World of Ancient Times* (New York: Charles Scribner's Sons, 1966), p. 83.

The Libyan family which became the royal family of Ethiopia had naturally been also Egyptianized by their surroundings at Napata, with its temple and priesthood. When they had added Egypt to Ethiopia, the Ethiopian kings imported a number of Egyptian craftsmen, especially for the building and decoration of the great temple of Amon at the Holy Mountain (Gebel Barkat). These included masons, sculptors in relief and in the round, scribes, jewellers, faience workers, and other craftsmen, and the traditions of Egypt became fixed as the traditions of Ethiopia. This is the basis on which rests the whole history of the culture of Ethiopia. The civilization was Egyptian, not native, and the subsequent history is one of loss, not of gain—of the gradual fading of the tradition of fine arts and crafts and of the knowledge of the Egyptian language and the sacred texts. For a century or so the degeneration was hardly noticeable. After three hundred years, the losses, especially in forms, in skills and in knowledge of Egyptian had become striking, but the main features of the old culture, although blurred, were still discernible. Then the sovereignty passed to Meroe and the development of the Meroitic culture begins with this Ethiopian version of the Egyptian culture, all being based on Egypt.[9]

Invaded by the Assyrians in the mid-seventh century B.C., Egypt was then successively conquered by the Persians (525 B.C.), the Alexandrian armies (332 B.C.) and the Romans (30 B.C.). The political, cultural, and religious influence of these foreign powers filtered through Egypt and into Nubia. When Egypt became Christianized, Egyptian missionaries carried the new faith up the Nile Valley, and Axum was largely converted by the fourth century A.D. When, after a controversy with Rome, Egypt adhered to the Monophysite (Coptic) church, Axum followed suit, and when Meroe was converted in the sixth century, the Coptic faith was also adopted there. Although Christianity did not spread to the Sudanic civilizations influenced by Meroe, it was so strongly established in the Nilotic Sudan that the area resisted Islam until the eleventh century.

9. "The Pyramids of Meroe and the Candaces of Ethiopia," *Sudan Notes and Records,* V (December, 1922), 177–78.

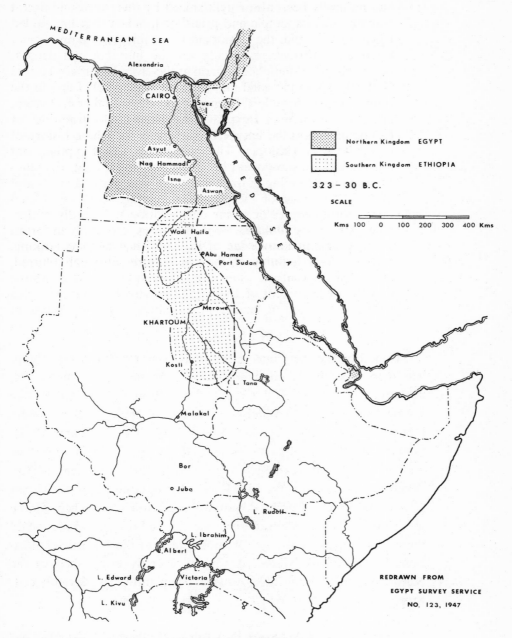

The Northern and Southern Kingdoms in the Ptolemaic Age

Evolution of the Policy

Trade relations in this period were for the most part restricted to the Nile Valley and were directed toward the Mediterranean, but trans-Saharan trade routes established in the fifth century B.C. continued to be in at least intermittent use up to the sixteenth century A.D., and trade connections from the Mediterranean powers and Egypt to the East African coast were operative in the first century A.D. By the fourth century, trade was well-developed as far south as Rhapta, on the Tanganyika coast. Cloth and metal items were brought from the north in exchange for spices and ivory; slaves were exported to Egypt from Opone, now Ras Hafun in Somalia.[10]

During the first half of the seventh century A.D., Caliph Omar ibn al-Khattab ordered Amir ibn al-As to conquer Egypt. With al-As came many tribes from Arabia. The subsequent Arab conquest of Egypt, and Egypt's ensuing Arabization and Islamization, marked the revival of Egyptian activity in Africa. Between the Arab occupation of Egypt in 639 and the Nubian war of 651–52, the Arabs extended the Egyptian boundary south as far as Aswan. Raids by Nubian forces led to a punitive expedition which defeated the southern kingdom and bombarded the Nubian capital of Dongola. A treaty was concluded between the Arab commander, Abdullah ibn Saad, and the Nubian king, which provided for trade and religious freedom. The subjects of each kingdom were to have freedom of travel and worship in the other domain, and the Nubians were to send slaves and gold to Egypt in exchange for wheat, cloth, and horses.[11] In the latter part of the seventh century, an Arab base was established at Kairouan, in southern Tunisia, by a nephew of Amir ibn el-As, but it was lost to a force of desert Berbers. After the Arabs had built a navy to protect the coast from Byzantine attacks and the Berbers had been subdued (about 705), the area of modern Tunisia was fully incorporated into the Arab empire. The rest of North Africa fell to the Arabs at the time of the conquest of the Iberian Peninsula. Religious disputes and divisions led to

10. See Gervase Mathew, "The East African Coast Until the Coming of the Portuguese," in *History of East Africa,* ed. Roland Oliver and Gervase Mathew (London: Oxford University Press, 1963), I, 94–96.

11. Abdul al-Fattah Ibrahim al-Sayid Baddur, *Sudanese-Egyptian Relations: A Chronological and Analytical Study* (The Hague: Martinus Nijhoff, 1960), pp. 17–21.

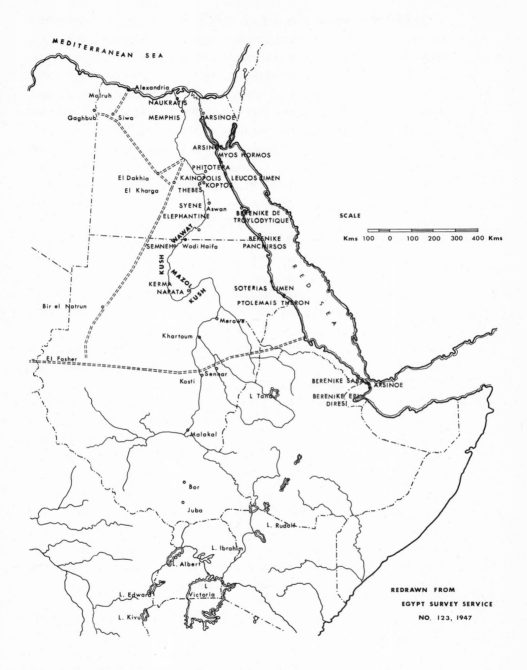

Nile Basin: Trade Centers and Caravan Routes in Ancient Times

11

a decline in the power of Egypt, and African Berbers placed the Fatimid Caliphs in power in Cairo in 973. The Fatimids turned their attention to the east, however, and lost contact with the Maghrib. In the late eleventh century, dominance over North Africa and Spain was established by the Almoravids, an African Islamic dynasty, who were superseded in the twelfth century by another group of Muslim Berbers, the Almohades. The Almoravids and Almohades, through the establishment and extension of trading settlements, carried Islam deep into Africa, and the faith penetrated most of the Western Sudan, at least among the upper classes.

Although little historical evidence is available for the East coast of Africa from the fourth through the tenth centuries A.D., it appears that traders from India and Arabia frequented the area and that more or less permanent trading bases were established there. From the tenth to the thirteenth centuries these trading posts became more important and were transformed into Islamic bastions which controlled the commercial routes into the interior of East Africa; trade probably extended as far inland as the Great Lakes. Among the most important towns were Zeila and Mogadiscio (Somali Republic), the island ports of Kilwa (Tanzania) and Mombasa (Kenya), Zanzibar, and Sofala (Mozambique). The Arab merchants carried their culture and civilization to East Africa and tied the people of Africa to the Arab centers outside the continent. Trade was also extended to West Africa through Timbuktu and Djenne (Mali) and Tekrur (Senegal).

From about the twelfth century Timbuktu was an Arab commercial center; it also became a center for Arabism and Islamic studies and large numbers of students and religious leaders (*ulamas*) were attracted to its schools and university. Djenne developed simultaneously with Timbuktu, and the number of *ulamas* who studied religion and language there reached 4,000. A great mosque was established in Djenne and this became the school of Arabism in Central Africa.[12] The rulers of Tekrur, whose influence extended to West and Central Africa, had very strong ties with Egypt, and a large number of students from Tekrur attended Al-Azhar Univer-

12. Ibrahim Ahmad al-Adawi, "Talai al-'Uruba fi Ifriqiya" [The vanguards of Arabism in Africa], *Nahdhat Ifriqiya*, no. 6, April, 1958, p. 34.

sity, which had been established in Cairo in the latter part of the tenth century as a center of Muslim learning. The Islamic influence also reached Uganda through the coast of Africa. King Amtiza of Uganda requested that the Egyptian administration in the equatorial region of the Upper Nile send two *faqihs* (religious scholars) to teach the inhabitants the Islamic religion.[13] Ghana and later Mali (both of which had large Arab settlements) had close religious, cultural, and commercial relations with Egypt. Mali's Muslim kings often stopped in Cairo on their frequent pilgrimages to Mecca.[14] Indeed, Ibn Battuta, the famous medieval Arab traveler, visited Mali in 1352 and commented in his writings on the ease of travel between Egypt and Central Africa.[15]

By the fourteenth century Egypt had thus acquired a position with a great potential for influence in Africa. Travel and trade were relatively easy, and the growing importance of Al-Azhar, in the context of the rapid expansion of Islam in Africa, had established Egypt as a great religious center. Under the Ayyubids, founded by Salah ad-Dinn Yusuf ibn-Ayyub (Saladin), and the Mamelukes who succeeded them, Egypt's interests turned to Asia, and until the sixteenth century its main service to Africa may have been essentially that of shielding the continent from foreign invasion. Although Egypt's military power under the Mamelukes was such that it was not surpassed until the reign of Muhammad Ali (1805–49), from the end of the fourteenth century the state declined; and after the Turks under Selim I occupied Egypt in 1517, Egypt's involvement in Africa was, until the nineteenth century, reduced to the cultural and religious spheres. (One exception to be noted in this tendency toward disengagement was the supply of arms and Turkish military instructors sent to the Islamic kingdom of Bornu, southwest of Lake Chad, at the end of the sixteenth century.)

Although direct Egyptian influence declined after the Ottoman

13. Ibrahim Ahmad al-Adawi, "Al-usul al-Arabiya fi takwin Yuganda al-siyasi" [The Arabic origins of the establishment of political Uganda], *Nahdhat Ifriqiya,* no. 11, September, 1958, p. 59.
14. See Nehamia Levtzion, "The Thirteenth and Fourteenth-Century Kings of Mali," *Journal of African History,* Vol. IV, No. 3 (1963), 341–53.
15. *Muhadhab rihlat Ibn Battuta* [Revised travels of Ibn Battuta] Cairo: Al-Matba'a al-Amiriya, 1933), II, 298.

invasion, refugees from Egypt migrated to the Sudan and fostered the expansion of Islam and Arabization.

> The rigorist Malikite Islam of the Mamelukes, which had made the Middle Nile an Egyptian territory, developed in African circles and won to itself more and more rulers in this Western region through close and profitable commercial relations established with Bornu. Owing to the infiltration of Egyptian Moslems, most of whom were Arabs, dynasties of colored Moslems were established in Darfur (sixteenth century), Wadai, and Bagirmi (seventeenth century).[16]

Thus, even as Egyptian political influence ceased, cultural and religious connections and similarities were developing.

Muhammad Ali, wanting to restore Egypt's Sudanic empire to its ancient geographic boundaries, revived the Egyptian political role in Africa after a hiatus of some three hundred years. In 1820 he began a campaign to unify the Nile Valley, and in 1839 an Egyptian base was established at Gondokoro, near the present Sudan-Uganda boundary. Muhammad Ali was granted legal control of the area by the firman sultani on February 13, 1841. The Ottoman sultan recognized Egyptian rule of the Sudan only during the lifetime of Muhammad Ali, but recognition was extended to his heirs by the firman of May 27, 1866, and under the Khedive Ismail (1863–79), Egyptian political influence once again extended deeply into Africa.

> Towards the close of Ismail's reign the Sudan extended southwards to the equator, including the Lakes of Albert and Victoria with the territory lying between them. The eastern boundaries reached the shores of the Red Sea and the Gulf of Aden, while the Sudan, on its southeastern boundary, touched the Indian Ocean, thus including Swakin, Mosawah, Teila, Barbara, Harar, and the northern coasts of Somaliland. All the western shores of the Red Sea from Suez in the north to Bab El-Mandab in the south were parts of Egypt. Egypt's dominion also extended to the shores of the Gulf of Aden

16. Norbert Tapiero, "Evolving Social Patterns," tr. Beata Dabrowska, in *Islam in Africa,* ed. James Kritzeck and William H. Lewis (New York: Van Nostrand-Reinhold, 1969), pp. 70–71.

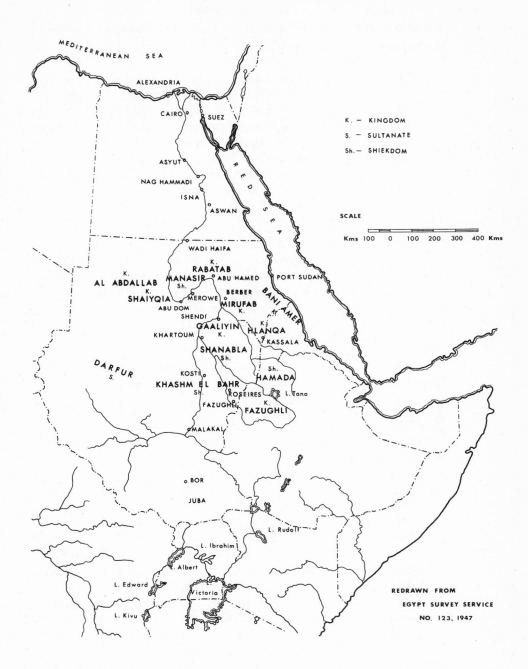

Sudan Emirates before the Egyptian Conquest

from Bab El-Mandab to Cape Cordafwi [Guardafui] and to Cape Hafoun. The Egyptian Empire extended westwards to the Kingdom of Wadai which lay to the west of Darfour.[17]

On the advice of General Gordon, then governor of the Egyptian administration in the Sudan, Ismail made an attempt to occupy Kismayu, on the East African coast, in order to establish a better route to the southern Sudan but was dissuaded from this object by the British; Egyptian moves to the south ended about 1877. Considering this Egyptian drive and the Zanzibari advance from the coast, Oliver and Fage conclude:

> Had there been no direct intervention of European power, the influence of the Arabs would have consolidated itself not only on the east coast and in the northern Sudan, but in the southern Sudan also, and in many parts of East Africa and the Congo. . . . Had full-scale European intervention been delayed fifty years, not merely the northern third of Africa, but the northern two-thirds, would have belonged culturally to the world of Islam.[18]

During the nineteenth century Egypt sent many scientific expeditions into Africa. Between 1839 and 1841, Egyptian Lt. Col. Salim Afandi made explorations along the Nile and brought back valuable information on the course of the river, the branches that feed it, and the tribes that were settled there. From 1860 to 1885 the Egyptian administration also encouraged expeditions by non-Egyptian explorers into Somalia, Harar, and all of East Africa. The Egyptian Geographic Society was founded in 1875 for the purpose of studying the geography of Africa and exploring its little-known regions. The Egyptian Staff College, also established during the 1870s, greatly contributed to the geographic exploration of the continent. Egyptian army officers were sent out to collect anthropological and geographical data. In 1870 Captain Salman Halawa completed a voyage around Africa in three months. General

17. Abdul Rahman al-Rafai Bay, *Egypt and the Sudan* (in Arabic), p. 83, quoted in *Egypt, Britain and the Sudan*, by Rashid al-Barawy (Cairo: Renaissance Bookshop, 1952), p. 4.

18. Roland Oliver and J. D. Fage, *A Short History of Africa*, 2d ed. (Harmondsworth, England: Penguin Books, 1966), p. 180.

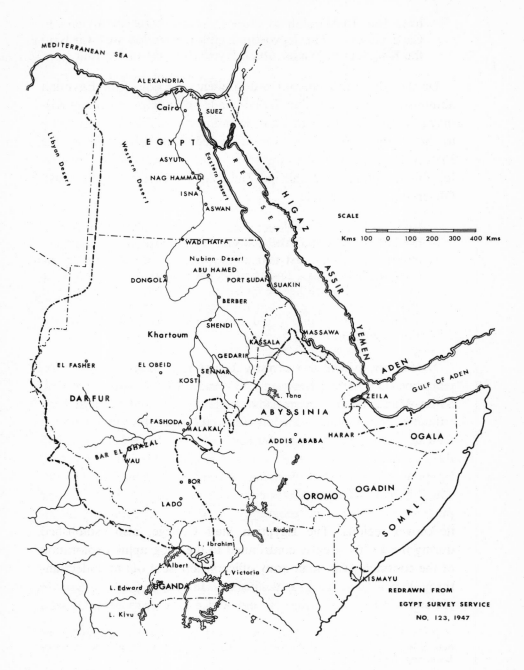

SCALE

Kms 100 0 100 200 300 400 Kms

MEDITERRANEAN SEA

ALEXANDRIA

Cairo SUEZ

Libyan Desert

Western Desert

E G Y P T

ASYUT

NAG HAMMADI

ISNA

Eastern Desert

ASWAN

H I G A Z

R E D   S E A

WADI HALFA

Nubian Desert

ABU HAMED

DONGOLA

PORT SUDAN SUAKIN

A S S I R

BERBER

Y E M E N

SHENDI

Khartoum

MASSAWA

KASSALA

GEDARIF

A D E N

EL FASHER

EL OBEID

SENNAR

GULF OF ADEN

KOST

L. Tana

ZEILA

D A R F U R

A B Y S S I N I A

FASHODA

MALAKAL

ADDIS ABABA HARAR

O G A L A

BAR EL GHAZAL

WAU

O R O M O

O G A D I N

BOR

LADO

S O M A L I

L. Rudolf

L. Ibrahim

L. Albert

L. Victoria

KISMAYU

L. Edward UGANDA

REDRAWN FROM

EGYPT SURVEY SERVICE

L. Kivu

NO. 123, 1947

Egypt 1882

17

Evolution of the Policy

Muhammad Mukhtar Pasha, a Staff College graduate and one of the pioneers of African geography, participated in the occupation of Harar in 1875 and drew a detailed map of that area and of Zeila. In 1877 he took part in drafting a map of the entire continent which was considered the most accurate one available at that time. The next year Pasha visited the coast of Somalia, then under Egyptian rule, to select a location for a lighthouse and mapped that area.[19]

From the time of the Mahdi rebellion at the end of the nineteenth century until the end of World War II, Egypt's influence in Africa remained primarily religious and cultural rather than political. The direct and indirect effects of the British occupation of Egypt, taken together with colonial enterprises in other parts of Africa, nearly eliminated direct Egyptian involvement in Africa. The British controlled Egyptian activities there and also the means by which these activities could be financed. Considering their interest in a stable Egypt and their position in East Africa, it could hardly be expected that the British would encourage Egyptian political involvement in the African scene.

However, the idea of the restoration of Egypt's ancient boundaries persisted. After a trip through the Sudan in 1940, Egyptian Prime Minister Ali Mahir (who also became the first prime minister after the 1952 revolution) stated in a speech before the Egyptian Parliament:

> It is my pleasure to renew together with you the memory of Egypt's greatness in the Pharaonic era and during the Ayyubid Dynasty when our forefathers extended Egypt's influence into Africa and flew the banner of progress on the banks of the Nile and its happy valley.[20]

After World War II, Egypt's revived interest and activity in Africa was focused mainly on the Sudan and manifested itself in the

---

19. See Mustafa al-Shihabi, *Al-Jughrafiyhn al-'Arab* [The Arab geographers] (Cairo: Dar al-Ma'arif, 1962), pp. 110–15; and Muhammad al-Mu'tasim Sayyid, "Misr al-kushuf al-Ifriqiya wa al-haditha" [Egypt and the modern African discoveries], *Nahdhat Ifriqiya*, no. 60, November, 1962, pp. 35–36.

20. *Al-Ahram*, March 12, 1940, p. 7.

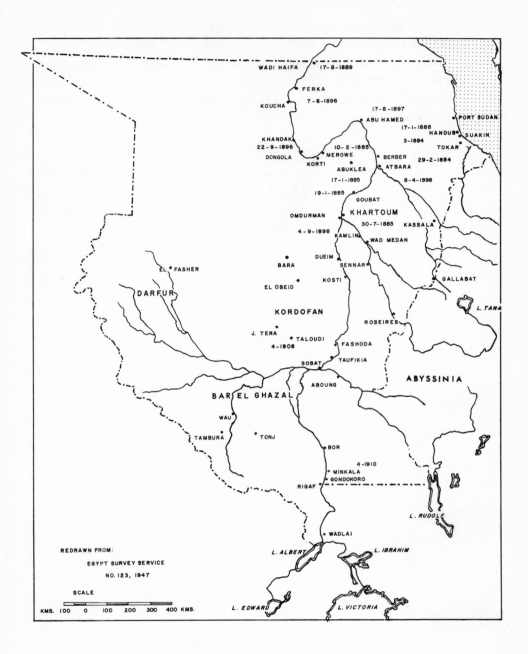

Egyptian Army Battles in the Sudan after 1882

Evolution of the Policy

"Unity of the Nile Valley" movement. Shortly before the 1952 revolution Ali Mahir drew up an outline for a national policy, entitled "Freedom Pact,"[21] in which he discussed Egypt's objectives in the Sudan but never referred to the rest of Africa, an omission indicative of Egypt's general lack of interest in the continent outside of the Sudan.

21. *Jabhat Misr* [*Egypt's front*] (Cairo: Al-Matba'a al-Amiriya, 1952), pp. 1–3. In November, 1945, Ali Maher announced the formation of the "Egyptian Front," and he later outlined its program and objectives in this book. He states that the "Egyptian Front" is not a party; it is a front for all Egyptians. "It's aim is to gather the dynamic power of the country, both individuals and groups, around the main principles for the internal and external social and economic policies" (p. 20).

Chapter Two

Contemporary Policy

The revolution of 1952 brought to power a group of young men, dedicated to the principles of Egyptian nationalism and sovereignty, who were faced with the consequences of the confused and uncertain policies of their predecessors. Among the manifold problems facing these men was the creation of a foreign policy that would at the same time establish Egypt's independence, restore to her a place of importance in regional and world affairs, and serve domestic needs. This problem could only be solved, for these pragmatic men, through a process of trial and error. Beginning from the principles of ending foreign occupation of Egypt and unifying the Nile Valley, the Revolutionary Command Council began to develop a policy quite unprecedented for an African or Middle Eastern state. The chief pitfalls facing the young officers were the danger that their inexperience might lead them into a disastrous confrontation with a stronger power and the possibility that failure to develop a foreign policy suitable for the attainment of revolutionary objectives might have serious repercussions in domestic politics. The evolution of Egyptian foreign policy was in the direction of an increasingly explicit ideology, and an increasingly active role in world affairs. This is nowhere better exemplified than in the slow and deliberate development of Egypt's African policy. In this chapter these developments will be traced through the shifting flow of events.

SEARCH FOR A POLICY: 1952-1954

The basis for Egypt's African policy was the new military regime's interest in a traditional area of Egyptian concern: the Nile Valley. The "Unity of the Nile Valley" theme remained an aspiration integral to Egyptian nationalism. Thus, while Nasser was occupied with Egypt's internal affairs in the early stages of the revolution, President Muhammad Nagib was primarily concerned with the Sudan question. His personal ties to the Sudan (where he was born and had spent his early childhood) and his strong belief in the unity of the Nile Valley diverted most of his efforts to the problems of the liberation of the area from British control and the subsequent unification of Egypt and the Sudan.[1]

Major Salah Salem (the first minister of national guidance, a member of the Revolutionary Command Council, and later the minister of Sudanic affairs) also had personal ties with the Sudan and shared General Nagib's preoccupation with the Sudan question. He, too, affirmed the continuing strength of the unity of the Nile Valley movement:

> We should fight firmly and offer sacrifice after sacrifice to become 30,000,000 free people [Sudan and Egypt], standing together to tell imperialism, "Stand still in your place. No imperialism after today. Leave our country and get out of this oppressed continent which hangs all its hopes on the nation of the Nile Valley."[2]

1. "My reform program," declared Nagib, "is the liberation of the Nile Valley and the restoration of complete independence and sovereignty to it." *Al-Ahram,* February 10, 1954, p. 8.

2. *Al-Ahram,* February 15, 1954, p. 7. Speeches made during the first year of the revolution indicate that General Nagib and Major Salah Salem were responsible for the main effort over the Sudan question. Until the resignation of Major Salah Salem in August, 1955, Nasser concentrated on the internal problems of

After the Anglo-Egyptian Agreement of February, 1953, on the Sudan, a new phase in Egyptian-African relations opened. Fundamentally, this began as an attempt to re-evaluate Egyptian-Sudanese relations within an African context.[3] However, the role Egypt could play on the continent as the largest and most economically developed independent African state, aside from the Republic of South Africa—and the only one with a modern nationalist at its head—was not overlooked. Nor was Egypt unaware of the importance of expanding relationships in a world community which was rapidly being consolidated by modern technology. Within this context, then, the political, strategic, and economic propinquity of Africa was being considered anew. "We look for a power which will protect Africa," proclaimed a Cairo newspaper. "We see no one but Egypt. It is the nearest African power with a personality that the world recognizes. It is necessary for Egypt to pursue a single African policy aiming at the enfranchisement of the continent."[4] Egypt's new military regime, then, was heralding an anti-imperialist policy on the African continent. Wing Commander Abdul Latif al-Baghdadi, a close associate and trusted friend of Nasser, explained Egypt's relationship to the anti-imperialist struggle in emotional terms:

> We are the nation which tasted the bitterness of slavery and appreciate the hopes of each nation in the struggle for the accomplishment of independence and the fight to win its rights . . . we encourage and support them; moreover, we will help them in their struggle.[5]

Egypt. (see Republic of Egypt, Armed Forces Public Relations Department, *Mithaq al-tharwa min aqwal rais wa a'adha majlis qiyadat al-thawra* [The Charter of the Revolution from the speeches of the president, vice-president and members of the Revolutionary Command Council] [Cairo, 1953], pp. 154–83; this section, which deals with the Sudan, does not contain even one speech by Nasser).

3. Egypt's role and objectives in the Sudan are examined in detail in Chapter Seven.

4. *Al-Akhbar,* March 24, 1953, p. 4.

5. *Al-Ahram,* February 22, 1954, p. 1. Wing Commander Abdul Latif al-Baghdadi was at that time minister of war, head of the Revolutionary Court, a member of the Egyptian delegation to the evacuation talks, the Egyptian delegate to the League of Arab States, representative of Egypt in the Council of the Common Arab Defense Pact, and a member of the Revolutionary Council.

Evolution of the Policy

The deteriorating situation in Morocco furnished the occasion in 1953 for Egypt to arrange an Afro-Asian conference to organize action and protest against "imperialism." The representatives to the conference concluded that

> Protest against the bloody massacres committed by France in Morocco will bear no fruit. The problem requires taking definitive steps because the era of protest is over. The world does not accept anything but practical methods which lead to the road of success and the accomplishment of goals.[6]

Although at this time Egypt's main foreign-policy interest lay in the Nile Valley and the Arab world, Egypt had "extended its hands to each nation that justly wants to be free and independent." In early 1954, therefore, President Nagib met with representatives of the Mau Mau and with the leaders of Uganda and Nigeria, and he invited the leaders of all national movements to meet in Cairo. He "assured them that Egypt, which vigorously opposes imperialism, wishes their countries success and prosperity." These leaders, it was reported, "left Egypt and each one of them entertained the idea of a conference in Cairo that would include all the leaders of anti-imperialism . . . and discussion of anti-discrimination on the African continent."[7]

Thus, by 1954 Egypt had indicated an interest in a broad policy of anti-imperialism and support for nationalist movements in Africa and the Middle East. However, at this time the objectives of this policy were vague and undefined. In 1954 Nasser wrote his celebrated book *The Philosophy of the Revolution*. Subsequent developments prove that this was a clear statement of Nasser's objectives. Commenting on the expansion of Egypt's foreign-policy interests, Nasser stated:

6. *Al-Ahram*, August 28, 1953, p. 1. The conference was held in the Indonesian Embassy in Cairo and was attended by the chargés d'affaires of India, Iraq, Pakistan, Lebanon, Syria, and the ambassadors to Cairo of Afghanistan, Indonesia, and Jordan. Also, the minister of Yemen attended. Ethiopia, Saudi Arabia, and Iran did not attend. Egypt's sizable delegation included Omar Lutfi, (then director of the Legal Office in the Foreign Office, who later became the Egyptian ambassador to the U.S.); Sami Abdul Futuh (undersecretary in the Foreign Office); and Ahmad al-Shuqayri (assistant to the general secretary of the Arab League).

7. *Al-Ahram*, January 13, 1954, p. 6.

The era of isolation is over. Gone also are the days when barbed wire marked the frontiers separating and isolating countries. Every country must now look beyond its frontiers to discover the sources of the currents that affect it and how to live with other countries, etc. . . . It has become imperative that every country look around to discover its position and environment, deciding what it can accomplish, what is its vital sphere, where is the scene of its activity, and what is its positive role in this troubled world.[8]

Misr wa risalatuha [Egypt and its mission], by Husain Muinis, a prominent Egyptian historian, was published during the same period and also attempts to define Egypt's "sphere of activity."[9] The book is significant because it carries an introduction by Nasser implying his approval of the views expressed. Nasser's sponsorship of the book indicates that he was already concerned about the importance of Africa to Egypt and was evaluating various alternatives for an African policy. However, Professor Muinis's views subsequently were disregarded by Nasser. The reason for such a change of mind might have been that Muinis outlined a policy for Egypt in Africa that would have resulted in closer cooperation with the West, making Egypt, in effect, merely a bridge from the West to Africa.

In his book, Muinis described three "dimensions of Egyptian history": (1) Africa, (2) the Middle East, and (3) the Mediterranean. He stated that Egypt is "on the crossroads between the Orient and the West."

We are the meeting point between three continents. We, and we alone, are the ones who are able to be the messengers between the two sides. . . . We are the door to Africa. Transfer to its people what we have and what others have and we will hold it out to all comers on this oppressed continent which has not been fairly treated by anyone.[10]

Regarding Egypt's role in Africa, Professor Muinis states that

8. *The Philosophy of the Revolution* (Cairo: The National Publication House [1954]), p. 51.

9. (Cairo: Al-Namudthajiyya Press [1954]).

10. *Ibid.*, p. 144.

The Europeans have attempted to build barriers and obstacles on this continent. But the people of the continent do not want that and they always turn toward us, copying from us, or saying they would like to do so if the circumstances permitted. It is our duty to carry the torch to their country. Their culture is our culture; their future is ours.[11]

Prior to 1954, however, outside of moral support given to national liberation movements and their leaders, Egypt's active participation in African affairs was confined to the Sudan and North Africa. After a series of meetings between Nasser and his foreign-policy advisers from December, 1953, to January, 1954, and Nasser's subsequent clarification of Egypt's ties with Africa (as expressed in *The Philosophy of the Revolution*), Wing Commander Abdul Latif al-Baghdadi made a firmer statement of Egypt's intentions, indicating that Egypt had established a clear policy direction and was prepared to participate actively through coordinated action with the African national liberation movements.[12]

Although Africa occupies a significant position in Egypt's "sphere of activity," as defined by *The Philosophy of the Revolution*, Egypt, from the early days of the revolution, was most deeply involved in Arab, primarily Middle Eastern, issues. In a discussion of Egypt's foreign relations in an article prepared sometime in early 1954, apparently before *The Philosophy of the Revolution*, Nasser regarded the Arab world to be the main concern in his foreign policy; he did not consider Africa, except with reference to a discussion of imperialism in general.[13] In *The Philosophy of the Revolution*, however, Nasser did emphasize the importance of Africa, as well as the Middle East, to Egypt.

So intense was Egypt's identification with the Middle East that Nasser described an Arab interest as the second aim of the revolution. "The first aim after evacuation is the support for the Arab

11. *Ibid.*

12. "Our policy," he said, "concentrates on action to achieve the goal. We have met and contacted the leaders of the struggling national forces to organize this effort and unify the plans which will lead to the expulsion of the imperialist" (*Al-Ahram*, February 22, 1954. p. 1).

13. "The Egyptian Revolution," *Foreign Affairs*, XXXIII (January, 1955), 209–11.

League in order to guarantee security and stability in an area that is the most sensitive area in the world."[14] On one occasion an ex-general secretary of the League of Arab States stated: "There is a malicious campaign . . . claiming that Egypt is an African state and has nothing to do with the countries situated in the Middle East. But this is vicious propaganda that died the day it was conceived."[15]

The Baghdad Pact presented one of the major challenges to Nasser's Middle East policy. To counteract the Baghdad Pact, and prompted by Israel's Gaza raid of February, 1955, Nasser attempted to form his own defense alliance. In early March, 1955, Egypt and Syria formed a "defense organization and mutual Arab cooperative to establish a permanent common command to execute the defense and supervise the war industry and economic cooperation."[16] Saudi Arabia endorsed the agreement,[17] and Yemen declared its support.[18] *Al-Ahram*, describing the purpose of the alliance, stated:

> What Egypt and Syria seek is the complete integration of the Arab world. . . . Politically the Arab world ignores the Iraqi-Turkish pact or any other non-Arab pact. Militarily the new Arab world should have an organization which takes care of its defense. . . . Economically . . . an Arab economic council will be formed to direct the economic policy.[19]

By mid-1955 it was apparent that Nasser had failed to rally the support of the Arab states behind the Arab Mutual Security Pact. Personality conflicts between Nasser and other Arab leaders were intensified. Furthermore, Nasser's active opposition to the Baghdad Pact created conflicts with the West. Although his efforts in the Middle East continued, Nasser was turning more toward Africa, as the Bandung Conference had indicated the importance of Africa in regional and world politics. Egypt's African policy in this period had grown from a narrow concern with the Sudan and North

14. *Al-Ahram*, September 3, 1954, p. 1.
15. *Al-Ahram*, August 31, 1954, p. 7.
16. *Al-Ahram*, March 7, 1955, p. 1.
17. *Al-Ahram*, March 8, 1955, p. 7.
18. *Al-Ahram*, March 7, 1955, p. 1.
19. *Al-Ahram*, March 10, 1955, p. 6.

Africa to a still tentative, but increasingly strong, interest in the sub-Saharan area as well.

FOUNDATION FOR A POLICY: 1955

The events of the Bandung Conference strongly influenced Egypt's foreign policy. Occurring during the period of the Baghdad Pact controversy, it encouraged Egypt's strong anti-West position. The conference afforded Nasser the opportunity to challenge the traditional leaders of the Middle East. These leaders were primarily pro-Western and relatively moderate in their demands on such Arab questions as Palestine and North Africa.[20] By winning Afro-Asian support for more radical solutions to Arab issues, Nasser hoped to gain the support of the Arab masses, and in order to effect that end he prepared a definite program of objectives to be achieved at the conference:

> The question of North Africa will be the most important question to be discussed at the conference. . . . Henceforth, President Nasser will struggle . . . for the liberation of North Africa. . . . As for the African continent, Egypt sympathizes with the independence movement in Kenya and with the demands for racial equality in Africa. The Egyptian government does not await and will not request any aid for the liberation movements in Africa and Asia from the Bandung Conference. But she believes that the condemnation of imperialism by 20 states in Africa and Asia which represent half the population of the globe . . . will have a significant impact on the liberation movements of Arabs and blacks. . . . Egypt will try to alienate the Afro-Asian states from Israel. . . . The second aim of President

20. The different stands taken by Egypt, Iraq, and Jordan on recommendations to the Council of the League of Arab States on issues to be discussed at the Bandung Conference are a good example of this contrast. The recommendations of Iraq and Jordan avoided directly challenging the West. They proposed that the conference discuss the following: (1) the Palestine refugees and their compensation and (2) Israel's treatment of its Arab population. In contrast, Egypt sponsored: (1) the question of Palestine, (2) the question of North Africa, (3) freedom of Africa, (4) discrimination in Africa, and (5) disarmament (*Al-Mutamar al-Asyawi al-Ifriqi al-awwal al-maaqud fi Bandung bi Indonesia* [The first Afro-Asian conference held in Bandung, Indonesia], 18–24 April, 1955 [Cairo: League of Arab States, 1955], p. 25–26).

Nasser will be his full support for the policy of . . . neutrality between East and West. . . . The official circles in Egypt declared that President Nasser will support Nehru in his condemnation of racial discrimination in South Africa. Egypt in her capacity as the leader of the African continent has continually objected to the policy of racial discrimination.[21]

Nasser realized from its inception the importance of the Bandung Conference. As early as January, 1955, the Egyptian newspapers, mobilizing and preparing public opinion, gave extensive coverage to the activities preceding the meeting. The official reports to the sponsoring governments "praised Egypt's attitude and the Arab countries' attitudes toward this conference. They mentioned the good propaganda in the Arab newspapers in general and in *Al-Ahram* in particular."[22]

Egypt's delegation to the conference was the largest, consisting of 50 persons. (The next largest were Indonesia with 40 and China with 26.) Nasser's delegation included three ministers, one deputy minister, the general secretary of the League of Arab States, and two professors of law and international relations, providing him with diverse and expert counsel.[23]

Nasser encouraged all the Arab states to send delegates to the conference so that he would have behind his proposals a bloc of votes which would afford him some bargaining power.[24] Egypt used her influence in the Political Committee of the League of Arab States to secure cooperation. At a meeting on December 11, 1954, the Council accepted the recommendation of the Political Committee and urged the following:

First—The participation of all Arab states in this conference with strong delegations that include political, economic, and cultural elements.

21. *Al-Ahram,* March 21, 1955, p. 1.
22. *Al-Ahram,* January 1, 1955, p. 6.
23. *Al-mutamar al-Asyawi al-Ifriqi al-awwal* [The first Afro-Asian conference], English Appendix.
24. See Abdul Aziz Rifai, "Ittijahatina al-siyasiya nahwa qarati Asiya wa Ifriqiya" [The direction of our politics toward the continents of Asia and Africa], *Egyptian Political Science Review,* no. 39, June, 1964, p. 125.

Second—Work to include on the agenda of the conference a discussion of the Arab questions and schedule the question of Palestine with the world problems such as anti-imperialism, opposition to racial discrimination, disarmament and nuclear proliferation, etc.

Third—Send a representative from the General Secretariat of the League to observe and follow the work of the conference in cooperation with the Arab delegations.[25]

Nasser achieved two significant victories at the conference: the first was the scheduling of the Palestine problem on the agenda and the support for a resolution calling for "the implementation of the U.N. decisions concerning Palestine," and the second was the success of the Egyptian-sponsored proposal of a protest against French "imperialism" in North Africa. Nasser's most important personal success was persuading Nehru to agree to discuss the Palestine problem. Nehru had previously objected to any such discussion because he felt it was a regional problem. Through Nasser's personal persuasion, Nehru allowed the issue to be placed on the agenda and he supported the resolution.[26] He also called for immediate peace talks between the Arab countries and their adversary. *Al-Ahram* proclaimed, "The campaign was led by President Nasser to win over the conference to the necessity of condemning Israel."[27]

By associating such Arab problems as Palestine and North Africa with the problem of imperialism, Nasser was able to keep these questions within the context of Afro-Asian issues and rally the support of the participating nations behind him. He "did not forget the objectives of the conference," noted a Cairo newspaper. "He always remembered . . . it was a conference for the Afro-Asian nations and nobody had the right to take it out of this context."[28] This was a carefully planned tactic, the foundation of which

25. *Al-mutamar al-Asyawi al-Ifriqi al-awwal* [The first Afro-Asian conference], pp. 19–20.

26. *Al-Ahram,* April 23, 1955, p. 1. Prior to the conference, Nasser succeeded also in having Israel excluded from participation.

27. *Al-Ahram,* April 22, 1955, p. 1.

28. *Al-Akhbar,* May 4, 1955, p. 1.

had been prepared in advance; in March, 1955, the Political Committee of the League of Arab States had made recommendations to the Council to achieve the following at Bandung:

A. Discuss the subject of imperialism in connection with the demands of the Arab countries that are struggling for their independence.

B. Request the Afro-Asian states to support the questions of Palestine and North Africa, especially Algeria . . . and all the problems of the non-participating Arab countries.

C. Representation of the general secretary in the conference and the attendance of delegates of non-participating Arab nations as observers.

D. Organize communications between the Afro-Asian bloc for the discussion of common problems that will be debated in the General Assembly of the U.N. . . . and coordinate . . . and cooperate to achieve membership for their regions in the U.N. and representation on her committees and specialized agencies.[29]

The conference was Nasser's first visit outside Egypt as prime minister. It gave him the opportunity to establish personal contact with the leaders of emerging Afro-Asian nations and helped to create a friendly atmosphere. The Arab League official publication described this effect:

This conference created a change in the atmosphere of Afro-Asian relations. . . . The exchange of opinions during the sessions of the conference and its committees and the private discussions that occurred outside the conference had a great effect on creating friendships and destroying the spirit of doubt and suspicion which overshadowed the relations between the states of this area of the world.[30]

Nasser increased his stature and power in the Middle East and Africa through his association which such men as Nehru, Sukarno,

29. *Al-mutamar al-Asyawi al-Ifriqi al-awwal* [The first Afro-Asian conference], pp. 24–25.

30. *Ibid,,* p. 8.

and Chou En-lai. His visits on the way to and returning from the conference and subsequent visits with other world leaders were diplomatic moves to supplement his success. Chou En-lai "launched a diplomatic courtship" with Nasser and "in effect" invited him to visit China.[31] In describing the importance of this meeting, *Al-Ahram* stated:

> Nehru was very successful in establishing friendly and cordial relations between President Nasser, the leader of the largest and strongest state on the African continent, and Chou En-lai, the head of the largest and strongest state on the Asian continent. The fight against and expulsion of imperialism on these two continents is strongly connected with the friendly and cordial relations between the Egyptian leader and the Chinese leader. Each of them played his role at the Bandung Conference with great success.[32]

As Nasser observed, the Bandung Conference was the first time that "the states of Africa and Asia met . . . without the participation of the powers that control them."[33] It not only gave these states an insight into the role they could play in international relations, it also gave Nasser a vision of the role he could play as spokesman for the African nationalist movements; at the conference he naturally appeared as their leader since he was the only modern African nationalist at the head of a sovereign nation. That Nasser consciously aspired to this role is indicated by an editorial in *Al-Jumhuriya* on the occasion of his return from the conference:

> Africa, our glorious homeland, meets you today . . . as it never met a revolutionary before. Did you not struggle for her peace and security and the rights of her people to live without imperialism?[34]

31. *New York Times,* April 16, 1955, p. 1.
32. May 1, 1955, p. 6.
33. *Al-Ahram,* May 3, 1955, p. 1.
34. May 2, 1955, p. 4.

FORMULATION OF A POLICY: 1956-1957

If the Bandung Conference had indeed indicated that "the age of Asia and Africa has begun," as *Rose El-Youssief* heralded,[35] then Egypt, at the crossroads of these two continents, was in a position to play a vital role in the Third World. To facilitate this, however, Egypt's foreign policy required a reorientation toward the south and east. Commenting on this, an Egyptian writer stated:

> Why don't we start today to establish a post of assistant minister of foreign affairs for the African continent? . . . We Egyptians should be the first to have closer relations with the nations of the conference. We should begin to concentrate a great part of our external political effort on improving our relations with the people of the two large continents through constant consultation, closer connections, exchange of . . . treaties, exchange of aid, and assistance . . . which will result in the end in the concentration of the power of the two continents. Therefore, Egypt should begin now to take the first practical steps in its foreign policy toward the two great continents.[36]

Enhancing this role for Egypt, and even surpassing it, was the mantle of leadership Nasser had assumed over the African nationalist movements. In pointing this out, an Egyptian delegate to the U.N. declared, "the destiny of Egypt is closely connected with the African continent because she became the leader and her leadership was recognized on this continent."[37] But Egypt's policy at this time was far too limited to offer effective leadership to the floodtide of nationalism awakening in Africa. "Africa will be swept away by floods of nationalism, and disturbance and disorder will continue during the year," observed *Al-Jumhuriya* in predicting the outlook for 1955. "The nationalists, black and white, will cooperate on the expulsion of imperialism and the destruction of the European

35. No. 1466, July 16, 1956, p. 3.

36. Tawfiq al-Shamali, "Nahwa al-sharq" [Toward the East], *Al-Ahram*, May 16, 1955, p. 9.

37. *Al-Jumhuriya*, April 18, 1956, p. 1.

colonies."[38] For Egypt to participate fully in this movement the formulation of a vigorous African policy was required.

These were the major considerations that resulted in the extension of Egypt's African policy. However, overriding even these issues was the failure of the Unity of the Nile Valley policy in the Sudan. The Sudanese Parliament's declaration of independence on December 19, 1955, a result of this failure, brought about a re-evaluation of Egypt's Sudan policy within an African context. As early as August, 1955, Major Saleh Salem's telegram to the Sudan government, congratulating them on the occasion of the beginning of this evacuation of British troops, indicated the new African orientation:

> We Africans should congratulate ourselves for the liberation of a spot on our continent from the foreign occupation which came to us a long time ago. In these critical moments in the history of the nations of Egypt and the Sudan our hearts are full of hope directed toward our brothers who are still living under the tyranny of imperialism and occupation on this African continent, wishing the Lord to lead them to success in their struggle.[39]

Thus, after the Bandung Conference Egypt moved rapidly toward the formulation of an effective African policy. In January, 1956, Nasser ordered the formulation of the Supreme Committee to Supervise African Affairs in order to draw outlines of Egypt's political, economic, social, and religious policy in sub-Saharan Africa. Egypt's highest-ranking government officials were appointed to the committee.[40]

The committee produced detailed recommendations for an African policy, including objective methods of implementation. In time, these recommendations actually became Egyptian policy. The program produced by the committee stated:

38. January 1, 1955, p. 3.

39. *Al-Ahram,* August 17, 1955, p. 1.

40. These included: Lt. Col. Zakaria Mohieddin, the minister of interior; Dr. Abdul Mun'im al-Qaisuni, the minister of finance; Lt. Gen. Muhammad Sayf al-Yazal Khalifa, ambassador to the Sudan; the economic chancellor of the Egyptian Embassy in Khartoum; and "others of those interested in African affairs that the committee deems can help" (*Rose El-Youssief,* no. 1442, January 30, 1956, p. 4).

Egypt has to plan its African policy on the basis of "Africa for the Africans" and to direct this policy to Africa's liberation from foreign influence, politically, economically, socially, culturally, and militarily. It must also defend the Rights of Man which claim liberty for all and an equality in rights without distinction of race, religion, or language. It must endeavor to unify the peoples of the continent and discover a tie to join them so that they may form a united bloc in economy, defense, and politics vis-à-vis the big blocs now existing in the world. It must also ensure that Africa with its peoples and resources shall be on the side of peace and not be an implement employed for warmongering, but stand together in international cooperation on the basis of liberty and equality and not as victims for exploitation.[41]

In February, 1956, Mahmud Fawzi, the minister of foreign affairs, began preparations for an African Affairs Section in his ministry to implement this policy. In July, 1956, Lt. Gen. Taha Fatih al-Din was appointed the director of this section. The appointment of such a high-ranking military official indicates the importance of the department to the Egyptian government.

Anti-imperialism was the "tie" sought by the Supreme Committee to Supervise African Affairs—the common thread with which Egypt would attempt to unite the African people. By the time of Britain's evacuation of the Sudan, Egypt was endeavoring to interpret each country's struggle for independence within the context of a broader struggle against imperialism. This was apparent in *Al-Ahram's* commentary on the independence of Sudan:

> We are picking the fruit of our common struggle today in the Khartoum; tomorrow we'll pick the fruit in the Canal, North Africa, and each corner of the revolutionary African con-

41. This material was actually published in the semi-official journal *Egyptian Economic and Political Review,* II (August, 1956), 21–24, under the title, "An African Policy for Egypt," written by "a special correspondent." In my opinion, these are, in fact, the recommendations of the Supreme Committee to Supervise African Affairs, for they reflect the policy followed by Egypt and are the basis of all later publications on African policy. The *Times* (London) stated: "A detailed program for the assumption by Egypt of leadership of the African Continent is suggested. . . . *The Egyptian Economic and Political Review* . . . article is anonymous but probably presents government policy" (October 2, 1956, p. 6); see Appendix I for the full text of this article.

tinent that every day offers a number of its sons as fuel for the fight for liberty—a small sacrifice on the altar of dignity and independence.[42]

At the Bandung Conference Nasser had met many African leaders and had offered them protection:

> This was accompanied by African leaders arriving in Cairo to escape from imperialism. . . . They found in Cairo security, comfort, and freedom of . . . action. African Bureaus were established in Cairo representing the nationalist movements in Kenya, Nigeria, Uganda, Somalia, Guinea, and others.[43]

Through the establishment of African Bureaus in Cairo, Egypt attempted to perpetuate and nurture anti-Western sentiments and rally African nationalists behind the anti-imperialist banner. For example, they used Cairo radio facilities to broadcast anti-Western propaganda throughout Africa. By allowing Cairo to become the headquarters of African liberation movements, Egypt attempted to become identified as the center for African liberation. An Egyptian journalist asserted that "Egypt's message in the second half of the twentieth century . . . is to become the freedom bridge of African liberation."[44]

In an ironic way the Western powers aided Egypt in its realization of this role. Because of the Anglo-French-Israeli aggression of October–November, 1956, Egypt became the tangible symbol of resistance to imperialism, even though, in reality, it suffered a military defeat. Oginga Odinga, a former vice-president of Kenya, summarized the African attitude toward the Suez fiasco:

> It was the abortive Suez adventure of 1956, the twentieth-century exercise in gunboat diplomacy, that failed, that united all Africa, and Africa with Asia and the Arab world, to give a great spurt forward to national independence. An African

42. August 9, 1955, p. 7.

43. "Al-Qahira al-haditha markaz li al-wa'y al-Ifriqi al-mustanir" [Modern Cairo is the center of African enlightened consciousness], *Egyptian Political Science Review*, no. 41, August, 1964, p. 6.

44. Mishal Kamil, *Al-Isti'mar fi Ifriqiya* [*Imperialism in Africa*] (Cairo: Nasr Publishing Organization, 1958).

state, backed by the socialist world, repulsed with ignominy the concerted attack of several of the world's leading powers of which even the United States was critical. Africa was never the same after Suez and the coming into play on the continent and in the world of the forces of Pan-Africanism.[45]

In early 1957, Egypt made an unsuccessful attempt to form a military alliance with Ethiopia and the Sudan. Visits among the three heads of state were made and close contacts maintained. In April, 1957, Emperor Haile Selassie of Ethiopia and Abdullah Khalil, prime minister of the Sudan, met in Cairo to "discuss a number of important questions which concerned the African continent."[46] The prospects of a "Cairo–Khartoum–Addis Ababa axis" were examined. Egypt apparently was seeking a "tripartite conference of the states of the Nile Valley to study the prospects of a union among the three."[47] It was hoped that such an alliance would serve as the nucleus for African unity and eventually develop into a "Greater State of the Nile Valley," encompassing the Sudan, Somalia, Ethiopia, Egypt, and Uganda.

By mid-1957, Egypt was preparing to take a positive role in African affairs. With the failure of the Cairo–Khartoum–Addis Ababa axis, Egypt began directing its African policy at the nongovernmental level. Its involvement in Africa was principally manifested in its attempts to unite the African liberation movements under its leadership. This policy direction was clearly stated by a government publication commemorating the fifth anniversary of the Egyptian revolution:

> Egypt's foreign policy is based on work for the benefit of Africa and the Africans. For this Egypt will strive to strengthen its relations with all the countries of Africa and continuously

45. *Not Yet Uhuru* (London: Heinemann Educational Books, 1967), p. 175.

46. *Rose El-Youssief*, no. 1505, April 15, 1957, p. 4.

47. Muhammad Kamal Abdul-Hamid, *Al-Sharq al-Awsat fi al-mizan al-istratiji* [The Middle East in the strategic balance] (Cairo: The Modern Publishing House, n.d.), p. 321. Nasser's attempt to form a "tripartite pact" was apparently partly motivated by his fear that Ethiopia would attempt to intervene in the Nile-waters agreement between Sudan and Egypt. At the end of 1957, Ethiopia did attempt to become part of those negotiations (*Rose El-Youssief*, no. 1536, November 18, 1957, p. 7). See Chapters Three and Seven for a fuller discussion of the alliance.

endeavor to tie the nations and states of this continent to it
and continue the effort toward the liberation of the continent
from imperialism and exploitation.[48]

In late 1957 the African Association was established in order
to consolidate the African Bureaus and more effectively coordinate
their activities with Egyptian policy. As the African states achieved
independence, the leaders of the liberation movements would constitute an influential factor in shaping their governments' policies.
By establishing rapport with them at that time, Egypt hoped to gain
influence in the future. The African nationalists in Cairo "continued
their activities . . . within the limits of the African Association."[49]

The African Association sponsored celebrations for African
states achieving independence, protests against imperialism, and
trips to Egypt by African dignitaries. It also published periodicals
such as the monthly journals *Nahdhat Ifriqiya* [Renaissance of
Africa] and *Al-Rabita al-Ifriqiya* [The African Association].[50] Such
activities on the part of the African Association not only made Cairo
appear to be the center of African nationalism but presented Nasser
as the spokesman for Africa's liberation.

IMPLEMENTATION OF THE POLICY: 1958-1960

The Afro-Asian Solidarity Conference, held in Cairo in December,
1957, represented Egypt's first major attempt to implement its
African policy of organizing the liberation movements under its

48. Republic of Egypt, Ministry of National Guidance, *Al-thawra al-Misrya fi
khams sanawat* [The Egyptian revolution in five years], Political Books Series
Special Issue (Cairo: Political Books Committee, 1957), p. 115.

49. Abdul Malik Auda, "Tatwor al-alaqat al-'Arabiya al-Ifriqiya fi ashar sanawat" [The development of Arab-African relations in ten years], *Egyptian Political
Science Review*, no. 16, July, 1962, p. 99.

50. Both journals are entirely devoted to African issues and are circulated
throughout the continent. The aims of *Nahdhat Ifriqiya*, as described on the first
page of each issue, are: "(1) promotion of African national consciousness; (2)
acquaintance between Africans in various regions and environments; (3) publication of private and public treatises of interest to Africans whatever their pur-
suits." *Al-Rabita al-Ifriqiya's* objective, as described on the cover of each issue,
is "to express the African nationalist point of view in an atmosphere of freedom
and understanding."

leadership within an Afro-Asian framework. Such a framework justified Egypt's involvement in both the Middle East and Africa. Also, the idea of an Afro-Asian community could provide Egypt with bargaining power in the international sphere. The scope and potential of such a movement was described by Anwar al-Sadat, the chairman of the Preparatory Committee for the Afro-Asian Solidarity Conference:

> We, the people of Asia and Africa, comprise 37 states which include three-quarters of the globe's inhabitants. . . . We are rising as a new force. . . . The foundations began at Bandung, but these foundations must grow and expand.[51]

The concept of Afro-Asianism was not new. However, the idea of an Afro-Asian movement at the nongovernmental party level was unique. The Afro-Asian Solidarity Conference was an attempt to "mobilize the nationalist forces in the Afro-Asian countries to fight imperialism in all its forms throughout the world."[52]

Youssief al-Sabai, general secretary of the Preparatory Committee, stressed the development of an Afro-Asian movement as the primary aim of the conference:

> The aims of this conference are to strengthen the solidarity of the Afro-Asian nations through the mobilization of the national forces in these countries . . . and to promote acquaintance among the people through cooperation in all . . . fields.[53]

Nasser also expressed a similar objective when he said, "I hope that this conference will play a great role in strengthening and supporting the relations between Afro-Asian countries."[54]

Egypt considered the international climate ripe for such a conference for several reasons: the policy of positive neutrality was considered successful; the "socialist camp" was believed to have

51. Quoted in "Ma'aradh al-shahr" [The exhibition of the month], *Nahdhat Ifriqiya*, no. 2, December, 1957, pp. 38–39.

52. Muhammad Anis, *Al-Mutamar al-Asyawi al-Ifriqi* [The Afro-Asian conference], We Choose for You Series, no. 44 (Cairo: We Choose for You Committee, n.d.), pp. 204–5.

53. Quoted in "Ma'aradh al-shahr" [The exhibition of the month], p. 39.

54. Quoted in *ibid.*, p. 38.

demonstrated superiority in the strategic and scientific fields; the nationalist movements in Africa and Asia were gaining strength; and the "imperialist" powers were departing from Africa and Asia.[55] To insure the success of the conference, Egypt attempted to make it broadly representative and unleashed a widespread propaganda campaign to popularize and publicize it: delegates were sent throughout Africa; handbooks on each country attending the conference were prepared; bulletins in Arabic and English were published; and radio programs and press campaigns were organized.[56]

The results of the conference were to bear witness to Egypt's influence and leadership, not only at the regional level but also at the international level. To insure the success of the conference and to avoid its becoming a mere debating session, Nasser appointed Egypt's highest-ranking intellectuals, publicists, and government officials to the Preparatory Committee.[57] In his opening address, Youssief al-Sabai, general secretary of the conference, emphasized that the conference should prepare a program to achieve tangible results in the development of Afro-Asian solidarity:

> When we call upon the peoples of Asia and Africa to unite for the realization of these glorious aspirations, we do not mean to call upon them to partake in dreams or to exchange compliments. We call upon them to act, to define our common objectives and to mark the road for reaching them, to mobilize our forces, to stand shoulder to shoulder and move forward toward these objectives inspired by faith, confidence and resolution.[58]

55. Anis, *Al-Mutamar al-Asyawi al-Ifriqi* [The Afro-Asian conference], pp. 20–22; see also, Abdul Mun'im Shmayis and Abdul Adhim Mahmud, *Tadhamun al-shu'ub al-asyawi al-Ifriqi* [Afro-Asian solidarity], Political Books Series, no. 45 (Cairo: Political Books Committee, 1958), pp. 226–27. Both books emphasized the importance of the "international climate."

56. *Mutamar al-shu'ub al-Ifriya al-Asyawi* [The Afro-Asian peoples' conference] *26 December 1957–1 January 1958* (Cairo: Afro-Asian Solidarity Council, n.d.), p. 21.

57. The members of the Preparatory Committee were Anwar al-Sadat, Youssief al-Sabai, Abdul Qader Hatim, Muhammad Hassanein Heikal, Muhammad Fuad Jalal, Khalid Muhiddin, Taha Hussain, Zakaria Lutfi Guma, Muhammad Fahmi al-Sayed, Najib Mahfudh, Ihsan Abdul 'Quddus, Salah Abdul Hafez, Ahmad Bahai al-Din (Anis, *Al-Mutamar al-Asyawi al-Ifriqi* [The Afro-Asian conference], p. 203).

58. *Mutamar al-shu'ub al-Ifriqiya al-Asyawi* [The Afro-Asian peoples' conference], p. 19.

40

To insure its leadership of the conference, Egypt attempted to maintain control of the various committees. Two of the five committees were headed by Egyptians: the Organizational Committee and the Cultural Committee. In addition, the Economic Committee was headed by a pro-Nasser Syrian, and the Social Committee, upon the insistence of the Egyptian delegation, had a rotating chairmanship. Also, on the recommendation of the Egyptian delegation, an Indian was appointed chairman of the Political Committee.

Although the conference had been organized in close cooperation with the Soviet Union, Egypt did attempt to keep it within the neutralist context. Zakaria Lutfi Guma toured Africa prior to the conference to assure African leaders that the conference would reflect a neutral orientation and would not be Communist dominated. However, the conference was successfully exploited by the Communist bloc, which was strongly represented.[59] Some of the African delegations, such as Sudan, Tunisia, Morocco, Ethiopia, and Ghana, were reported to have become "angered at the heavy overtones of communist propaganda emanating from the first day's proceedings."[60] In the end, the final resolutions of the conference reflected this influence rather than a neutralist orientation. This somewhat discredited the conference among neutral and Western nations. Also, the friction between the many factions represented at the conference (which Egypt attributed to imperialism)[61] limited its success in organizing a strong Afro-Asian movement.

Egyptian propaganda, however, ignored these problems and presented the conference as a successful continuation of the results achieved at Bandung. Comments by the Egyptian cabinet members emphasized this. Kamil al-Din Husain, the minister of education, declared: "We consider that the Afro-Asian Solidarity Conference opened a new chapter in history that will be a continuation to the

59. *New York Times,* December 28, 1957, p. 1. Iran, Turkey, Pakistan, the Philippines, Saudi Arabia, and Iraq refused to allow delegations to attend the conference because of the strong Communist influence (*Rose El-Youssief,* no. 1543, January 6, 1958, p. 3). For a fuller discussion of the Communist activities at the conference, see Chapter Three.

60. *New York Times,* December 27, 1957, p. 1.

61. *Rose El-Youssief,* no. 1543, January 6, 1958, p. 3.

41

chapter that was opened by the Bandung Conference." Ali Sabry, the minister of presidential affairs, stated that

> The conference accomplished its purpose. . . . It will have tremendous influence on the future, no less than did the Bandung Conference. That was a connection between the Afro-Asian governments, but the Afro-Asian Peoples' Conference is a connection between the people.

In fact, the conference did represent a success for Egypt. It was the first major attempt to organize Afro-Asian movements at the party level, and it brought international prestige to Cairo. As Abdul Latif al-Baghdadi, president of the National Assembly, stated: "This is a beginning that will be followed by progress . . . for the nations of this area. In the near future they will become a power . . . that will be counted."[62]

More significantly, the conference increased Egypt's prestige among the African nations as a potent force against imperialism. At the conference Egypt established important contacts throughout the continent. The establishment of the Cairo based Afro-Asian Solidarity Council, with an Egyptian as president, gave Egypt control of the only Afro-Asian organization and provided a strong propaganda tool for Egyptian policy.

Egypt also attempted to seek international support for its struggle to create a unified African liberation movement under its leadership. The Egyptian delegation to the U.N. was given full authority to sponsor African issues. Egyptian diplomacy and propaganda sought support in the name of humanity and liberty. An Egyptian journalist observed:

> The liberation of Africa . . . is an international question. For its success we have to coordinate the African liberation movements and support the collective struggle between the nations of Africa and consolidate all the forces that support African liberation whether in the socialist camp or even among the Western nations. . . . In this respect, Egypt has a great responsibility.[63]

62. *Al-Ahram,* January 2, 1958, p. 1.

The Egyptian attempt to establish leadership over Africa did not go unchallenged. In April, 1958, Nkrumah sponsored the Conference of Independent African States in Accra in an attempt to increase the international prestige of Ghana and his own personal influence among African leaders.

Nkrumah presented a direct threat to Nasser's objectives for several reasons. First, in contrast to Nasser's policies, Nkrumah maintained friendly relations with the West. Ghana also maintained friendly relations with, and received economic and technical aid from, Israel. Second, Nkrumah was eager to organize a Pan-African movement, and such a movement could undermine Egypt's role both in the Middle East and in Africa. In his address to the Accra conference, Dr. Mahmud Fawzi, minister of foreign affairs and head of the U.A.R. delegation, reminded the delegates of Egypt's dual responsibilities: "The U.A.R. assures you humbly and firmly that she realizes her dual responsibilities as both an African and an Asian state."[64]

However, the potential threat of the Conference of Independent African States to Egypt's policy was minimized by two occurrences. First, the international importance of the conference was reduced when it descended from the summit to the foreign ministers' level. Nasser dropped out first, followed by Bourguiba and the Libyan prime minister. (The only head of state to attend other than Nkrumah was Tubman of Liberia.)

The second development that affected the Accra conference was the unexpected attendance of Algerian and Cameroonian nationalist representatives.[65] (Three of these four representatives worked within

---

63. Kamil, *Al-Isti'mar fi Ifriqiya* [Imperialism in Africa], p. 1. The U.A.R. government yearbook of 1959 declared that the main objectives of the U.A.R.'s foreign relations "stand on the principle of working for peace and a ban on nuclear weapons, and disarmament for the benefit of humanity. This policy aims at the achievement of positive principles in the life of the Afro-Asian nations especially. These principles are (1) support for self-determination; (2) support for the nations in achieving their independence; and (3) work to stop power politics" (U.A.R. Information Department, *Al-Kitab al-sanawi* [The yearbook], *1959* [Cairo: 1959], p. 55).

64. *Al-Ahram,* April 16, 1958, p. 1.

65. The four nationalists were Muhammad Yahya, Liberation Front representative in Cairo; Muhammad Yazid, Algerian National Liberation Front representative in New York; Rashid Gayd, general secretary of the Confederation of

the framework of the African Association in Cairo.) Their arrival embarrassed Ghana because at that time it had not yet recognized the Algerian Provisional Government. The Algerian problem united the delegates and overshadowed basic divisions such as those between the pro- and anti-Western factions, black and Arab Africans, and Anglophonic and Francophonic Africans. The arrival of these representatives, however, was most advantageous to the U.A.R., for the Algerian issue kept Nasser's increasing conflict with Sudan and Tunisia from rising to the surface and focused the attention of the conference on French imperialism in Arab North Africa. The result was that four out of the five sessions of the conference were devoted to this problem. The U.A.R.'s official publication on the conference stated that

> Although the Accra conference was called because of the efforts of Nkrumah, the prime minister of Ghana, its meetings will be held under the shadow of Nasser and in general under the shadow of the five Arab states represented in the conference which will have the majority of the votes when decisions are made.[66]

The U.A.R. used the conference to improve its contacts with African leaders. Dr. Fawzi held private consultations with all the delegates, and stated that "One of the results . . . of this conference is that it is the prelude to more communication, consultation, and exchange of information between the African states."[67] Although the final resolutions were much more moderate than those of the Afro-Asian Solidarity Conference, they appeared as a sequel to the Cairo conference resolutions rather than as a uniquely African approach to world problems. The general secretary of the Afro-Asian Solidarity Council declared that

---

Algerian Workers, who was living in exile in Cairo; and Felix Moumie, president of the Union of the Cameroonian Populations, who also lived in exile in Cairo (*Rose El-Youssief,* no. 1559, April 28, 1958, p. 12).

66. U.A.R. Ministry of Foreign Affairs, *Nashra khassa al-mutamar al-duwal Ifriqiya al-mustaquilla* [Special bulletin on the Conference of Independent African States] (Cairo, May 25, 1958), p. 27.

67. *Ibid.,* p. 59.

The Accra conference has special importance because it was held in the first African colony to win independence. Its resolutions came as extensions to the resolutions of the Bandung conference and the Cairo conference and represent all the hopes that motivated us when we met in Cairo. It created the African tool on the governmental level to execute the resolutions of the Cairo conference.[68]

Throughout 1958, rivalry was developing between Nasser and Nkrumah for leadership of African nationalism. This rivalry was most clearly manifested in the propaganda campaign against cooperation with Israel and the West that Cairo radio transmitted to Ghana. However, the rivalry was also revealed in other more subtle ways. For example, when the Conference of Independent African States designated April 15 as Africa Freedom Day, the Afro-Asian Solidarity Council, in a move that Nkrumah regarded as an attempt to detract from Africa Freedom Day, designated December 1 as Quit Africa Day.

In June, 1958, Nkrumah visited Cairo. In spite of their wide political differences, especially with regard to Israel and the West, apparently neither Nasser nor Nkrumah wanted to create an open clash. Nasser attempted to minimize the discord by extending special personal courtesies. *Rose El-Youssief* made note of Nasser's unique attendance at Nkrumah's arrival in the following manner:

> It is usually the custom that the president only greets heads of state. It is customary to send a representative, vice-president, or minister to greet a head of government. The reason for this special treatment is Dr. Nkrumah's image as one of the leaders of the revolutionary movements in Africa.[69]

During Nkrumah's visit, plans for closer economic and cultural ties were developed. Nasser agreed to buy more of Ghana's cocoa; it was agreed to establish regular maritime links between the two countries (in spite of the fact that Ghana and Israel operated a joint shipping line); and the U.A.R. proposed to establish a regular

68. *Ibid.*, p. 60.
69. No. 1566, June 16, 1958, p. 9.

airline schedule to Ghana and also to supply Ghana with teachers and books.

When addressing Nkrumah during the June, 1958, visit, Nasser made clear that Egypt's involvement in Africa extended to the entire continent:

> We pledge you, here and now, that the United Arab Republic and the people of the United Arab Republic shall strive, as I have mentioned, with all determination and firmness for the sake of the liberation of Africa, and for the cause of supporting liberty and the peoples who struggle for the liberation of Africa, and for the freedom of their countries.[70]

Ghana's union with Guinea in November, 1958, to form a "nucleus for a Union of African States" was considered a challenge to Nasser's leadership. Shortly after the union, however, Nasser devoted a speech to the denial of the existence of rivalry. He claimed that there was no basis for rivalry since "we are in Northeast Africa while he is in Western Africa."[71]

In December, 1958, Nkrumah sponsored an All African Peoples' Conference. This conference, unlike the Conference of Independent African States held in Accra in April, was at the party level. Sixty-two organizations, including unions, from twenty-eight African countries and eight independent states sent official representatives.

At the announcement of the conference there was some question whether the U.A.R. should attend. However, Nasser decided to send a strong delegation of intellectuals and publicists that could overshadow even Ghana's delegation. The *New York Times*, in describing the delegation, stated:

> Their task at Ghana obviously is to see that the conference does not show too strong a Western feeling and to keep prominently before the delegations the name of Nasser and his role as freedom leader of Africa and the Middle East.[72]

70. Speech delivered on June 21, 1958 (*President Gamal Abdel Nasser on Africa*, comp. and trans. U.A.R. Information Department [Cairo, n.d.]).
71. Speech delivered on November 27, 1958 (*ibid.*, p. 12).

The rivalry between Nasser and Nkrumah was evident at this conference. There was an attempt to undermine Egypt's participation in African affairs by differentiating between North Africa and Black Africa and by stigmatizing Egypt's motives. Ahmad Bahai el-Din, a member of the Egyptian delegation, complained that "a great effort was made to isolate the U.A.R. at the conference. . . . These attempts were concentrated in a poisoned propaganda campaign . . . which asserted that the U.A.R. is an Arab, not an African, state."[73] Black Africans were suspicious of Egypt's intentions. This suspicion was intensified because Egypt was considered to have sent invitations to nationalist exiles living in Cairo and to the Afro-Asian group, although Egyptian officials denied it.

In January, 1959, Nkrumah made another visit to Cairo. When asked his opinion of Arab nationalism, he stated, "I believe in Afro-Arab nationalism, strong, united, and dynamic."[74] However, his attempts at unification were confined to Black Africa. In July, 1959, Ghana formed the Community of Independent African States with Liberia and Guinea. In December, 1960, Nkrumah met with Modibo Keïta and Sékou Touré. This meeting resulted in the formation of a special committee which met in Accra in January, 1961, to discuss proposals for a Ghana-Guinea-Mali union. In April, 1961, a charter was agreed upon. The U.A.R. was not included in any of these negotiations. In his book *Africa Must Unite*,[75] Nkrumah virtually ignored the U.A.R.'s role in African affairs. Nonetheless, both Nasser and Nkrumah continued to support one another verbally until Nkrumah's downfall in 1966.

---

72. November 30, 1958, p. 19. The ten-member delegation included Muhammad Fuad Jalal, president of the Arab Graduates Association; Ihsan Abdul Quddus, chief editor of *Rose El-Youssief;* and the editor of the Cairo morning newspaper, *Al-Sha'ab.* The remainder were university professors of high standing. Two were from Syria.

73. *Rose El-Youssief,* no. 1593, December 22, 1958, p. 3. The change in Egypt's policy orientation is apparent when this statement is compared with the statement made in 1954 by the Egyptian general secretary of the Arab League: "There is a malicious campaign . . . claiming that Egypt is an African state and has nothing to do with the countries situated in the Middle East region. But this is vicious propaganda that died the day it was conceived" (*Al-Ahram,* August 31, 1954, p. 7).

74. *Al-Ahram,* January 10, 1959, p. 5.

75. (New York: Praeger, 1963).

Evolution of the Policy

The Afro-Asian Youth Conference of January, 1959, had essentially the same purpose as the Afro-Asian Solidarity Conference —to establish Egyptian contact with an important segment of African society. Egypt recognized the "close association between the future and the youth."[76] The youth "spread through all sectors of society and constitute a dynamic force."[77] Emphasizing this idea, a well-known journal stated: "It is now the role of the youth to carry . . . complete responsibility . . . for the political and economic liberation of the two continents."[78]

The Afro-Asian Youth Conference was attended by delegations representing fifty-four Asian and African states. The final resolutions of the conference emphasized the main principles of Egypt's foreign policy: positive neutrality, Afro-Asian solidarity, and a denunciation of imperialism. The Egyptian press dramatized the importance of the conference. Kamil al-Din Husain, the central minister of education, made the conference the subject of the first lesson which he broadcast throughout Egypt via Radio Cairo after the mid-year vacation. Nasser himself addressed the opening session and stressed the significance of youth to the future. He even compared the conference in importance to the Bandung Conference and stated that it was a confirmation of the Bandung principles.[79] The U.A.R. government organized a very impressive program to entertain the delegates, and this aura of consequence which was given to the conference and to the role of youth in Asia and Africa could not but have had some impact on the youthful delegates.

By 1959, the U.A.R.'s primary foreign-policy activity had shifted to Africa. Ihsan Abdul Quddus, a prominent Egyptian journalist, stated that "the year 1959 will be the year of Africa. The center of activities will be transformed from the Middle East to the heart of the African continent."[80] There were several reasons for this

76. *Al-Ahram,* February 3, 1959, p. 1.

77. Mustafa al-Khudhari, *Al-shabab fi mujtama'una al-ishtiraki* [Youth in our socialist society], We Choose for the Student Series, no. 109 (Cairo: We have Chosen for the Student Committee, n.d.), p. 9.

78. *Al-Ahram al-Iqtisadi,* no. 83, February 1, 1959, p. 6.

79. *President Gamal Abdel Nasser's Speeches and Press Interviews, 1959,* comp. and trans. U.A.R. Information Department (Cairo, n.d.), p. 9.

80. "Bila khawf" [Without fear], *Rose El-Youssief,* no. 1604, March 9, 1959, p. 9.

development. Nasser's bid for leadership in the Arab world had been frustrated by formidable opposition, especially in Iraq, Tunisia, and Jordan. Also, Nkrumah's bid for African leadership and the increase of Israel's activities in Africa had caused the U.A.R. to meet these challenges by increasing and intensifying its own enterprises. Of even greater significance, however, was the growth of Africa's importance in the international domain.

The addition of thirteen African nations to the U.N. in 1960 could have resulted in an upheaval in the balance of power if they had voted as a bloc with the neutral Asian nations, and, indeed, the U.A.R. believed at that time that Africa would have a strong influence on international politics. Egyptian mass media described the fifteenth U.N. General Assembly session as the "African session":

> The African question . . . will be among the great questions to be discussed at this session. . . . All world opinion has agreed to give special importance to Africa's great effect on the future of humanity and the future of international peace. The fast and continuous development that was witnessed on the African continent this year proves the importance of the problems of this continent for the whole world.[81]

Nasser made his bid for leadership of the new African nations at this fifteenth U.N. General Assembly session in September, 1960. His decision to lead the U.A.R. delegation to the Assembly, along with world leaders representing the three major international blocs, was hailed as a "master stroke" by U.A.R. news media[82] and was considered a confirmation of the importance of the U.A.R. in the international domain. Mahmud Fawzi described Nasser's purpose at the U.N., stating, "The important international issues are not exclusive to the big powers. We . . . should participate in solving them."[83] In cooperation with Tito and Nkrumah, Nasser attempted to organize the African and Asian nations into an effec-

81. *Al-Ahram,* September 12, 1960, p. 6.
82. Nassir al-Din al-Nashashibi, "Dharbaa qadhiya" [A master stroke], *Al-Jumhuriya,* September 11, 1960, p. 1.
83. *Al-Ahram,* September 12, 1960, p. 1.

tive bloc. He appeared as the spokesman for them. Considering Nasser, the *New York Times* reported: "Almost unknown five years ago, today he is a spokesman to whom world leaders listened closely."[84] His speech to the assembly was described by a Cairo radio commentary as a proposal to internationalize the Bandung principles.[85]

The U.A.R. continued its bid for leadership of the new African states in the U.N. by championing African causes. For example, the U.A.R. delegation to the Technical Assistance Committee of the U.N. sponsored resolutions recommending that the Economic and Social Council issue a decision urging the secretary-general to increase the social aid offered to member states, particularly the African states.[86] Also, the U.A.R. insisted that the U.N.'s 1960 estimated budget for the African Economic Committee was not adequate and persuaded the Administrative and Budgetary Affairs Consultative Committee to agree to the figure the U.A.R. felt was sufficient. "The delegates also explained that the U.N. should employ all practical means for economic development of all African states and the raising of the living standards."[87]

Nasser's speeches in 1960 markedly stressed Africa. The pace of the U.A.R.'s diplomatic activities in Africa also indicated the shift in policy emphasis. In 1960, the U.A.R. sent delegations to the following African conferences: (1) the All African Peoples' Conference in Tunis in January; (2) the Emergency Accra Conference of April, at which the explosion of nuclear weapons in the Sahara was protested; (3) the Afro-Asian Solidarity Conference in Conakry in April; (4) the Conference of Independent African States in Addis Ababa in June; and (5) the Leopoldville Conference on Foreign Affairs in August.[88]

84. September 28, 1960, p. 16.

85. *Arab Observer,* October 9, 1960, p. 25.

86. U.A.R. Information Department, *Al-kitab al-sanawi* [The yearbook] *1960,* (Cairo, 1960), p. 821.

87. *Scribe* (Cairo), February 22, 1960, p. 93.

88. "The state participated in 1960 in the conferences that were held in the African continent. . . . At these conferences we declared our opinion clearly and candidly to support the just and help the nations to achieve independence and support their freedom" (U.A.R. Information Department, *Al-kitab al-sanawi* [The yearbook] *1961* [Cairo, 1961] pp. 210–13).

Also during 1960, many heads of state arrived in Cairo to confer with Nasser. In January, Mohammed V of Morocco arrived for a ten-day visit; in April, Sukarno of Indonesia arrived for a four-day visit; in July, President Ibrahim Abboud of the Sudan arrived for a week's visit; in October, King Mohammed Dahar Shah of Afghanistan arrived for a nine-day visit; and Muhammad Ayub Khan of Pakistan arrived for a week's visit in November. In all these meetings the heads of state affirmed the main principles of the U.A.R.'s foreign policy of nonalignment, Afro-Asian solidarity, aid for African liberation, and work for peace and disarmament.

> In Cairo the sons of Africa met, studying their problems and planning their future. . . . African leaders started coming to Cairo to strike with Abdel Nasser the future blow on the structure of imperialism.[89]

In July, 1960, Nasser held a conference with the U.A.R.'s ambassadors in Africa. Main items of discussion were the African activities of Israel, the conditions and potentialities of the countries about to become independent, and the attitude to be adopted by Egyptian embassies toward national movements in countries that were still "dominated by Colonialist rule."[90] Shortly thereafter, Nasser affirmed his support of the nationalist movements and the newly independent African states and offered them "commercial, cultural and military aid."[91]

These ideas were well expressed at the time by Ihsan Abdul Quddus:

> The U.A.R. is the center of liberalism radiating to all Africa. . . . The U.A.R. is not a negative state. It plays a positive role in supporting the fighting peoples. . . . It helps with its experienced counsel, arms, and aid.[92]

89. Arab Agency for Publications and Press, *Tisa sanawat tahta al-shams* [Nine years under the sun] (Cairo, 1961), p. 180.

90. *Arab Observer,* July 10, 1960, p. 20.

91. *Arab Review* (Cairo), I (September, 1960), 13.

92. "Al-Qadda al-'Arab fi Ifriqiya" [Arab leaders in Africa], *Rose El-Youssief,* no. 1699, January 2, 1961, p. 3.

51

Evolution of the Policy

One event indicative of the role played by the U.A.R. in the African liberation movements occurred in August, 1960. Josep Kiwanuka, chairman of the Uganda National Congress, rushed to Cairo to "expose a plot of British colonialism" which he claimed was attempting to arrange for the secession of Buganda Province. A stream of cables was sent out from Cairo to the British colonial secretary and the British governor of Uganda "strongly protesting against the British maneuvers to stage another Katanga farce."[93]

Meanwhile, the considerable increase in the number of independent African states had an even greater significance for the U.A.R.'s role in African affairs. There were several reasons for this. After the Suez crisis, the U.A.R. had appeared as the only champion of freedom and liberation in Africa, and the liberation movements had looked to it for support. The U.A.R. also had helped focus world attention on Africa by appearing as its spokesman at the international level. However, as independent governments, the former liberation movements no longer required the U.A.R.'s support. They appeared as their own spokesmen, and through strength in numbers alone they overwhelmed the international realm. The fifteenth and sixteenth U.N. General Assembly sessions were dominated by African issues, and the African states held the majority of votes in the Afro-Asian bloc (twenty-five to twenty-one). Their support was coveted by all factions, and the big powers courted the Afro-Asian states with prodigious amounts of aid and assistance. No longer would the U.A.R. appear as their mentor against colonialism but as their ally against imperialism. Nasser indicated such adjustment when he stated:

> In Africa, the year 1960 was one of festivity for the achievement of independence, and the year 1961 must be one of assiduous efforts for the protection of this independence and the consolidation of African cooperation.[94]

By the end of 1960, the independent African nations appeared to be coalescing into two informal groupings based on policy orientation and colonial background. This trend became apparent at the

93. *Arab Observer,* August 28, 1960, p. 18.
94. *Arab Review* (Cairo), I (January, 1961), 87.

Addis Ababa Conference of Independent African States of June, 1960. Cleavages between the African states developed because of their different approaches to the problems of colonialism, imperialism, and, most basic of all, African unity itself. The two groups that appeared could be broadly classed as "moderate" and "radical." The disparity between the two groups intensified during the fifteenth U.N. General Assembly session. The "moderate" African nations supported U.N. action in the Congo; the "radical" nations opposed it. The moderate states were represented by the Sudan, Nigeria, Ethiopia, Togo, Liberia, and Cameroon; the radical, or anti-imperialist, states were represented by the U.A.R., Ghana, Guinea, and Mali.[95]

The coalition of French-speaking African states, formed at the Brazzaville Conference of December, 1960, established the first formal grouping. The members shared a common language, a similar colonial background, and economic and political interests. The conference established the principles of economic cooperation and nonalignment in foreign policy.[96] The Brazzaville Group was composed of the Republic of Cameroon, Central African Republic, Congo Republic (Brazzaville), Dahomey, Gabon, Ivory Coast, Madagascar, Mauritania, Niger, Senegal, Chad, and Upper Volta.[97]

In January, 1961, the Casablanca Conference was called together by King Mohammed V of Morocco in order

> to organize the role which will be played by the independent African countries to help the Congo and Algeria in their struggle against imperialism and to study the special case of the African states that will achieve independence in the near future and also to discuss the aid that should be offered to these newly independent states.[98]

95. See A. K. Barden, "The Evolution of African Unity," *Voice of Africa* (Accra), III (February; March; April, 1963), 29–31.

96. See Doudou Thiam, *The Foreign Policy of African States: Ideological Bases, Present Realities, Future Prospects* (New York: Praeger, 1965), pp. 53–54.

97. Thomas F. Brady, discussing this tendency, in an article in the *New York Times*, saw two blocs developing—radical and moderate. He stated: "There is a wide separation between the radical and the moderate African states on most issues except that of Algeria" ("Africans' Dream of Unity Fading," January 1, 1961, p. 13).

98. *Al-Ahram*, December 21, 1960, p. 1.

Evolution of the Policy

Although invitations were sent to most African countries (with the exception of the French Community states), the only heads of state to attend were Nasser, Nkrumah, Touré, and Keïta. Ferhat Abbas represented the Algerian Provisional Government, Libya sent its foreign minister, and the Ceylonese ambassador to Cairo was an observer. The countries represented at Casablanca were generally considered more radical in their approach to anti-imperialism and nationalism in Africa than were those who attended the Brazzaville Conference. In commenting on the Casablanca Conference, *Al-Ahram* stated:

> The Casablanca bloc is the first meeting of free Africa that includes the heads of the states that affirmed their independence and protected it from any bond . . . which might affect its free will. It is the voice that comes purely from the conscience of Africa nd speaks in its name.[99]

The conference issued a comprehensive program in the form of an African Charter to specify "the means by which . . . [the countries participating in the Casablanca Conference] can destroy anything that threatens sovereignty, freedom, security, peace, and material growth of Africa's nations."[100] It proposed the creation of an African Consultative Assembly composed of representatives from every African state. The Assembly was to maintain permanent headquarters and hold regular sessions. The Charter provided for the establishment of political, economic, and cultural committees "to coordinate the policies of African nations in these fields." It also provided for a joint African High Command made up of the chiefs of staff of independent African countries. A Liaison Office was to be established to coordinate the activities of the committees. The resolutions supported Lumumba and called for the withdrawal of troops from the U.N. command in the Congo. The resolutions embodied the following objectives:

1. Liquidation of colonial regimes and liberation of colonial territories

99. December 28, 1960, p. 6.
100. *Al-Ahram*, January 2, 1961, p. 6.

2. Elimination of all forms of racial segregation in Africa
3. Resistance against all forms of old and new colonialism
4. Consolidation of mutual defense of new African states
5. A build-up of African unity
6. Reaffirmation of Africa's neutralism
7. Evacuation of all occupation troops from Africa
8. The exclusion of all nuclear experiments from Africa
9. The prevention of foreign intervention in African affairs
10. Action to consolidate world peace.[101]

The African Charter guaranteed the U.A.R. a voice in African affairs. According to *Al-Jumhuriya,*

> The feeling of solidarity between African nations liberated from imperialism was an established fact. But it was not an effective fact because it lacked the organization that would turn it into a positive element in the achievement of comprehensive African liberation. The Casablanca Conference laid down the general principles and established the necessary machinery to turn the feeling of African solidarity into a positive and effective force.[102]

Agreement on the broad aspects of the African Charter was attained through compromises on specific issues, for each nation sought recognition for its individual problems: Morocco wanted support for its claim to Mauritania; Ghana sought support for its Congo position; and Guinea, Mali, and Ghana desired an alliance vis-à-vis the Brazzaville Group of African nations.[103] It was in this context that the U.A.R. was able to achieve the far-reaching condemnation of Israel as "the instrument of imperialism and neo-colonialism in the Middle East, Africa and Asia."[104] As an official of the Arab League described it,

> The resolution . . . concerning the Israeli question is by itself an historic event recording a great victory for the Arab position.

101. *Times* (London), January 5, 1961, p. 9.
102. January 9, 1961, p. 1.
103. See Thiam, *The Foreign Policy of African States,* p. 62.
104. *Arab Review* (Cairo), I (January, 1961), 10.

> This victory . . . makes our struggle with Zionism a part of the Afro-Asian struggle against imperialism, discrimination and capitalism.[105]

However, the resolution had little effect on Israel's friendly relations with Ghana and Guinea.

The Casablanca Conference presented Nasser with an opportunity to keep the U.A.R. associated with African issues as well as for more contact with sub-Saharan African governments.[106] It was the first African conference that Nasser personally attended, and he was accompanied by an impressive delegation of the U.A.R.'s highest-ranking government officials.[107] In his address to the conference Nasser emphasized the development of a realistic "African personality" and stated his desire for a united African action.[108] In a speech before the U.A.R. National Assembly, Nasser outlined the U.A.R.'s position at the conference and described the points laid out by the U.A.R. delegation: (1) the problems of Algeria and the Congo as a part of the struggle against imperialism on the African continent; (2) the problems of Africa as problems of world peace; (3) socioeconomic development of Africa as the base for political freedom; (4) the importance of the U.N. in the liberation of Africa; (5) the usefulness of the U.N. as an instrument to keep the Cold War out of Africa; (6) the importance of unity to the African struggle; (7) the importance of working within a realistic framework of capabilities and goals.[109] The type of role that Nasser sought

105. Clovis Maksud, "Mutamar al-aqtab al-Ifriqiyyin wa Israil" [The African summit conference and Israel], *Al-Ahram al-Iqtisadi,* no. 130, January 15, 1961, p. 9.

106. It also gave Nasser the opportunity to meet Mobido Keïta and Sékou Touré personally for the first time. See *President Gamal Abdel-Nasser's Speeches and Press Interviews, 1961,* comp. and trans. U.A.R. Information Department (Cairo, n.d.), p. 2; hereafter referred to as *Nasser's Speeches, 1961.*

107. The delegation consisted of Dr. Mahmud Fawzi, minister of foreign affairs; Zakaria Mohieddin, central minister of the interior; Ali Sabry, minister of presidential affairs; Mahmud Riadh, the president's advisor; Dr. Murad Ghaleb, former ambassador to the Congo; Asa'ad Mahassin, ambassador to Morocco; and Muhammad Fayek, director of African affairs at the presidency of the republic (*Scribe* [Cairo], January, 1961, p. 16).

108. *Nasser's Speeches, 1961,* p. 2.

109. *Majmu'at khutab wa tasrihat wa bayanat al-Rais Gamal Abdel Nasser* [Collection of speeches, statements, and remarks of President Gamal Abdel Nasser], *Part III, February, 1960–January, 1962,* comp. U.A.R. Information Department

for the U.A.R. in African affairs is apparent from these points. An Egyptian African specialist described the conference as "an extension of the struggle to strengthen our national and international existence on the basis of Arab and African solidarity."[110] An official journal of the U.A.R. government described the Casablanca Conference as "The U.A.R.'s big drive in international politics."[111]

During the Casablanca Conference, the participants launched an "appeal to all independent African states" to associate themselves with the actions of the conference for the "consolidation of liberty in Africa."[112] It was hoped that the conference had indicated "a direction for action" around which other African states would coalesce. The Casablanca Group anticipated the creation of a broad front from which "Africa would enforce her will."[113] The Casablanca Conference, as Nasser stated, "in itself carried many far-reaching historic meanings of grave importance."[114] The African Charter was the focal point of these aspirations, as it represented the most significant attempt to that date to set up formal machinery for the implementation of African unity.

However, the conference's narrow representation, a representation restricted to the more "radical" anti-imperialist states, limited its appeal and cast upon the African Charter ideological overtones. Rather than representing a rallying point for all African nations, the conference signaled the polarization of differences between the informal African groupings. Instead of associating with the Casablanca Group within the framework of the African Charter, the majority of independent nations, including the Brazzaville Group, formed a rival organization. That organization's principles of cooperation, especially in the political field, and the essential elements of its constitution were established at the Monrovia Confer-

---

(Cairo, n.d.), p. 365; hereafter referred to as *Nasser's Speeches, February, 1960–January, 1962.*

110. Rifai, "Ittijahatina al-siyasiya" [The direction of our politics], p. 136.

111. *Scribe* (Cairo), February, 1961, p. 3.

112. *New York Times,* January 8, 1961, p. 1.

113. *Al-Ahram,* January 5, 1961, p. 6.

114. *Nasser's Speeches, 1961,* p. 8.

ence of May, 1961. At a subsequent meeting in Lagos in January, 1962, concrete measures to formalize this cooperation were taken, and the draft of a charter was proposed.

Because of the participation of 20 African states encompassing British and French-speaking Africa as well as North, Central, East, and West Africa, the Monrovia Conference more truly represented the aspirations of the majority of independent African states and resulted in the isolation of the Casablanca Group. The U.A.R. however had channeled its policy into the framework of the African Charter. The isolation of the Casablanca Group thus reflected the failure of its own policy.

Within this context, it is worthwhile to examine the basic differences that existed between the Casablanca and Monrovia Groups. On the one hand, the Casablancans' vitriolic anti-imperialism caused them to be thought of as "radical anti-imperialists"; they were less moderate than the Monrovians on the subject of decolonialization; and they proclaimed political unity to be "the necessary prelude to the creation of the extended field for which integrated plans for development in the economic and social spheres can be worked out."[115] On the other hand, the Monrovia Group considered economic cooperation to be the essential requirement of political unity.

It should be noted, however, that Nasser appeared to be sympathetic toward the economic cooperation approach to African unity. One of the tasks of the U.A.R. delegation at the Casablanca Conference, as described to the U.A.R. National Assembly by Nasser, was to establish the importance of the socioeconomic development of Africa as the base for political freedom.[116] This view certainly is in line with the Monrovia Group's contention that economic cooperation must be the foundation of African harmony. Also, the fact that the U.A.R. was already politically united with Syria but was experiencing difficulty with the economic aspects of that merger could not have made Nasser enthusiastic over the idea of political unity as advocated by the Casablanca Group. Nkrumah's strong belief in political integration as a base for unity prevailed at

115. Nkrumah, *Africa Must Unite*, p. 147.
116. *Nasser's Speeches, February, 1960–January, 1962*, p. 365.

the Casablanca Conference, probably as a compromise measure to preserve the aura of harmony and singularity of purpose within the group. Nevertheless, this very point was one of the basic differences between Nasser and Nkrumah.[117]

Another very significant difference between the Monrovia and Casablanca Groups was their attitude toward Afro-Asianism. The Casblanca Group had invited Asian countries to attend, including India and Indonesia, but all except Ceylon, which sent its Ambassador to Cairo as an observer, declined. Nasser clearly expressed the sentiments of the Casablanca Group when he declared on this occasion that agreement "in the first place with the peoples of Asia was a vital matter in the bringing of the struggle in Africa nearer its goal."[118] But in contrast to the Casablanca Group's active solicitation of Asian participation and cooperation, the Monrovians rejected Afro-Asianism in favor of the formation of "a distinct and independent group" of African states within the United Nations. A resolution by such a large number of African states had serious implications for Nasser's Afro-Asian policy.

Major differences also existed between the Casablanca and Monrovia Groups in approaches to problems on which there was basic agreement. For example, both groups supported the Algerian people in their struggle for independence from France. However, the Monrovia Group, for the most part, favored a negotiated solution between France and the FLN, while the Casablanca Group wanted the conflict to be internationalized. Another example is the Congo problem. The Monrovia Group largely supported U.N. action, but the Casablanca Group proposed withdrawal of their troops from the U.N. command.

---

117. Nkrumah's book *Africa Must Unite* indicates his preoccupation with the political integration of Africa as his ultimate goal. "The ultimate goal of a United States of Africa must be kept constantly in sight amidst all the perplexities, pressures and cajoleries with which we shall find ourselves confronted, so that we do not permit ourselves to be distracted or discouraged by the difficulties and pitfalls which undoubtedly lie ahead" (p. 143). Henry Tanner, in a *New York Times* article entitled "Nkrumah Steps up Nkrumahism," considered this factor an "obsession." He wrote "President Kwame Nkrumah passionately believes that the independence of Ghana is meaningless unless it is linked up with the total liberation of the African Continent" (January 14, 1962, Sec. 6, p. 13).

118. Quoted in Thiam, *The Foreign Policy of African States,* p. 70.

Evolution of the Policy

There were divergences within the Casablanca Group itself that also limited its potentiality. For example, although the Algerian Provisional Government was a member of the group, Ghana did not extend recognition to it until the Belgrade Conference of September, 1961. Another inconsistency became apparent when Ghana, prior to the Casblanca Conference, supported, in the United Nations General Assembly, Mauritania's independence. After the conference, the Mauritanian president made a visit to Ghana, and Nkrumah officially extended recognition to that state. It is difficult to reconcile the contradiction between these actions and Ghana's acceptance of the Casablanca resolution which stated that Mauritania was an "artificial state" created by France to further her own ambitions in Africa. The resolution condemning Israel is yet another example of the inconsistencies within the Casablanca Group. Although they had passed the resolution, Ghana, Guinea, and Mali continued their friendly relations with that state as recipients of aid. Here, too, these factors were causes contributing to, and perhaps to some degree resulting from, the friction between Nasser and Nkrumah.

Not only, then, was the Casablanca Group isolated but its internal disparities caused its paralysis. This was evident at the Casablanca Political Committee meeting of August, 1961. (In accordance with the Charter, the Political Committee was composed of heads of state.) Neither Nkrumah nor Touré attended. They reportedly were vacationing in Yalta.[119] With the meeting thus hamstrung, the heads of state left after only one session, and the foreign ministers continued the meeting. Nasser's disappointment with this outcome was reflected not in the content but in the length of his address to the Casablanca Charter Political Committee in August, 1961. The usually verbose Nasser gave one of his shortest recorded speeches. Realizing the difficulties involved in forming an effective African bloc, Nasser stated:

119. *Times* (London) reported that one of the reasons Nkrumah did not attend was his dissatisfaction with the results of the African High Command meeting. He also influenced Touré to boycott the meeting (August 29, 1961, p. 7). However, Nkrumah apparently wanted to paralyze the group because he also avoided the next summit meeting of the Casablanca Group in June, 1962 (*New York Times,* June 16, 1962, p. 6).

In my opinion it is not easy to achieve unity between the African states because of the existence of different nations. However, in my opinion, reaching African solidarity is a great victory. We were able in the Casablanca Charter to create an African Association and this is one of the ways to destroy the obstacles in the path.[120]

Without Nkrumah's and Touré's participation, the Casablanca Group became a Muslim organization, primarily of North African countries, but including Mali. The tendency toward isolation of the Arab countries also occurred within the Monrovia Group. Tunisia, Libya, and the Sudan, participants in the Monrovia Conference, boycotted the Lagos Conference because the Algerian Provisional Government was not invited. The Casablanca Group members declined to participate for the same reason. Thus, no North African state attended the Lagos Conference.

ADJUSTMENT OF THE POLICY: 1961-1968

In March, 1961, the third All African Peoples' Conference was held in Cairo. (The previous two had been held in Accra in December, 1958, and in Tunis in January, 1960.) About 200 delegates, representing more than 50 political and labor organizations and 31 African territories, attended. Nasser himself addressed the opening session and emphasized the "necessity of unifying African nationalist ranks against new imperialism."[121] The final resolutions of the conference denounced neocolonialism, which was defined as indirect "domination by political, economic, social, military, or technical means." The delegates considered the U.S., the Federal Republic of Germany, South Africa, and France to be the main perpetrators.[122] The resolutions were considered "a practi-

---

120. U.A.R. Documentation Research Center, *Dairat al-ma'arif al-siyasiya al-Arabiya: nashrat al-wathaiq* [The Arab political encyclopedia: bulletin of documents], X (August, 1961), Section of the President, 55; hereafter referred to as *Nashrat al-wathaiq.*

121. *Times* (London), March 27, 1961, p. 9.

122. *Al-Ahram,* March 31, 1961, p. 1.

61

cal expression . . . of the aims of the conference" and proof of the vitality of Cairo as a liberal force in Africa.[123]

However, the significance of this conference lay not in the final resolutions, which were not new, but in Nasser's attempt to clarify the U.A.R.'s activities in Africa. He told the delegates that the U.A.R.'s support of African nationalist movements stemmed from a dual concept of "principles and responsibility." Nasser asserted that the principles were based on the U.A.R.'s anti-imperialist policy and that it was the responsibility and the duty of those nations who had achieved freedom to aid the newcomers.[124] This concept of Egypt's policy in Africa as a reflection of the application of the broader principles of its foreign policy was clearly manifested after 1962.

By September, 1961, the reorientation of the U.A.R.'s African policy was evident. As early as April, 1961, there had been speculation in the Egyptian press about convening another Bandung Conference.[125] In May, the Egyptian papers reported that a nonaligned nations conference would be held at the U.N. the following September, and it was hoped that it would be organized under the auspices of the U.N. Secretariat.[126] The Conference in fact was held in Belgrade in September and was sponsored by Tito, Nasser, Sukarno, Nehru, and Ayub Khan. The U.A.R., through the conference, attempted to consolidate its position in the Third World and increase its prestige in Africa.[127]

The conference dealt extensively with the problems of colonialism, disarmament, underdevelopment, and reorganization of the U.N. However, the primary concern was with the easing of East-West hostilities. It was hoped that the nonaligned countries could

123. *Al-Ahram,* April 1, 1961, p. 8.

124. *Al-Ahram,* April 13, 1961, p. 1.

125. *Rose El-Youssief,* no. 1714, April 17, 1961, p. 4.

126. *Rose El-Youssief,* no. 1720, May 29, 1961, p. 4.

127. Afghanistan, Burma, Cambodia, Ceylon, Cuba, Ethiopia, Ghana, Guinea, India, Indonesia, Iraq, Mali, Morocco, Nepal, Saudi Arabia, Somalia, Sudan, United Arab Republic, Yemen, the Algerian Provisional Government, and an observer from Brazil attended the preparatory meetings held in Cairo in June, 1961. In addition, Nigeria, Togo, Upper Volta, Lebanon, Brazil, Mexico, Ecuador, and Bolivia were invited to participate in the conference (*Nashrat al-wathaiq,* X [July, 1961], Section of International Affairs, 3).

effectively mediate between the two camps to bring about an easing
of tensions. It is significant within the context of the U.A.R.'s role
in international affairs that the conference adopted Nasser's proposal to send representatives to try to persuade Khrushchev and Kennedy of the imperative need for talks. Nehru and Nkrumah were
chosen to carry the message to Khrushchev, and Sukarno and Keïta
carried the message to Kennedy.

Nasser's address to the assembly at the Belgrade Conference
dealt with the problems menacing the world and with the responsibility held by the nonaligned nations to maintain peace. He identified two factors which he felt posed the greatest threat: tensions
existing between East and West and tensions between North and
South, that is, between the colonialist powers and the colonies
and ex-colonies.[128] The most significant aspect of Nasser's speech
was his denunciation of the formation of a third bloc in international affairs. There would appear to be a correlation between this
and the Monrovian rejection of an Afro-Asian bloc, especially in
light of Nasser's previous attempts to form such a front (as at the
September, 1960, U.N. General Assembly session and in the Casablanca Group). Nasser made this statement at the Belgrade Conference:

> I believe I would not be exceeding my limits if I said that
> there should not be in the method of our approach, in the
> resolutions we reach, or in the effects it may leave on world
> public opinion, that which might insinuate directly or indirectly
> that the states following the policy of non-alignment are by
> their activities creating a third world bloc. We live in a world
> suffering from the strife between two blocs and we cannot
> imagine that a third bloc should enter the arena and increase
> the tensions of this strife instead of easing them.[129]

The isolation of the Casablanca Group was the culmination of
the failure of the U.A.R.'s African policy. There were a number of
basic factors which had contributed to the exclusion of Egypt from
the mainstream of African initiative for cooperation and unity. The

128. *Arab Observer,* September 10, 1961, p. 4.
129. *Arab Observer,* September 10, 1961, p. 6.

following were especially significant: (1) The U.A.R.'s policy in
the Congo had proven ineffectual in influencing the course of events
there and was in opposition to that of the majority of the African
states, which supported U.N. action. (2) Nkrumah's rivalry with
Nasser for leadership of Africa contributed to a dissipation of Nasser's influence on the continent. (3) The U.A.R.'s radical anti-
Westernism and cooperation with the Soviet Union alarmed the
more conservative African states, and (4) racism in African politics
threatened to isolate North Africa from Black Africa. Finally, (5)
the injection of Arab issues into African politics, especially the Israeli issue, created a frequent source of tension. (It should be noted
that Egypt's foreign policy had proven to be ineffective in that the
U.A.R. had failed to curb Israel's activities in Africa and the Monrovia Group had rejected Afro-Asianism.)

But the U.A.R. was experiencing difficulty not only in Africa.
Syria's secession from the U.A.R. had a great impact on Nasser
personally and on the U.A.R.'s Middle Eastern objectives in general. Nasser cited the Syrian case as an important factor in his
decision to re-evaluate the U.A.R.'s policies.[130] There were also
grave internal problems confronting Nasser. An economic crisis
within the U.A.R. and widespread corruption in government were
sources of discontent among the Egyptian masses.

By November, 1961, Nasser called for a complete re-evaluation
of Egypt's internal and external policies and the drawing up of a
National Charter as a "guide for action."[131] Nasser appointed a
Preparatory Committee for the National Conference of Popular
Forces to draw up the Charter. The National Conference of Popular
Forces was to consist of 1,500 delegates selected from all walks
of life.[132] In May, 1962, the Charter was ratified by the assembly

---

130. *Nashrat al-wathaiq,* XIII (January–March, 1962), Section of the President, 18.

131. *Nashrat al-wathaiq,* X (November, 1961), Section of the President, 108.

132. Some of the members of the Preparatory Committee who had been deeply
involved in Egypt's African policy were Ihsan Abdul Quddus, Ahmad Bahai al-
Din, Bahaia Karam, Taha Husain, Dr. Iz al-Din Farid, Muhammad Hasanain
Heikal, Muhammad Fuad Jalal, Zakaria Mohieddin, and Anwar al-Sadat (*Nashrat
al-wathaiq,* X [May–June, 1962], Section of the Popular Forces Conference, 53).

of the National Conference of Popular Forces and adopted as national policy. Explaining the nature of the Charter, Nasser stated:

> The Charter is . . . a framework for action. . . . It is the result of the experience and experimentation of ten years, 1952 to 1962. . . . That was a period of trial and error. . . . Henceforth, the Charter is nothing but a framework for a plan for social, economic, political, and popular action for the future. This framework naturally does not include the means of execution.[133]

The Charter had important implications for the U.A.R.'s African policy. First of all, Arab unity was treated as an internal matter and was clearly specified as the center of activities. Section 9 of the Charter, entitled "Arab Unity," dealt exclusively with this problem and clearly defined Egypt's role. It stated:

> If the United Arab Republic considers it her calling to strive for complete Arab Unity, attainment of this objective would be promoted by the clear-cut methods that must, at this stage of the Arab struggle, be defined in a decisive and binding manner.[134]

Africa was identified as an external problem and discussed rather briefly in Section 10, which was entitled "Foreign Policy." The Charter identified Egypt's interest in Africa in association with the problem of Israel: "Our pursuit of the Israeli policy of infiltration in Africa is only an attempt to limit the spread of a destructive imperialist cancer."[135] Egypt's relationship to Africa was identified as geographically based: "Our people live in the northeastern gate of struggling Africa and cannot be isolated from its political, social, and economic development."[136] The Charter affirmed the U.A.R.'s support for Pan-Africanism and Afro-Asianism: "While our people believe in Arab unity, they also believe in a Pan-African move-

133. *Nashrat al-wathaiq,* X (May–June, 1962), Section of the Popular Forces Conference, 53.
134. U.A.R. Information Department, *The Charter* (Cairo, [1962]), p. 93.
135. *Ibid,* p. 100.
136. *Ibid,* p. 104.

65

ment and an Afro-Asian solidarity."[137] However, its relationship to these forces was not defined, as in the case of Arab unity. The ambiguity of Egypt's relationship to Pan-Africanism and Afro-Asian solidarity gave it the option to practice a pragmatic policy within the framework of its foreign-policy principles. The Charter outlined three factors as the most important concepts of Egypt's foreign policy: (1) the fight against imperialism; (2) the struggle for peace; and (3) the attainment of international cooperation. The Charter also outlined the spheres of political action: (1) Arab unity; (2) Pan-Africanism; (3) Afro-Asian solidarity; (4) a tie with the Islamic world; and (5) loyalty to the U.N. and the U.N. Charter.[138]

The Charter did not indicate any major change in the U.A.R.'s policy, but it did mark the beginning of a new phase in African-U.A.R. relations and it represented an attempt to cope with the changing scene in a newly independent Africa. No longer could the U.A.R. make an outright bid for leadership in Africa. An effective role in African politics required the U.A.R. to reconsider its policies and bring them into line with those of the majority of the African states, that is, those of the Monrovia Group:

> The U.A.R. believes . . . in the necessity of the establishment of an African League that includes all the independent states. Its aim should be the creation of a free and united African will.
>
> The U.A.R. believes that the circumstances which the African continent is experiencing at the present time requires the creation of this African will.[139]

This adjustment was clearly reflected at the meeting of the Political Committee of the Casablanca Charter in Cairo in June, 1962. The final communiqué of that meeting declared:

137. *Ibid,* p. 103.

138. U.A.R. Information Department, *Al-Tandhim al-siyasi* [Political organization] (Cairo, n.d.), p. 24.

139. Muhammad Hafiz Ghanim, "Al-Thawra fi al-maiden al-Alami" [The revolution in the international sphere] in *Adh wa 'ala al-thawra* [Reflections on the revolution], ed. 'Ain Shams University, Public Relations Department (Cairo: 'Ain Shams University Press, 1963), p. 59.

The heads of state call for African solidarity embracing all African states, the nucleus of which would be the grouping of African independent states. This can be discussed at a conference comprising all African states.[140]

At the conclusion of this meeting, Sékou Touré flew to Addis Ababa to propose to Emperor Haile Selassie a summit conference of all African states; he sent a number of his "faithful colleagues" to twenty-one other African states to gain support for such a conference.[141]

At the subsequent Addis Ababa Conference of May, 1963, Nasser's new approach to Africa was "made . . . crystal clear."[142] Nasser broached all of the major problems of the U.A.R.'s African policy. In dealing with one of the main sources of divergence between the Casablanca and the Monrovia Groups, Nasser aligned the U.A.R. with the majority of African states by advocating the establishment of economic cooperation as a prelude to African unity. This was in opposition to Nkrumah's proposal for the immediate establishment of an African federal government.[143] At the initial conference of foreign ministers Dr. Mahmud Fawzi attempted to lay to rest the issue of the U.A.R.'s dual loyalties as both an African and an Arab state. He pointed out that "the U.A.R. was truly an Afro-Asian country in that she was geographically on both continents and racially involved in both."[144] However, such assertions did not succeed, as Dr. Fawzi intended, in "squashing forever the imperialist-propagated idea that there is some contradiction in being an Arab and an African state at the same time."[145] Indeed, the U.A.R.'s constant injection of the Israeli issue into African politics served to point up the fact that the U.A.R.'s attempt to maintain dual loyalties was a source of conflict. The U.A.R. had unsuccessfully pushed the Israeli issue at every conference

140. *Al-Ahram,* June 18, 1962, p. 1.
141. Rihda Khalifa, "Wathaiq an al-wahda al-Ifriqiya" [Document on African unity], *Nahdhat Ifriqiya,* no. 66, May, 1963, p. 30.
142. *Arab Observer,* July 22, 1963, p. 45.
143. *Scribe* (Cairo), August, 1964, 67–68.
144. *Arab Observer,* July 19, 1965, p. 41.
145. *Ibid.*

and in so doing had alienated many of the African states.[146] Realizing this, Nasser decided to keep the Arab-Israeli conflict out of African politics. In his speech to the conference, he declared:

> We have come here without selfishness. Even the problem which we consider to be our most serious problem—namely the problem of Israel, and one on which the group of Casablanca member states rightly shared our view that it is one of the tools of imperialist infiltration to the continent and one of its bases of aggression—we shall not submit this problem for discussion at this meeting, in the conviction that the progress of free African endeavor will, through trial, reveal the truth day by day and lay it unmasked before the African conscience.[147]

This decision was "appreciated and admired" by the delegations. They considered it proof that Nasser "objectively put the aims of the conference above all other considerations."[148]

Past experience had indicated that the formation of blocs could result in the division of Africa along ideological, regional, linguistic, or racial lines. Such an occurrence would clearly not be in the interests of the U.A.R. Thus, Nasser rejected this concept in his address to the conference:

> This does not mean for one moment that Africa should become an international bloc or that African endeavor should be isolated from the march of human progress as a whole. This is the last thing we think of or ask for. Rather, we consider reaching that extent to be fanaticism, the responsibility of the outcome of which we cannot bear.[149]

146. The 1960 Conference of Independent African States held at Addis Ababa presented an example of this. The U.A.R. tried very hard to win conference support for sanctions against Israel. This even caused a delay in the final plenary session and annoyed some of the African delegations (*New York Times,* June 25, 1960, p. 7).

147. *Nashrat al-wathaieq,* XI (March–June, 1963), Section of the President, 21.

148. U.A.R. Information Department, *Mutamar al-qumma al-Ifriqi* [The African summit conference] *22–25 May, 1963* (Cairo, n.d.), p. 9.

149. *President Gamal Abdel Nasser's Speeches and Press Interviews, 1963,* comp. and trans. U.A.R. Information Department (Cairo, n.d.), p. 97; hereafter referred to as *Nasser's Speeches, 1963.*

Thus, at the 1963 Addis Ababa Conference, Nasser modified the U.A.R.'s African policy, assuming the position of a moderating influence within the African community. A government publication declared: "The biggest breakthrough in U.A.R.–African relations has come this year, with President Nasser's signing of the African Charter at the Addis Ababa Heads of State Conference in May."[150] Ali Sabry, the president of the Executive Council and a member of the U.A.R. delegation to the conference, described the importance of the conference to the U.A.R. as follows:

> First, from the point of view of personal contact, the U.A.R. delegation held fruitful conferences of great usefulness with all presidents and leaders and members of the African delegations. Second, this conference will result in cooperation . . . in the political, economic, and social spheres in the African continent.[151]

The U.A.R's dual interests in Africa and the Middle East presented a continuing dilemma in its relations with Africa. For example, in 1963, a Kenyan journalist asked Nasser if the U.A.R. was "working for Arab unity or African unity." Nasser replied:

> I can see no contradiction between Arab unity and African unity. . . . Unity covers a wide scope ranging from unity of aims to constitutional unity. I cannot imagine that constitutional unity will be established in Africa today since African countries have to know each other in the first place and in the meantime, unity of aim will come about and an African League will be formed as in the proposal made by the Addis Ababa summit conference. We consider this as a step towards unity. I speak as an African and as the president of the U.A.R.[152]

The salient point of the problem for the U.A.R. lay in the fact that a large part of its Arab aspirations were in fact manifested in Africa:

150. *Arab Observer,* July 22, 1963, p. 45.

151. *Nashrat al-wathaiq,* XI (March–June, 1963), Section of African Affairs, 94.

152. Speech delivered October 1, 1963, *Nasser's Speeches, 1963,* p. 250.

> The Arab question in general cannot be separated from the African problem especially if we realize that 73 per cent of the Arab land is situated in the African continent and two-thirds of the people of the Arab states live in Africa.[153]

But despite such figures, sub-Saharan Africa, for the most part, did not want to be entangled in Middle Eastern problems. The announcement that the Arab League was planning to open information offices in West African countries caused an adverse reaction. As one West African stated, "The decision of the League must be resisted because it is a subtle device to involve us more directly with the frenetic politics of the Middle East." Dr. John Karefa Smart of Sierra Leone went even further in stating that "African members of the League will have to decide soon where they stand. Are they in the Middle East or in Africa?"[154]

A primary problem of the U.A.R.'s policy here was the attempt to integrate Afro-Arab policies. Whenever African and Arab interests took divergent courses, Egypt's loyalty was clearly with the Arabs. In order to solve the problems posed by an integrated Afro-Arab policy, Nasser, after 1962, dealt separately with these two primary areas and worked through the broader channels of Afro-Asianism and nonalignment to link them loosely together. That this separation of policies was successful was indicated at the 1963 Addis Ababa Conference. Tom Mboya of Kenya stated:

> In speaking of Pan-Africanism, one refers to the whole continent and often the question is asked: "What about the Arabs in North Africa? Do you think of them as Africans? Do they consider themselves Africans?" I cannot answer the last question for them, but can only say that, from my experience at Pan-African conferences and observing their interest in Pan-African matters, I have come to believe that the great majority of Arabs in North Africa look on themselves as African. From our side, there has been increasing recognition and acceptance of the Arabs as Africans. Presidents Nasser, Ben

153. Abdul Aziz Rifai, "Thawrat 23 Yuliyo 1952 wa harakat al-taharrur fi Ifriqiya" [The revolution of July 23rd, 1952, and the revolutionary movements in Africa] *Egyptian Political Science Review,* no. 28, July, 1963, p. 237.

154. *Arab Observer,* March 9, 1964, p. 32.

Bella and Bourguiba demonstrated fully at the Addis Ababa conference their commitment to Pan-Africanism.[155]

The several conferences held in Cairo during 1964 again emphasized this separation of African and Arab policies. In less than six months, three summit conferences were held in the U.A.R.: the first was the Organization of African Unity summit conference in July, which was attended by three kings and the heads of state of thirty-three countries; the second was the Arab summit conference held in September, which brought together fifteen leaders of Arab states; and the third was a nonaligned nations conference held in October and attended by the kings and heads of state of sixty-four nonaligned countries. President Nyerere of Tanganyika considered the O.A.U. conference to have been "proof of the unity of the African continent and [a refutation of] . . . the false propaganda which divided it into black Africa and Arab Africa."[156]

It was clear that the U.A.R. considered its best interests to be served by working within the framework of the larger African community rather than as the nucleus of a small group. This was exemplified by the U.A.R.'s attempts to establish friendly relations with the rather conservative French-speaking states during 1963–64. Prior to 1963 the U.A.R. did not even have diplomatic relations with any of the former French colonies. By 1964, however, Nasser had established relations with Senegal, Congo (Brazzaville), Dahomey, and Niger.

The U.A.R's efforts within the O.A.U. also point up this intention to remain in the mainstream of African affairs and to become a moderating, rather than radical, influence. When that organization was threatened by internal divergence, Nasser attempted to mediate in order to preserve its solidarity. This was evident at the O.A.U. summit conference in Cairo in 1964. Tshombe, who had become prime minister of the Congo shortly before that, wanted to take his seat at the conference. Algeria, Morocco, and the U.A.R. strongly opposed this. Madagascar supported Tshombe. For the most part, the other states were "divided . . . between their

155. Tom Mboya, *Freedom and After* (London: Andre Deutsch, 1963), p. 231.
156. Peter Mansfield, *Nasser's Egypt* (Baltimore: Penguin Books, 1965), p. 104.

hostility toward the person ~~of~~ the former leader of Katanga and their care not to interfere in the internal affairs of the Congo."[157]

In an attempt to avoid a confrontation on this issue at the O.A.U. summit conference held at Accra in July, 1965, Nasser proposed that Kasavubu lead the Congo delegation. He also attempted to settle other disruptive issues in advance by sending a special envoy, Muhammad Fayek, on a twenty-five-day trip to East and West Africa to prepare for the 1965 conference. One of Fayek's missions in West Africa was to attempt to mediate between the French-speaking African states and Ghana. These states had refused to attend the conference if it took place in Accra because of Ghana's alleged interference in their internal affairs.[158]

Despite Nasser's efforts, however, the 1965 Accra conference was not entirely successful, as Muhammad Hassanein Heikal's rather grim assessment would seem to indicate: "The national revolutionary movement in general lives now in severe crisis."[159] At the conference, Africa again appeared to be separating along the lines of the earlier groupings, that is, the Brazzaville Group, the Monrovia Group, and the Casablanca Group. It was the issue of support for the Congo rebels that precipitated this deterioration of the O.A.U.'s solidarity. Ben Bella, Keïta, Touré, and Nkrumah, "with Nasser's blessing," gave their support to the rebels.[160] It is significant to note here that whereas in the past Nasser usually played a leading role in such issues, after the 1963 Addis Ababa Conference he preferred to take a back-seat position on the disruptive issues. This was also apparent at the O.A.U. summit conference in Cairo in July, 1964. Nasser did not push the Israeli issue, but Ben Bella and Bourguiba did.[161]

Since the 1961 reappraisal of its foreign policy, the U.A.R. has not attempted to play a role of political leadership in Africa. The policy emphasis has shifted to cooperation, especially in the eco-

157. Philippe Herreman in *Le Monde Diplomatique*, VII (April, 1965), 4.

158. *Rose El-Youssief*, no. 1955, July 12, 1965, pp. 8–9.

159. *Mulhaq al-Ahram*, November 12, 1965, p. 1.

160. Herreman, *Le Monde Diplomatique*, 4.

161. Assemby of the Heads of State and Government of the O.A.U., *Speeches Delivered at the Assembly, 17–21 July, 1964,* comp. U.A.R. Information Department (Cairo, n.d.), pp. 25, 50.

nomic sphere. Egypt's head start in industrialization over the other independent African states (except for the Republic of South Africa) offers it the possibility of becoming a major supplier of manufactured goods to the continent. The realization of this goal is still in the future, and Egypt faces keen competition from the major industrial powers of the world in its pursuit of the African market. But this is where Egypt's real opportunity lies, and indeed in economic cooperation lies Africa's best opportunity to free itself from economic, and thus political, dependence on the industrial nations.

Egypt is playing still another role in Africa. Under Nasser Egypt has moved from a client state to a free and sovereign nation, has achieved internal political stability and freedom of maneuver in foreign affairs, and has made tremendous progress in economic growth. The Egyptian example has been of great significance to emerging African states intent upon seeking their own identity in a world dominated by big powers. Peter Mansfield noted that

> several African leaders were inclined to link [Egypt's economic progress] . . . with political stability and consequently with Egypt's lack of political parties. One of the first things that Jomo Kenyatta did on his return to Nairobi was to announce that he wanted Kenya to become a one-party state. All this tends to confirm that Egypt's role in Africa is likely to be one of example and inspiration.[162]

Since the June, 1967, war with Israel, the pattern of U.A.R.– African relations has been modified somewhat, due chiefly to the drain on physical and diplomatic resources necessary to continue cultivating African ties. However, the pattern has been set, and it may be expected that as the situation in the U.A.R. is stabilized, Egypt will renew its pursuit of African friendship. The results of the U.A.R.'s African policy may be seen from the reaction of the African states to the Arab-Israeli conflict. Immediately after the war, at a meeting in Cairo on July 1, 1967, some forty-five Afro-Asian states expressed their support of the Arab

162. *Nasser's Egypt,* p. 106.

cause. In the United Nations African (sub-Saharan) voting was mixed. Ten states voted consistently with the U.A.R. on two of the major resolutions (Yugoslav and Latin American), while eight voted consistently in opposition.[163] Although this is not evidence of solid support for Nasser south of the Sahara, it does indicate that the active policy of the U.A.R. has produced results, both positive and negative, and that Arab affairs are of concern to African states. A further example of this concern is a proposal made by President Senghor of Senegal in May, 1969, in which he linked the achievement of peace in Africa to a complete arms embargo on all countries of the Middle East.[164] At an O.A.U. conference held in Kinshasa in September, 1967, the Israeli issue was not discussed, at the request of President Nasser. But at the O.A.U. Algiers conference a year later the African states voted a resolution supporting the Arab states against Israel.[165]

Even more recently, there have been indications that African leaders are sympathetic to the Arabs in the Arab-Israeli dispute. The *Christian Science Monitor* reported that Mali's chief of state recently visited Cairo. And President Bongo of Gabon recalled his ambassador from Israel after Prime Minister Golda Meir failed to receive Mrs. Bongo. Even more disturbing to Israel have been the visits to Cairo and Moscow of President Bokassa of the Central African Republic, whose country is an important source of diamonds for Israel's thriving diamond trade.[166] During an April, 1970, visit to Cairo, President Bokassa made a personal visit to Nasser's home. In a subsequent communiqué he "assured President Nasser of his country's support for the Arabs and the necessity of a complete Israeli withdrawal from occupied Arab lands."[167]

In a news conference held at the conclusion of the Foreign

163. Burundi, Congo (Brazzaville), Guinea, Mali, Mauritania, Senegal, Somali Republic, Uganda, Zambia, and Tanzania voted with the U.A.R. Botswana, Gambia, Ghana, Lesotho, Liberia, Malagasy Republic, Malawi, and Togo voted in opposition (*New York Times,* July 5, 1967, p. 3).

164. Russel Warren Howe, "Senghor Offers Plan for Peace in Africa: Arms Embargo Urged," *Christian Science Monitor,* May 20, 1969, p. 6.

165. *New York Times,* September 18, 1968, p. 4.

166. July 16, 1970, p. 1.

167. *Al-Ahram,* April 17, 1970, p. 1.

Ministers Conference of Nonaligned Nations at Dar-es-Salaam in April, 1970, President Nyerere of Tanzania gave a clear statement of his views of the Arab-Israeli dispute. When queried by a West German television correspondent, "Why don't you accept Israel as a member of the nonaligned nations?" Nyerere laughed and stated in a loud voice, "You occupy the lands of three states; you aggress against three nations and expel from their homes the indigenous populations; and you speak after this of nonalignment." The journalist responded by stating, "But Egypt gets Soviet arms." Nyerere answered in a grave tone "You [the West] created the problem and you want the Arabs to refuse arms from any source. Israel is an aggressive state and conquers land. But when *we* accept arms to defend ourselves, you describe us as Communists. You cooperated in the Second World War with the Communists to stop Hitler. Egypt accepts the arms and it's her right to liberate her land."[168]

Other areas of foreign policy are more pressing for the U.A.R. at present than sub-Saharan Africa, but it is apparent that Egypt has important interests there, and it can be expected that when more attention can be devoted to this matter the U.A.R. will again actively seek political involvement in Black Africa.

168. *Al-Ahram,* April 19, 1970, p. 1.

Chapter Three

The U.A.R.'s East-West Relations

Egypt's African and Middle Eastern policies, which embody Egypt's principal foreign involvement, have influenced its relations with the great power blocs. In fact, the development of Egypt's alliance with the Soviet Union has been, in part, a ramification of the deterioration of its association with the West. This deterioration has been caused by a clash over African and Middle Eastern strategy. This chapter will trace the history of Egyptian-Western conflicts subsequent to the revolution and the parallel development of Egyptian-Soviet relations and will indicate the implications of this for Africa.

EGYPTIAN DIPLOMACY AFTER THE REVOLUTION

Egypt's policy after the revolution was anti-British and anti-French. However, Nasser apparently hoped that Egyptian-American relations would develop independently, especially since America had no history as a colonial power. Nasser may even have expected America to be sympathetic toward the revolution.

However, Nasser was not able to gain America's support nor was he able to come to terms with Britain over the Suez question (the "first aim" of the revolution). So he attempted to bargain with the West, using Egyptian cooperation in the international sphere as the negotiable commodity. According to an interview published in 1953, Nasser warned, "Egypt intends to take a neutral stand between the Western and Eastern blocs if the Egyptian question [evacuation of the Suez] is not solved as soon as possible."[1]

At a series of meetings held between December, 1953, and January, 1954, with the Egyptian Ambassadors to Washington, London, Moscow, New Delhi, and Karachi, Nasser re-evaluated Egypt's foreign policy. Neutrality was declared in world politics: "The meaning of neutrality from the Egyptian point of view is that Egypt will not accept cooperation with any state except on the basis of the recognition of its rights and on the basis of equal treatment and dignity."[2]

This declaration of neutrality put Egypt in a better bargaining position by placing the West in competition with the East. The Soviet Union had been looking for an avenue of penetration into Africa and the Middle East, but it had been largely unsuccessful because of the relationships—political, cultural, and economic—that the West (especially Britain and France, and later America) had already established in the area. The superiority of Western technology and the availability of technical assistance in agriculture and industry contributed to the success of the West in this area. In addition, since the African elite spoke French and English and the basic economic structure of the African states was capitalistic in orientation, cultural and business relations with the West were further facilitated. At the same time the deviations and tensions within the Communist world weakened its effort to gain significant influence in Africa.

---

1. *Al-Ahram,* December 8, 1953, p. 1. In this interview, Nasser was questioned regarding a note Dr. Ahmad Hussain, ambassador to Washington, supposedly delivered to Mr. Dulles making this threat. Nasser declared that there was no written note to Dulles on the subject but that there had been a conversation to that effect between himself and Ambassador Hussain. When asked if the Soviet government had been notified, Nasser replied, "No."

2. *Al-Ahram,* January 27, 1954, p. 1.

Evolution of the Policy

The growing nationalist movements in Africa were often anti-Western, but they were also wary of Communist motives and big powers in general. Thus, the Egyptian declaration of neutrality and Egypt's active solicitation of Soviet support presented one of the first indications that relations with the Soviet Union were being pursued outside Communist circles, even though the U.S.S.R. had habitually supported nationalist issues in opposition to the West. *Al-Ahram* described Egypt's effort to utilize Soviet support:

> Egypt will try to make the Soviet Union and its allies support the Egyptian question and the Arab question in the international field. . . . As a matter of fact, the Soviet Union never stopped supporting these questions in the U.N. On the other side, the record of the U.N. sessions reflects nothing but the opposition of the big Western powers—particularly Britain—to any effort for liberation and independence.[3]

In seeking Soviet support, however, Egypt attempted to justify its opposition to local and regional Communist activities by creating a distinction between the government and the party. Egypt, wrote *Al-Ahram,* "distinguishes between the political system of the Soviet Union and the government of that Union. She strongly opposes Communism and fights the Communists. But her connection with the Soviet government is a diplomatic connection."[4]

By mid-1954 Egyptian-Soviet diplomatic ties were cordial. The Egyptian newspapers published accounts of the Soviet Union's efforts to reconsider its policy toward Israel, of U.S.S.R. assistance to Arab causes, and of Soviet progress in the fields of science.

Nasser apparently intended to use the Soviet Union only to help establish an equilibrium in Egyptian-Western relations. He expected that Egypt's primary ties would remain with the West and that arms and aid would continue to be supplied by the West, Thus, Nasser believed that once the Suez question was settled, Egyptian-Western relations would normalize. He stated that "After the Suez Agreement there is nothing to stand in the way of our good relations with the

3. December 30, 1953, p. 7.
4. December 30, 1953, p. 7.

78

West."[5] However, Egyptian-Western relations did not improve after the Suez Agreement. America, through its support of French and British policies, had become identified with the "imperialist" West.[6]

The Baghdad Pact, first suggested in 1953, precipitated a bitter struggle between Egypt and the West for dominance in the Middle East. However, in reacting to the challenge, Nasser made it clear that he did not intend to let Egypt become a Soviet "satellite." In commenting on this situation *Al-Ahram* stated: "The official [Egyptian] circles pointed out that President Nasser's resistance to imperialism and his objection to Western pacts will not throw him into the arms of the Eastern bloc because of his policy of neutralism."[7]

Nasser attempted to minimize Egypt's dependence on the West, thereby neutralizing Western pressure. His government developed economic ties with the Eastern bloc, such as the agreement between Egypt and Rumania in 1954 which arranged the exchange of crude oil for cotton (the first of numerous major trade agreements with Communist countries) and the similar agreement reached with the U.S.S.R. in April, 1955. Communist influence was minimal since the Communist organization inside Egypt had been brought under control and the Soviet Union had no reservoir of influence within Egypt outside of the Communist Party.

Thus, by the time of the Bandung Conference, held in 1955, Egyptian-Western relations were strained. A degree of rapport had been established between Egypt and the U.S.S.R., but it was at the Bandung Conference, where the Soviet Union strongly supported and encouraged Nasser's neutralism, that closer Soviet-Egyptian ties were initiated. Ironically, it was the issue of the Baghdad Pact, the instrument through which the West intended to combat the threat of Communism in the Middle East, that the Soviet Union utilized. On the first day of the Bandung Conference, the Soviet Union attacked the attempts of the West to establish

5. *JANA* (Colombo, Ceylon), September, 1954, p. 16.

6. "The U.S. in its support of imperialism . . . lost a great portion of her reputation as a state defending the freedom of nations" (*Al-Ahram,* July 25, 1954, p. 1.).

7. March 21, 1955, p. 1.

a defense system. According to *Al-Ahram,* the Soviet reaction in the Warsaw Pact Meetings of May, 1955, was stressed: "Bulganin protested the pressure from the West on the Arab states. He deplored the attempts of the Western states to force Egypt, Syria, Iran, and Afghanistan to join military pacts."[8] After the Bandung Conference, long meetings were held between Nasser's aides (especially Major Salah Salem) and the Soviet ambassador, and Egyptian-Soviet relations at the economic and cultural levels measurably increased.

In February, May, and August, 1955, the Israeli Army raided Gaza. The superiority of Israel's military equipment intensified Egypt's efforts to purchase arms from the West, but Nasser was unable to come to terms in negotiations. In September, Nasser met with the Soviet ambassador for more than an hour.[9] By the end of that month Egypt announced the arms agreement with Czechoslovakia.

The Czech arms deal was a major victory for Soviet policy and a blow to Western diplomacy throughout Africa and the Middle East. The Soviet Union quickly followed up the Czech arms agreement with economic and diplomatic aid, including support for the Arabs in the Arab-Israeli conflict. The Soviet Union also offered to finance the Aswan High Dam project, and Russian economic and cultural missions were reported to be preparing to visit Egypt.[10]

With the culmination of the eventful year 1955, Nasser felt that Egypt had achieved true independence. At the Bandung Conference, Nasser had successfully established Egypt's role in the neutralist community, and the trade agreements with the Soviet bloc had reduced Egyptian economic dependence on the West. Also, the Czech arms deal neutralized the remaining vestige of Western predominance. *Al-Jumhuriya* stated:

8. May 12, 1955, p. 1.

9. *Al-Ahram,* September 16, 1955, p. 6. It was unusual for a diplomat to stay so long on a routine courtesy call with Nasser. Considering the earlier visits between this diplomat and Nasser's aides and the subsequent developments between Egypt and the Communist bloc, it may be concluded that the main topic of discussion was Egyptian armament.

10. *Al-Ahram,* October 11, 1955, p. 1.

Gamal Abdel Nasser said that Egypt has been liberated from all foreign influences . . . she handles her external and internal policies on the principle of her interest and the interests of her sisters, the Arab states. Egypt refuses foreign pacts because she sees in them a bond on her freedom and a tie with the wheel of imperialism. Egypt avoids foreign camps, East or West. . . . She fights her best for the sake of world peace and security. . . . This is Egypt's policy clearly stated . . . as it was declared by President Gamal Abdel Nasser . . . on more than one occasion.[11]

Nasser's policies were clashing with Western policies not only in the Middle East but also in Africa. As early as 1954, Great Britain had protested against Egypt's activities in the Sudan and against Egyptian broadcasts to East Africa.[12] In September, 1955, France temporarily stopped arms shipments to Egypt because of its interference in North Africa. Nasser, who since the Bandung Conference considered himself spokesman for African liberation movements, challenged the Western nations regarding their policies toward individual countries. *Al-Ahram* reported that Nasser requested the American ambassador to relay the following message to his government:

The Egyptian government considers the use of the French forces under the NATO command and the use of NATO military equipment against the citizens of North Africa as an aggressive act directed toward all Arabs not from France alone but from all the countries participating in NATO which permitted this action by France.[13]

Even after promoting Egypt's dependence, the Soviet Union did not interfere in Egypt's internal or external affairs. Soviet aid never had explicit "strings" attached to it and was extended entirely on Egypt's terms. Ideology was never an issue, even when Nasser was suppressing the local Communists. Nasser remarked, "The Russians are very clever. They know what I want to say and they please me

11. January 1, 1956, p. 6.
12. *Al-Ahram,* July 22, 1954, p. 6.
13. August 27, 1955, p. 1.

by saying it."[14] The result of this policy was the consolidation of Egyptian-Soviet friendship.

Nasser, however, was cognizant of the danger involved in becoming too dependent on the Soviet Union. He did not want to replace Western influence with Soviet predominance but hoped to maintain an equilibrium from which he could bargain with both and thus minimize both influences. In May, 1956, therefore, Egypt's foreign minister conferred with the British ambassador in an effort to restore good relations. In spite of American and British attempts to reach a rapprochement, as exemplified by their offer to finance the Aswan High Dam project, Nasser continued his policies of support of the African and Arab nationalist movements,[15] of Radio Cairo's anti-Western campaign, and of Egypt's close ties with the Communist bloc.

THE SUEZ AND AFTER

In July, 1956, America withdrew its offer to finance the Aswan High Dam project; Britain and the International Bank for Reconstruction and Development quickly followed suit. Nasser declared that the offer was revoked because "we have refused all the conditions through which they want to impose domination on us, politically and economically, because we do not want to sell our freedom and independence."[16] In retaliation, and to secure financing for the High Dam, Nasser nationalized the Suez Canal. The Egyptian newspapers also accused America and Britain of attempting to disturb the relationship between Egypt and Ethiopia, Uganda. and the Sudan by pressuring those countries to object to the High Dam project and "threatening to stop the flow of the Nile waters from its sources."[17] The Egyptian government asserted that France, Britain, and America were

14. *New York Times*, April 2, 1956, p. 3.
15. See Chapter Two for a discussion of Egypt's support for the African nationalist movement.
16. *Al-Jumhuriya*, July 27, 1956, p. 1.
17. *Al-Jumhuriya*, July 26, 1956, p. 1.

establishing a wall around Egypt . . . aiming to isolate . . . or to impose restrictions on her until she is subjugated to the West . . . in order to establish an iron curtain around [her] . . . as they attempted to do before with the Soviet Union and the People's democratic states. . . . [They] will fail for sure.[18]

The results and consequences of the Suez crisis are still being evaluated and debated, but several factors that are immediately pertinent to this study have been well established. The first ramification was Nasser's unprecedented ascension to the role of hero of the Arab masses,[19] a role to which he had been aspiring since the Bandung Conference. Another significant result was that America was considered primarily responsible for the intensification of the Suez crisis. Egypt accused America of manipulating events for its own political and economic advantages. America was also accused of "looking for a mask" to establish its influence in Egypt.[20]

The Soviet Union gave full diplomatic and moral support to Egypt. It quickly offered to finance the High Dam project "without a bond or condition, if Egypt requested that."[21] The Soviet ambassador assured U.S.S.R. support and "carried a message from Shepilov, the foreign minister of the Soviet Union, which stated that the Soviet Union had decided to support Egypt in the nationalization of the Canal."[22] Nasser consulted frequently with Soviet representatives throughout the development of the Suez crisis, and four days after he gave his nationalization speech in Alexandria he held an hour-and-a-half-long meeting with the Soviet ambassador. Apparently, details for the defense of the Suez area were discussed. In December, 1956, Nasser called for closer ties with the Soviet Union, citing Soviet support as an "important factor in Soviet-Egyptian friendship."[23] Thus, positive neutrality no longer meant nonalignment. Conditioned by the events of 1955 and 1956, Egypt's policy had developed into hostility toward the West and cooperation

18. *Rose El-Youssief,* no. 1468, July 30, 1956, p. 4.
19. See William R. Polk, *The United States and the Arab World* (Cambridge: Harvard University Press, 1965), p. 265.
20. Fathi Khalil in *Rose El-Youssief,* no. 1474, September 10, 1956, p. 5.
21. *Al-Jumhuriya,* July 25, 1956, p. 1.
22. *Al-Jumhuriya,* July 31, 1956, p. 1.
23. *New York Times,* December 28, 1956, p. 3.

with the Communist bloc, as long as such cooperation could continue on a voluntary basis with no "strings" attached.

DE FACTO FOREIGN-POLICY ALLIANCE

The Soviet Union's interest in the Middle East and Africa was based on political rather than economic goals. In 1955 Krushchev declared, "We value trade least for economic reasons and most for political purposes."[24] The Soviet Union made a substantial economic contribution to Egypt, mainly through aid, technical assistance, and loans, during the period 1955 through 1957. The investment was made to win confidence throughout the area; and the Soviet Union's interest and activity in Africa actually developed in correspondence to the success of this policy. Krushchev himself indicated the extent of the U.S.S.R. commitment and interest when he stated that

> The Soviet Union places a great importance on the struggle of the nations of Africa and the Middle East and its policy on this is to participate in supporting the political and economic independence of the independent states until their freedom is secure, and we will support all who struggle for their freedom until they achieve complete independence.[25]

The growth of the Soviet embassy in Cairo reflects the increasing importance the Soviet Union gave to the development of Egyptian-Soviet relations and the nature of these relations. Until June, 1954, the U.S.S.R. maintained only a legation in Egypt; but then it raised the status to embassy, and did the same to Israel to avoid involvement in the area conflicts. Then, during August 1956, at the height of the development of the Soviet Union's commitment to Egypt in the Suez crisis, two Middle Eastern specialists arrived.[26] By the summer of 1957 the Soviet Embassy in Cairo was the largest of

24. U.S. Department of State, *The Sino-Soviet Economic Offensive in the Less Developed Countries* (Washington, D.C.: Government Printing Office, 1958), p. 6.

25. *Al-Ahram,* November 22, 1957, p. 1.

26. *Rose El-Youssief,* no. 1470, August 13, 1956, p. 19.

the Russian Embassies in the Middle East and Africa, and to bolster its effectiveness, two more counselors in political affairs were added.[27] At the end of 1957 the U.S.S.R. Foreign Office strengthened its Middle East Section and transferred the political secretary of the U.S.S.R. Embassy in Cairo to the Foreign Office Middle East Section.[28] The Soviet ambassador to Egypt was promoted to head the Middle East section of the Soviet Foreign Office.

The Afro-Asian Solidarity Conference of December, 1957 to January, 1958, was the first manifestation of a Soviet-Egyptian foreign-policy alliance. But each country had different aims: Nasser hoped to establish his role as a leader of the African liberation movements, and the Soviet Union wanted to open a new economic and political offensive in Africa and the Middle East. However, both countries hoped to establish friendly contacts among the nationalists, and as these goals were not incompatible, the two countries found it expedient to cooperate.

At the conference, the Soviet Union extended the scope of the policies that had proven so successful in establishing ties with Egypt, and it offered unconditional aid to all independent African and Asian nations and support to all liberation movements. Sharaf R. Rashidov, the head of the Soviet delegation to the conference, declared:

> We are ready to help you as brother helps brother. Tell us what you need and we will help you and send, to the best of our capabilities, money in the forms of loans and aid. . . . We can build for you institutions for industry, education and hospitals. . . . We can send economists to you, or you can send economists to our country. Follow the route you consider best. . . .
>
> We don't ask you to join any blocs or change governments or change your internal or foreign policies. . . . Now is the time to break the unbalanced and unnatural international economic relationships and substitute another relationship based on equality.[29]

27. *Rose El-Youssief,* no. 1516, July 1, 1957, p. 15.
28. *Rose El-Youssief,* no. 1530, October 7, 1957, p. 5.
29. *New York Times,* December 28, 1957, p. 1.

85

Evolution of the Policy

The reason for the importance that the Soviet Union gave to the conference was evident from its membership. Organized on the nongovernmental level, the conference was attended by 577 delegates representing 46 Communist and non-Communist Asian and African countries. The 27-member Soviet delegation was reportedly the best organized of all. The delegation, headed by Sharaf R. Rashidov, president of the Presidium of the Uzbek Soviet Republic and a vice-president of the Supreme Soviet's Presidium, consisted predominately of Muslim and Asian members. Representatives from Soviet broadcasting stations and correspondents from all the major Soviet newspapers were also included. And the Soviet Union supported the conference with a strong propaganda drive.

The conference was generally considered to be a success both for Egypt and the Soviet Union. It provided an opportunity for the Egyptian and Soviet delegations to make friendly contacts throughout Africa. The most tangible result was the establishment of the Afro-Asian Solidarity Council, which would help foster these contacts. Both the Soviet Union and Communist China held important permanent posts on the secretariat.[30] The establishment of the Afro-Asian Solidarity Council gave the Soviet Union a base in Africa through which it could channel funds and propaganda, and it gave to Nasser leadership of the only Afro-Asian organization that incorporated both independent countries and liberation movements. Thus, the policy of collaboration had proved successful for both the Soviet Union and Egypt.

However, there was evidence of friction at the conference. Nasser had hoped to steer the conference along a neutralist line to help establish his role as a leader of Africa. Two months prior to the conference, his representative, Zakaria Lutfi Guma (a member of the National Assembly and writer for *Al-Jumhuriya*), had toured Africa to assure this. However, the conference discussions were Communist-influenced, and in the resolutions approved by the final plenary session, Nasser's neutralist doctrine was ignored.[31] Nas-

---

30. A ten-man secretariat was established. The secretary-general was to be nominated by Egypt and the others chosen from the Cameroons, Communist China, Ghana, India, Indonesia, Iraq, Japan, Sudan, Syria, and the Soviet Union (*New York Times,* January 4, 1958, p. 5).

ser was apparently dissatisfied with the Soviet Union's control and with its disregard for his policy of neutrality. Thus, though he was expected to address the opening meeting, he instead sent at the last moment a "terse and non-commital" message; furthermore, the Egyptian press minimized the role played by the U.S.S.R. at the conference.[32]

The Soviet Union, in an apparent effort to restore Nasser's confidence in its good will, took great care to appease Nasser on his visit to Russia in April, 1958. One week prior to the visit, the Soviet ambassador to Cairo declared, "My government will do its best to make the visit of President Gamal Abdel Nasser to the U.S.S.R. useful and fruitful."[33] Egyptian-Soviet relations were the main topic of discussion during the visit. Dr. Murad Ghaleb, Nasser's adviser for political affairs and a member of the U.A.R. delegation, accompanied Nasser and declared:

> Our relationship with the U.S.S.R. is a normal relationship . . . based on the principle of true friendship. . . . This . . . is the mutual interest and exchange of benefits and assistance and the most important feature of this friendship . . . has been based on complete equality. It is not founded on pressure or political, military, or economic subjugation. This type of normal relationship should continue and grow stronger as time passes. It will not weaken if our relations with the U.S.A. improve and will not grow stronger if our relationship with the U.S.A. worsens.[34]

In an address delivered at the Kremlin, Nasser clarified the basis and the nature of Soviet-Egyptian relations: "Your assistance to

31. *New York Times,* January 2, 1958, p. 2. The only delegations that Nasser received privately after the conference were the Communist Chinese and Soviet (*Times* [London], January 3, 1958, p. 6).

32. *New York Times,* December 30, 1957, p. 1. For example, the Ministry of Foreign Affairs published a special issue on the conference that summarized world press reactions to the conference country by country but significantly omitted the press comments of the Soviet Union and Communist China (U.A.R. Ministry of Foreign Affairs, *Nashra kha'sa: Mutamar al-tadhamun al-Ifriqi al-Asyawi* [Special issue: the Afro-Asian Solidarity Conference] (Cairo, Ministry of Foreign Affairs, 1958).

33. *Rose El-Youssief,* no. 1560, May 5, 1958, p. 4.

34. *Rose El-Youssief,* no. 1563, May 26, 1958, p. 8.

us did not hinge on any condition or commitment . . . there has never been interference of any kind. You respected the policy of positive neutrality which we proclaimed." At the same time, he also reaffirmed Egypt's determination to follow a line of positive neutrality:

> We fought to keep out of the spheres of influence of the imperialist countries. We decided to pursue an independent policy inspired by the dictates of our own conscience. In cooperation with you during the past four years, my friends, we adhered to the liberation policy which we had formulated and those years have only strengthened our determination to stick to it. That cooperation was a victory for the Bandung Conference principles of peaceful co-existence and cooperation among nations regardless of their different social systems.[35]

Commenting on the result of Nasser's visit, Dr. Ghaleb declared: "The most important result of the president's trip, in my opinion, is the support of the U.S.S.R. for the policy of positive neutrality and nonalignment, and assurance that it will respect this policy and its agreement to offer aid and assistance according to this policy."[36]

Although Nasser resisted Soviet attempts to subordinate Egyptian policy to Soviet interests, the Egyptian-Soviet foreign-policy alliance continued to develop. The Soviet Union apparently regarded the U.A.R. as a liaison with the Afro-Asian nations. In early January, 1958, Bulganin wrote Nasser a forty-page letter requesting "a detailed survey of international relations and the problems which cause tension in the world." The letter contained Bulganin's suggestion that Egypt should participate in the world summit conference to be held in Geneva.[37] Subsequently, on January 27, 1958, Egypt asked fourteen Afro-Asian states for their views on international problems. The deputy minister of Arab and Afro-Asian

35. *President Gamal Abdel-Nasser's Speeches and Press Interviews, 1958,* comp. and trans. U.A.R. Information Department (Cairo, n.d.), pp. 153–54.

36. *Rose El-Youssief,* no. 1563, May 26, 1958, p. 8.

37. *Al-Ahram,* January 12, 1958, p. 1.

affairs relayed the request to the heads of the Afro-Asian missions in Cairo.[38]

THE NATURE OF DE FACTO ALLIANCE

By 1958, close cooperation was a reality of Egyptian-Soviet foreign policies. However, this understanding was never ideological. Instead, it was a "marriage of convenience" that developed and was adhered to only insofar as Egyptian-Soviet interests happened to coincide, and was abandoned whenever their interests clashed.[39] A government journal describing the alliance declared:

> Arab-Soviet cooperation was not confined to bilateral relations but was also found in common action in the service of peace, and in bringing peoples closer to each other, a new field of collaboration and understanding. Joint or parallel efforts were exerted in this direction, such as in the case of decolonization, disarmament and the economic and social development of countries and men. Everything collaborates to consolidate friendship and extend bilateral or international cooperation between Moscow and Cairo governments, both of which are determining factors in respect to the predominant role which the two countries play in world affairs. Everything calls for this consolidation: the past action, the present cooperation and the effort directed towards the future. All of these come under the heading of common basic principles and major objectives.[40]

Nasser's anti-imperialist and anti-West policies were the most important factors in Soviet support for the U.A.R. An editorial in *Pravda* clearly summarized the government's attitude toward anti-imperialist movements: "The unity and solidarity of all progressive anti-imperialist forces constitute the most powerful barrier to the aggressive ambitions of the imperialists."[41] And Khrushchev

38. *Al-Ahram,* January 28, 1958, p. 4.
39. See Oles M. Smolansky, "Moscow-Cairo Crisis, 1959," *Slavic Review,* XXII (December, 1963), 713–26, for a fuller treatment of this idea.
40. *Scribe* (Cairo), June, 1964, p. 5.
41. April 24, 1965, p. 1.

affirmed this as an important element in U.S.S.R. support when he commented on

> the role played by the United Arab Republic and President Gamal Abdel Nasser in combating colonialism in all its ancient and new forms, and in struggling against foreign domination, which constitutes the greatest menace to the liberty of the people who recently acquired independence.[42]

The U.A.R., however, played a greater role in Soviet policy because of its strategic position vis-à-vis Africa and Asia. Kosygin noted this when he stated that among the factors of importance in the anti-imperialist movement "is the creation of . . . a progressive state such as the U.A.R., which occupies a special geographic position . . . on the crossroads between Africa and Asia."[43]

The U.A.R.–U.S.S.R. alliance had important implications for Africa. The Soviet Union's "unconditional" aid and support to the U.A.R. greatly increased its prestige among African nationalists as the friend of underdeveloped nations and of liberation movements, and thus some of the suspicion of Soviet motives was offset and the door for increased Soviet activity in Africa was opened. Kosygin indicated the importance of the U.A.R. as an example or model of Soviet policy when he stated that

> The experience of the U.A.R. under the leadership of the proficient fighter against imperialism, President Gamal Abdel Nasser, attracts . . . a large number of the countries that achieved national independence and the countries that are still struggling for freedom.[44]

Nasser's Afro-Asian movement thus supplied the opportunity for Soviet participation in African affairs: it was at the 1957–58 Afro-Asian Solidarity Conference that the U.S.S.R. opened its economic and political offensive. The conference gave the Soviet Union a permanent channel by which to funnel aid and propaganda

42. *Scribe* (Cairo), August, 1964, p. 29.
43. *Al-Jumhuriya*, May 18, 1966, p. 5.
44. *Al-Akhbar*, May 17, 1966, p. 13.

throughout the continent. The conversion of the Afro-Asian Solidarity Council into a tricontinental organization demonstrated Egypt's willingness to participate in an action that would be of little benefit to Egypt (considering its limited connections with Latin America), and the organization's choice of Havana, "40 kilometers from imperialism," as the site for the January, 1966, conference was of significant propaganda value to the Soviet Union. The Afro-Asian Youth Conference of January, 1959, had indicated how important these conferences could be in establishing extensive contacts in Africa. (The Youth Conference was also used as a "dress rehearsal" and recruiting ground for the World Communist Festival at Vienna the following spring.)[45]

The African Association also helped to bring the U.S.S.R. into the African network. Through the association, it courted the liberation movements with support and aid, and it gave scholarships to African students for study in the Soviet Union. The association also provided a liaison with the nationalist leaders. For example, in July, 1962, it was reported that members of the association representing Northern Rhodesia, Southern Rhodesia, South Africa, Kenya, and Mozambique were in Moscow.[46]

The need for U.A.R. support to prevent isolation of the Soviet Union from the Afro-Asian movement was demonstrated by the Afro-Asian Economic Conference of December, 1958. Nasser strongly resisted Soviet attempts to use the conference to its advantage. In an abortive attempt to steer the conference along anti-imperialist, anti-Western lines, the U.S.S.R. introduced a political resolution condemning Western action in the Middle East. The resolution was overwhelmingly defeated by twelve votes (including that of the U.A.R.) to four, with four abstentions. Another resolution introduced by the Soviet Union proposed that Afro-Asian countries pool their raw materials to keep prices stable. This resolution also received an unfavorable reaction.[47]

Perhaps the greatest evidence of Egypt's importance to the Com-

---

45. *Times* (London), January 31, 1959, p. 5.

46. *Arab Observer*, July 23, 1962, p. 33. The purposes of their visits were not reported.

47. *Times* (London), December 11, 1958, p. 10.

munist world as a bridge to Africa came to light in the course of the preparation (and subsequent cancellation) of the "Second Bandung"—the second Afro-Asian Conference scheduled for November 5, 1965, at Algiers. Occurring as it did under the shadow of the Sino-Soviet dispute, both Communist China and the U.S.S.R. sought U.A.R. support. For the Soviet Union, Egyptian support was necessary in order to get its candidature for the conference accepted. Communist China sought the U.A.R.'s support to keep the Soviet Union out of the conference.[48] In the end, the U.A.R. supported the Soviet candidature, but not without considerable bargaining.[49] The significant point here is that both nations considered the conference of importance to their respective roles in Africa and considered Nasser's support for their position at the conference to be of primary importance.

Soviet support was also an important factor in Egypt's African policy. Nasser used the Soviet Union to counteract Western predominance and to give potency to the U.A.R.'s policy and activities in Africa. Soviet participation in the Afro-Asian conferences increased their prestige and broadened their scope.

The prodigious amount of aid supplied by the Soviet Union bolstered the U.A.R.'s economy, modernized its army, and pre-

48. The Sino-Soviet dispute, including its ramifications in Africa, is outside the scope of this investigation, except insofar as it affects Egyptian policy. A French periodical reported that Chou En-lai visited Egypt on four occasions in an attempt to secure Egypt's cooperation against the Soviet Union. The first occasion was in April, 1965. In June he visited Nasser on his way to and returning from Tanzania. Chou En-lai failed to enlist Nasser's support against the Soviet Union, and at the conclusion of the third visit, relations between the U.A.R. and China were strained. The final visit was occasioned by the fall of Ben Bella. Serious and extensive negotiations took place during Chou En-lai's twelve-day visit. The results were that Nasser agreed to maintain neutrality in the Sino-Soviet dispute and to support China on certain other issues of importance to it. In return China agreed to coordinate its policy in the Arab World with Egypt, to recognize the U.A.R.'s role as spokesman for the neutral nations, and to support the U.A.R. on other issues of importance to it. (Nichola Lang in *Est et Quest*, no. 351, 16–30 November, 1965, pp. 5–6).

49. It was reported that in September, 1965, Nasser went to the U.S.S.R. During this visit, the Soviet Union agreed not only to step up work on the Aswan Dam but also to participate to the amount of 350 million rubles in the construction of a sawmill and prospecting and substructure operations. In return, Nasser stated that he would support the U.S.S.R.'s candidature at the Algiers conference. No doubt his dealings with Chou En-lai played an important part in these negotiations (*ibid,*. p. 6).

sented Egypt as a model for African nationalism. The Czech arms deal, the Suez War, Aswan Dam, and the repression of Communism inside Egypt (without affecting its alliance with the U.S.S.R.), increased Nasser's prestige as well as the Soviet Union's. No doubt Soviet support was an important factor in Nasser's policies. Without it, Nasser most likely could not have declared that "The U.A.R. shall liberate Africa."[50] This was amply demonstrated by the Suez crisis. Nasser acknowledged the power of the U.S.S.R. when he stated:

> We believe with confidence that the revolutionary movements for the nations of Africa and Asia against imperialism and backwardness owe a great number of their victories to the existence and power of the Soviet Union which became the real factor in deterring the imperialists' ambitions and in creating a valuable opportunity for the progressive revolutionary to play an effective role on a larger scale in the struggle for progress and independence.[51]

The final communiqué of Nasser and Kosygin in May, 1966, clearly reflects the nature of the U.A.R.–U.S.S.R. alliance in Africa:

> The two sides surveyed the situation in Africa and agreed that the imperialists are aiming to create an atmosphere of political tension on the African continent and to interfere in the internal affairs, intensifying their subversive activities in an attempt to enforce their control over the nations of the continent.
> Because of these circumstances, the Afro-Asian peoples' unity should be consolidated in order to support the anti-imperialist powers in the African states and to create close cooperation among them and other states fighting old and new imperialisms.[52]

50. Abdul Mun'im Shmayis, *Thaman sanawat taht' al-shams* [Eight years under the sun] (Cairo: The Arab Agency for Press and Publications, 1960), p. 328.
51. Muhammad Mandur, "Al-alaqat al-'Arabiya al-Sovyetiya wa tatawwarha" [The development of Arab-Soviet relations], *Egyptian Political Science Review*, no. 39, June, 1964, p. 79.
52. *Al-Jumhuriya*, May 19, 1966, p. 3.

Evolution of the Policy

SINCE THE 1967 JUNE WAR

The nature of the tacit U.A.R.–U.S.S.R. alliance in Africa was altered by the 1967 June War. Nasser required Soviet aid in large amounts to recoup his losses, but the disastrous defeat at Israeli hands had cost Nasser much of his prestige in Africa. Unable to repay the Soviets in money, Nasser placed himself in the debt of the Soviet Union and as a consequence lost some freedom of action. Nasser did attempt to offset this, however. For example, he made a series of approaches to the West, particularly Britain, in late 1967 and early 1968,[53] but continued problems with Israel and with militant Arab guerrillas have prevented the U.A.R. from moving much closer to the West. It was reported in early 1969 that Nasser was attempting to revitalize nonalignment in order to neutralize Soviet influence.[54] Further, the removal of Marshal Amir and a subsequent military purge have had the secondary effect of insulating the Egyptian regime from increased Soviet influence in the military.

It has been suggested that the U.S.S.R. may have encouraged the June War in order to strengthen its hold on Egypt.[55] Whether or not that is true, Egypt has become more dependent upon the U.S.S.R. since the war, and that dependence has led to greater Soviet involvement in the Middle East. For example, on July 9, 1967, units of the Soviet Mediterranean Fleet began visiting Port Said and Alexandria, and both then became regular ports of call. Soviet naval strength in general was increased in the Mediterranean during 1967 and 1968.[56] Also, the Russians are making more direct moves into Africa, especially in the Sudan, which moved away from

53. John K. Cooley, "Nasser Looks to the West," *Christian Science Monitor,* October 14, 1967, p. 2.

54. John K. Cooley, "Egypt Reinvokes 'Nonalignment'?" *Christian Science Monitor,* January 9, 1969, p. 1.

55. Lt. Gen. Sir John Bagot Glubb, "Power Grab in Mideast?" *Christian Science Monitor,* November 11, 1967, p. 1.

56. Bertram B. Johannson, "What Is the Soviet Up To?" *Christian Science Monitor,* November 13, 1967, p. 9; and "Can the U.S.S.R. Penetrate Deeper into Mideast?" *ibid.,* December 30, 1967, p. 9; see also John K. Cooley, "U.S. Units Face Soviet Buildup," *ibid.,* November 19, 1968, pp. 1, 5.

94

the West after June, 1967.[57] It is apparent that the Soviet Union intends to take a more direct hand in this area and that the role of Egypt may thereby be reduced. In any event, the pattern of relations established by 1966, which allowed an uneasy partnership between the U.A.R. and the U.S.S.R., was disrupted by the June War, although Nasser denies any fundamental change. However, he has readily acknowledged the U.A.R.'s debt to Russia, stating that

> A fact we should know and understand is that without the Soviet Union we would have found ourselves facing the enemy without arms, forced to accept the conditions of America which was not willing to give us even one bullet and was giving Israel everything from tanks to planes to rockets. The Soviet Union gave us arms. . . . As a matter of fact, to this time we haven't paid a penny. In fact, . . . we don't have any money with which to buy and pay for more arms. . . . The Soviet Union gave us some as a gift and the rest will be paid in long-term installments.

In reaffirming the basis of the Soviet-Egyptian alliance, Nasser declared:

> One aim is common between us and the Soviet Union: that is the resistance to imperialism. We don't want any foreign influence in our part of the world. . . . We have a national and ideological interest in resisting imperialism and the Soviet Union has an ideological and strategic interest. I want to tell you frankly and clearly that the Soviet Union never tried even in our most pressing moments to dictate conditions or demand anything.[58]

Through 1968 and 1969 the extent of Soviet influence in Egypt remained a moot question, and the significance of increasing numbers of Soviet personnel resident in Egypt was unknown. In fact, estimates of the numbers of military and civilian advisers and technicians sent to Egypt from the Soviet Union varied widely. By

57. John K. Cooley, "Sudan: Impact of Soviet Arms," *Christian Science Monitor,* September 21, 1968, p. 1.
58. *Al-Ahram,* July 24, 1968, p. 1.

Evolution of the Policy

1970, the continued inability of the Egyptian army and air force to provide an adequate defense was emphasized by escalating Israeli offensives along the Suez Canal. The Soviet Union began providing Egypt with SAM-2 and SAM-3 surface-to-air missiles for anti-aircraft defense between the Canal Zone and Cairo, and increasing air activity led to rumors of participation of Soviet pilots in combat with Israeli air forces.

Whatever the case, Africans will watch Soviet policy in Egypt closely as a measure of the Soviet Union's willingness to honor commitments. Soviet prestige in Africa is allied to its policy in Egypt, and it is apparent that this alliance has had important effects upon Egyptian, Soviet, and African policies.

Part II

Substance
of the
Policy

Chapter Four

Principles
of the Policy

President Gamal Abdel Nasser is solely responsible for, and maintains close supervision over, Egypt's foreign policy.[1] Therefore, Egyptian public statements on Africa are generally a reflection of Nasser's attitudes and, as such, show a remarkable continuity.

Nasser's own conception of Egypt's relationship to Africa has remained consistent with the views expressed in his book *The Philosophy of the Revolution*. There he stated:

> We cannot under any condition, even if we wanted to, stand aloof from the terrible and terrifying battle now raging in the heart of that Continent between five million whites and two hundred million Africans.

> We cannot stand aloof for one important and obvious reason —we ourselves are in Africa.

> Surely the people of Africa will continue to look to us—*we* who are the guardians of the Continent's northern gate—*we* who constitute the connecting link between the Continent and the outer-world.

1. See Appendix II.

> We certainly cannot, under any conditions, relinquish our
> responsibility to help spread the light of knowledge and civil-
> ization up to the very depth of the virgin jungles of the Con-
> tinent.

He further stated:

> It is undeniable that Africa is now the scene of a strange and
> stirring commotion. The white man, who represents several
> European nations, is again trying to change the map of the
> Continent. We cannot under any condition stand as mere
> onlookers, deluding ourselves into believing we are in no way
> concerned with these machinations.[2]

In these statements, which can be considered valid throughout
the period of Nasser's leadership of the U.A.R., three main principles that actuate Egypt's African policy are apparent: (1) anti-
imperialism, (2) Africanism, and (3) leadership.

ANTI-IMPERIALISM

Anti-imperialism is the most dominant and persistent concept of
Egypt's foreign policy. It is the underlying theme of *The Philosophy
of the Revolution* and is described in the National Charter as one
of the "three deep channels in which the foreign policy of the
United Arab Republic runs and which express all the national principles." The Charter summarizes this principle as follows:

> War on imperialism and domination. Fighting against imperial-
> ism with all the country's potentialities and in every possible
> way, exposing it in all its shapes and masks and waging a bat-
> tle on it in all its dens.[3]

Nasser views imperialism as the main source of many of Egypt's
internal and external problems. In a volume entitled *Al-Isti'mar min
aqwal al-Rais Gamal Abdel Nasser* [Imperialism from the speeches

2. (Cairo: National Publication House [1954], pp. 69–70.
3. *The Charter* (Cairo: U.A.R. Information Department, 1962), p. 97.

100

of President Gamal Abdel Nasser] Nasser attributes most of Egypt's difficulties to imperialism and considers its liquidation Egypt's mission.[4] Anti-imperialism thus constitutes the main element in Egypt's African policy. In the early stages of the revolution, Egypt announced its "participation in Africa's anti-imperialist drive."[5] As Egypt's interest in Africa developed, Nasser declared, "We work for the liberation of Africa and to safeguard it from the domination of imperialism."[6] Egypt's involvement with the national liberation movements was based on this principle. As the African states achieved independence and colonialism declined, Nasser exposed new "imperialist plots" for Egypt to fight against. At the Addis Ababa Conference of 1963, he declared:

> There exists that colonialism which has not totally and fully been eradicated from all parts of the continent. There exist those attempts at forging new colonialist tools which infiltrate under the banner of the U.N. and which brought the Congo its violent crisis.[7]

Another function of anti-imperialism and its broader application to the unity of all anti-imperialist movements was apparent in Egypt's pursuit of Afro-Asian solidarity, especially after the 1955 Bandung Conference. On the basis of this solidarity, Egypt attempted to justify its dual involvement in both Africa and the Middle East. Nasser declared: "We cannot support freedom in one place and deny it in another place. It is my duty to support freedom everywhere, and it's our duty as a nation that suffered from imperialism and aggression to denounce aggression in any place."[8] Many conferences held in Cairo attempted to achieve Afro-Asian cooperation on a wide scale. Egypt's creation and sponsorship in 1958 of the Afro-Asian Solidarity Council is a clear manifestation of

4. Comp. U.A.R. Information Department (Cairo, 1964).

5. *Arab Observer,* July 19, 1965, p. 58.

6. *Al-Ahram,* July 23, 1959, p. 1.

7. *President Gamal Abdel Nasser on Africa,* comp. and trans. U.A.R. Information Department (Cairo, n.d.), p. 48.

8. *Al-Ahram,* December 24, 1964, p. 1.

101

this policy. In 1959 Nasser declared: "We play our part in building Afro-Asian solidarity, both objectively and physically."[9]

Nasser cited the unity of all freedom-fighters as an important factor for the success of any revolutionary movement.[10] By showing how Afro-Asian solidarity had been an important factor in defeating the Anglo-French-Israeli forces during the Suez War, Nasser explained its importance: "We were helped . . . by the solidarity of the people of Africa and Asia and the free people all over the world."[11] And Kamil al-Din Husain emphasized the same point in his address to the Afro-Asian Youth Conference held in 1959: "The bright face of our present is very closely connected with this solidarity. If we have hopes for a bright future it is also connected . . . with this solidarity."[12]

AFRICANISM

In *The Philosophy of the Revolution,* and as confirmed later by the National Charter, Nasser identified three "circles" in Egypt's "sphere of activity:" (1) the Arab world, (2) Africa, and (3) the Muslim world. In actuality, Africa overlaps the other two spheres. The total area of the Arab land is approximately 11 million square kilometers: 28 per cent, or 3,159,340 square kilometers, are in Asia, and 72 per cent, or 8,049,552 square kilometers, are in Africa. The Arab circle is inhabited by 82 million people: one-third, or 27,125,000, are in Asia, and the remaining two-thirds, 55,043,-000, are in Africa. In the Muslim circle there are over 120 million Muslims living in Africa. Except for central and southern Africa they permeate the continent with heavy concentrations across the Sudanic belt and along the coast of East Africa. It is apparent, then, that Egypt is intrinsically involved in Africa, even if the idea of the African circle were eliminated.

9. *President Gamal Abdel Nasser's Speeches and Press Interviews, 1959,* comp. and trans. U.A.R. Information Department (Cairo, n.d.), p. 257.

10. *Al-Ahram,* April 3, 1961, p. 1.

11. *Al-Ahram,* February 3, 1959, p. 1.

12. *Al-Ahram,* February 3, 1959, p. 1.

Prior to the revolution, Egypt identified itself with the European powers and hoped to play an equally significant role in Africa. *Al-Ahram* declared: "Egypt is a nation that has an importance in the African continent which qualifies her for a leading role . . . because her lands extend to the tropical regions of it."[13]

After the revolution, Egypt found herself in the precarious position of not being accepted as an Arab nation by the Middle East and not being accepted as an African nation by sub-Saharan Africa. Up until the time of the Bandung Conference Nasser concentrated on establishing Egypt's Arabism and, for the most part, neglected sub-Saharan Africa. After the Bandung Conference, in direct correlation with the rapid rise of Africa's importance in the international sphere and pressured by the inroads Israel was making on the continent, Nasser increasingly turned toward Africa, attempting at the same time to establish Egypt's Africanism as a justification for its activities there. Egypt based its claim to Africanism on historic experiences that established the (a) cultural unity, (b) geographic unity, and (c) political unity of the continent.

The major causes of Egypt's isolation from sub-Saharan Africa were the racial and cultural dissimilarities between Arab North Africa and Black Africa. To overcome these dissimilarities, Egypt attempted to identify its ancient civilization as African in origin. Egyptian spokesmen emphasized the racial mixture that is apparent in Upper Egypt. They contended that this racial intermixing occurred through centuries of migration from the Sudan, Somalia, and Uganda into Upper Egypt. They also claimed that the "supposed racial difference between Africa south of the Sahara and Arab Africa in the north" was a tool of imperialism to create a rift and a division. This attempt to establish a common racial identification was clearly manifested at the Conference of Independent African States held at Monrovia in August, 1959. Husain Zulficar Sabri, deputy prime minister and chairman of the U.A.R. delegation to the conference, declared:

> Here I want to state quite emphatically that Arab North Africa, and history attests to it, has always had relations with

13. February 8, 1948, p. 3.

103

countries south of the Sahara, and *vice versa.* The Egyptian region of the United Arab Republic was freely intermixed with peoples all along the River Nile, up to the innermost heart of Africa, in the Great Lake Region. We have mixed blood in our veins. I shout it to the world and I am proud of it.[14]

Islam was considered to have reinforced the cultural bonds between Africa and Egypt. The influence of Arabic on African languages, especially Swahili, and the influence of Arabic culture generally were also cited as further proof of the interrelationship of the two regions.

Along with the assertion of Egypt's Africanism, there was a need to create an African consciousness among the Egyptian people. The suggested program of an African policy for Egypt published in 1956 specified that "the success of Egypt's African policy necessitates drawing the attention of all Egypt's people to Africa."[15] As early as 1956, the government set Egyptian educators and publicists the task of creating an African identity and of making the public aware that Egyptians "live in Asia and Africa."[16] In 1956 Cairo University's political science department, in compliance with Republican Decree No. 216, introduced a new subject called "The Problems of Africa."[17] Inexpensive and simply written publications spread the content and meaning of Nasser's speeches to all levels of the literate population. These included, for example, such series as Political Books, National Books, We Choose for the Student, We Choose for the Soldier, We Choose for You, Arab Books, Africa for Africans, East-West Series, and The Thousand Books Series.

Abdul Ghany Abdallah Khalaf Allah, a professor in the Higher Teachers College and later chairman of the English department,

14. Government of Liberia, Department of State, *Conference of Independent African States Held at the Capitol* (Monrovia: Library Information Service, 1959), p. 44.
15. "An African Policy for Egypt," *Egyptian Economic and Political Review*, II (August, 1956), 21–24; see Appendix I for the full text of this article.
16. See Kamil Zuhary, "Nahnu na'ish fi Asiya wa Ifriqiya" [We live in Asia and Africa], *Rose El-Youssief*, no. 1542, December 30, 1957, p. 17.
17. See Abdul Malik Auda, *Al-Siyasa wa al-hukum fi Ifriqiya'* [Political systems in Africa] (Cairo: Anglo-Egyptian Bookshop, 1959), p. 5.

complained in 1957 that educators in Egypt neglected "one of their holy responsibilities—the duty of preparing the new generation for the greatest task of tomorrow and of nourishing their growing minds with the right idea about the role of the nation in Africa."[18] Muhammad Audah, still more recently, in his introduction to Mishil Kamil's book, also cited the need for an African consciousness among the Egyptian public.[19] In 1959, it was reported that there would be an increase in literature on Africa.[20] Indeed, there was. From 1959 to 1961, the two series We Choose for You and Political Books were in large part devoted to African problems. In 1960 Cairo University reported that more attention would be given to African languages.[21] Attempts were also made to rewrite school and university textbooks, especially geography and history books, to fit the new image the U.A.R. wanted to create of its relationship to the continent.

To clarify the question of Arabism and Africanism for the Egyptian public, Dr. Murad Ghaleb, a member of the National Committee of Education and undersecretary of foreign affairs, stated:

> We are Arabs . . . Arab nationalism is one aspect of African nationalism. . . . The Arab countries include the Northern Africans; we are then a part of the African continent. . . . Imperialism attempted to separate or distinguish between Arab nationalism and African nationalism. . . . As we are connected to African nationalism, we are also tied to Asian nationalism.[22]

18. *Mustqbal Ifriqiya' al-siyasi* [The political future of Africa] (Cairo: Muassasat al-Matbuat al-Haditha, 1957), pp. 390–91.

19. *Al-Isti'mar fi Ifriqiya'* [Imperialism in Africa] (Cairo: Nasr Publishing Organization, 1958).

20. Muhammad Fathi al-Tobji, *Al-Tayyarat al-siyasi fi Ifriqiya'* [Political trends in Africa], Political Books Series, no. 112 (Cairo: Political Books Committee, 1959), p. 3.

21. *Rose El-Youssief,* no. 1675, August 18, 1960, p. 5.

22. *Al-Ahram,* February 2, 1960, p. 3. The Committee on National Education was established in 1959 and has fifteen members representing "the growing forces in politics, science, and nationalism." The general secretary of the committee is the general secretary of the central government. Its membership in 1960 included Dr. Murad Ghaleb, undersecretary of foreign affairs; Dr. Hilmi Abdul Rahman, undersecretary of planing; Dr. Abdullah Alarian, professor of international law;

The Socialist Union was one of the main instruments employed to spread an African consciousness, and Africa was one of the most important topics on the agenda of the General Conference of the Socialist Union in 1960. Dr. Ghaleb, along with Fuad Jalal, chairman of the foreign relations committee of the Socialist Union, led the discussion. The Union not only supported the government's policy in Africa, but suggested that further steps be taken to protect the continent.[23]

A second aspect of Egypt's claim to Africanism was a renewed emphasis on its location on the African continent and an attempt to minimize the concept of the Sahara as a barrier separating North Africa from Black Africa. The cultural interplay between the two regions in the past was used as verification that the Sahara had not inhibited the continent's historic unity. In *The Philosophy of the Revolution* Nasser emphasized that the salient fact was that Egypt was in Africa and therefore could not be isolated from it.

Further, Egypt's claim to the historic experience of political unity was based on the concept of "unity of destiny" which was primarily a function of geography. Husain Muinis emphasized this point:

> Our destiny will finally be decided in Africa because we can never ignore the great principle fact that is our country's geography; that is, we are an African state. We are neither from the Orient nor from the West, although we have a share in each of them. We are Africans and if the balance on this continent is disturbed, the disaster will be on us.[24]

Egypt claimed that as the "guardian of the northeastern gate," it had defended Africa from foreign invasion since the early stages of history. Africa was overcome by "imperialism" only when Egypt itself fell under the yoke of imperialism.[25] The Egyptian revolution

---

Dr. Rafat al-Magjub, professor of economics; Amir Fahmi, engineer; and Ahmad Mukhtar Qutub, lawyer (*Al-Ahram*, February 5, 1960, p. 3).

23. *Al-Ahram*, July 11, 1960, p. 4.

24. *Misr wa risalatua* [Egypt and its mission] (Cairo: Al-Namudhajiyya Press [1954]), p. 144.

25. *Arab Observer*, July 22, 1963, p. 46.

was considered the vanguard for African freedom and was considered to have strengthened "the unity of the African struggle."[26]

LEADERSHIP

The concept of leadership, rather than constituting a clear principle in Egypt's African relations, is more of an attitude. It is evident from Nasser's *The Philosophy of the Revolution* that he considers Egypt to have a "responsibility" to Africa. A publication by the U.A.R. Information Department traced the idea of responsibility directly to Nasser's book.[27] Another Egyptian author, Muhammad Abdul Fatah Ibrahim, has also attempted to explain this concept, using *The Philosophy of the Revolution* as his source.[28]

Egypt considered itself "the leading African state."[29] Its duty, then, was to "lead the African nations against imperialism."[30] Nasser emphasized Egypt's role as the leader of Africa, not only in *The Philosophy of the Revolution* but also in numerous speeches: "Our people must carry the responsibility as the vanguard of freedom. Our republic must carry the responsibility as the base of freedom."[31]

Nasser considered it Egypt's duty not only to lead Africa to freedom but also to "safeguard the unity of the African march."[32] It is clear that Egypt considered its leadership to extend beyond just liberation. As one government publication stated, "The U.A.R.

26. See Muhammad Abdul Aziz Ishaq, "Thawrat 23 Yuliyo wa atharuha 'ala Ifriqiya" [The 23rd of July revolution and its effects on Africa], *Nahdhat Ifriqiya,* no. 56, July, 1962, p. 5.

27. *Ifriqiya min aqwal al-Rais Gamal Abdel Nasser* [Africa in the speeches of President Gamal Abdel Nasser], comp. U.A.R. Information Department (Cairo, n.d.), p. 5.

28. *Ifriqiya' min al-Sinighal' ila Nahr Jubba* [Africa from the Senegal to the Juba River] (Cairo: Anglo-Egyptian Bookshop, 1961), p. 8.

29. See Appendix I.

30. See Kamil, *Al-Isti'mar fi Ifriqiya* [Imperialism in Africa], p. 104.

31. *Majmu'at khutab wa tasrihat wa bayanat al-Rais Gamal Abdel Nasser* [Collection of speeches, statements, and remarks of President Gamal Abdel Nasser], *Part III, February, 1960–January, 1962,* comp. U.A.R. Information Department (Cairo, n.d.), p. 322.

32. *Al-Ahram,* January 24, 1961, p. 1.

cannot leave its leading role as a progressive, developed African state. It can participate in the liberation of the African continent . . . and help them in all fields of political, economic, and social life."[33]

Egypt always attempted to emphasize that it was "fate" that placed it in this role.[34] Nasser stated that Africa looked to Egypt for guidance; thus, it was Africa's "will" to be led by Egypt.[35] *Al-Ahram* declared: "Egypt cannot do anything but accept the will of these nations in achieving their national goals."[36] Dr. Tharwat Akashah, minister of culture and guidance and a close associate of Nasser, explained this role:

> The U.A.R. has a great responsibility toward these nations forced [on her] . . . by the nature of the leading role that is played by our republic [before] . . . the nations that are liberated but are still less developed than we economically and culturally.[37]

Nasser emphasized Egypt's responsibility on many occasions. For example, he declared, "Egypt realizes that she has a responsibility for the future of Africa and we will perform it."[38] The clearest manifestation of this responsibility was Egypt's attitude toward the liberation of Africa. Nasser stated, "As the vanguard of freedom, it is the duty of Egypt to carry this responsibility in order to liberate the African continent."[39] The article "An African policy for Egypt" elaborated this point:

33. Fathi al-Mahallawi, *Arba'a duwal fi rakb al-huriyya* [Four states in the freedom caravan], Political Books Series, no. 143 (Cairo: Political Books Committee, 1960), pp. 20–21.

34. See Ahmad Mahrawish, "Limadha tadhl al-Qahira markaz quwwa" [Why Cairo remains the center of power], *Rose El-Youssief,* no. 1042, August 30, 1965, p. 4.

35. *The Philosophy of the Revolution,* pp. 109–10.

36. January 13, 1954, p. 6.

37. Masuliyyatura al-thaqafiya nahwa Ifriqiya'" [Our cultural responsibility toward Africa], *Nahdhat Ifriqiya,* no. 50, January, 1962, p. 3.

38. U.A.R. Documentation Research Center, *Dairat al-ma'arif al-siyasiya al-Arabiya: nashrat al-wathaiq* [The Arab political encyclopedia: bulletin of documents], XII (November–December, 1963; January–February, 1964), Section of the President, 3; hereafter referred to as *Nashrat al-wathaiq.*

39. *Al-Ahram,* December 16, 1960, p. 1.

108

Egypt finds itself called upon to shoulder the great burdens thrown on it, to endeavour strongly and resolutely to liberate these peoples, to raise them from the deep abyss into which they have been driven by the power of foreign colonialism, and to help them by all possible means in all political, economic and social fields, so that the peoples may regain their freedom and become strong and united. Africa will then be for the Africans.[40]

It is evident in surveying Egyptian publications, however, that the idea of responsibility goes much deeper than just the liberation of Africa. Often implied, but seldom clearly stated, Egypt considers that its role in Africa is that of a sacred mission and historic duty. According to a close associate of Nasser, Anwar al-Sadat, "The men of the revolution have a mission in Somaliland and in Africa itself."[41] There are many examples from Nasser's own speeches that demonstrate that he considered Egypt's mission a historic one. He has declared:

Our people stood throughout long history at the entrance of the continent performing . . . their duty with responsibility and love. On the northeastern gate of the continent our nation stood, with all its power and trying to shield Africa and protect her.[42]

At the Addis Ababa Conference of 1963, he stated:

The U.A.R. comes here with an open heart and mind, with an appreciation of her responsibility . . . and she is ready to bear fully her historic responsibility toward the African continent.[43]

Furthermore, Egypt's mission was not only to lead the liberation movements but also to be the harbinger of the African awakening. "We represent the connection between Africa and the outside

40. *Egyptian Economic and Political Review,* II (August, 1956), 21.
41. *Al-Ahram,* January 25, 1955, p. 6.
42. *Nashrat al-wathaiq,* X (March–April, 1962), Section of the President, 165.
43. *Khutab al-Rais Gamal Abdel Nasser fi mutamar al-qumma al-Ifriqi fi Addis Ababa* [The speech of President Gamal Abdel Nasser in the African summit conference at Addis Ababa] *24 May 1963* (Cairo: U.A.R. Information Department, n.d.), p. 14.

109

world," it was asserted.[44] *Al-Ahram* declared that Egypt had a duty in the "awakening" of Africa.[45] There are many publications that attempt to show that Egypt has had this effect on Africa throughout history.[46] Mishil Kamil considered Egypt to be the only country that actually carried modern civilization to the heart of Africa during the nineteenth century.[47] Dr. Abdul Malik Audah also attempted to prove Egypt's historical influence in awakening Africa by tracing a cultural relationship between the Arabs and Africa.[48] In the textbook on African political systems used by Cairo University, Dr. Audah declares that "In 1960 the U.A.R. will stay as she has always been: a torch of light, liberation, and revolution in Africa."[49]

However, this concept as a factor in Egypt's present African policy is seldom emphasized by the government because of the obvious delicacy of the subject. Nasser himself gave it the clearest expression when he wrote that "Our responsibility is to help spread the light of knowledge and civilization.[50] On another occasion he stated, "Our people try to become the bridge of civilization and culture."[51] But the attitude does creep into other publications. An example is this statement: "The continent is in great need of thoughts that were created in the north, such as the concepts concerning freedom, unity, socialism, and the way of continuous organization."[52]

44. Shawqi Iqladius, *Yaqadhat Ifriqiya'* [The awakening of Africa], Political Books Series, no. 125 (Cairo: Political Books Committee, n.d.), p. 38.
45. March 28, 1961, p. 6.
46. See Muhammad al-Mu'tasim' Sayyid, "Dhaaw 'ala dawri Misr al-hadhari fi Ifriqiya [A light on Egypt's cultural role in Africa], *Nahdhat Ifriqiya,* no. 72, November, 1963, pp. 15–16.
47. *Al-Isti'mar fi Ifriqiya* [Imperialism in Africa].
48. See *Al-Ahram,* March 28, 1961, p. 6.
49. *Al-Siyasa wa al-hukum fi Ifriqiya,* [Political systems in Africa], p. 556.
50. *The Philosophy of the Revolution,* pp. 69–70.
51. *Nashrat al-wathaiq,* X (March–April, 1962), Section of the President, 165.
52. Abdu Badawi in *Nahdhat Ifriqiya,* no. 66, May, 1963, p. 2.

Chapter Five

The Policy Objectives

"The effort and capital inside our country are worthless if the country is surrounded from the south and west . . . by that which would threaten our existence and prosperity." This statement, published in an Egyptian newspaper in 1965, explains the objectives of the U.A.R.'s foreign policy in Africa.[1] Of course, as with any nation, the U.A.R.'s foreign policy is constructed within a hierarchy of interests. On a geopolitical basis the areas nearest to Egypt would be at the top of the hierarchy. Africa, then, particularly those regions bordering on Egypt and Sudan, are of primary importance. Egypt regards it essential to maintain friendly relations with the neighboring African countries in order to secure its frontiers and strategic interests and to insure the protection of the vital sources of the Nile River. The following statement portrays well the relationship between Egypt's strategic interests and the policy of anti-imperialism in terms of that hierarchy of interests. It explains, for example, the reasons for the U.A.R.'s active anti-imperialist policy in Africa (as opposed, for instance, to its passive policy in East Asia):

1. *Al-Jumhuriya,* January 21, 1965, p. 6.

Substance of the Policy

> We believe that our freedom is in danger as long as there is
> any colonized nation. Our prosperity is in danger as long as
> there are exploited nations. . . . We should secure our frontiers
> and we should consider that they are located wherever im-
> perialism exists. Whenever a battle against imperialism occurs,
> Egypt will support it and bless it, and if it can, Egypt will
> participate in it because of our interests, idealism, and history.[2]

That Egypt regards Africa as a primary area of concern cannot
be doubted. It has been stated by Nasser and confirmed by official
statements on many occasions. In an early period of policy development *Rose El-Youssief* summarized this concern accordingly:

> Egypt's vital sphere and future are in Africa. We should give
> more attention to the establishment of an Egyptian front in
> Africa. We should be more concerned about our important
> situation in Africa wherein lies our future and the future of
> the whole continent.[3]

Egypt's African policy itself can also be viewed as a hierarchy
of objectives ranging from minimum to maximum. These objectives
are not different in nature but represent differences in the degree
to which Egypt attempts to safeguard its strategic position.

THE MINIMUM OBJECTIVE

The minimum objective of Egypt's policy is to protect the Nile
water resources and to safeguard its other strategic and economic
interests in the Sudan.[4] Nasser has explained the geopolitical importance of Africa, tying it not only to Egypt's fate but to the fate
of the whole Arab world:

> The land of this Arab nation is situated in Africa. Also, in the
> northern part of this continent live other Arab nations. . . .

2. "Misr fikra wa laysat dawla" [Egypt is an idea, not a state], *Rose El-Youssief,*
no. 1451, April 2, 1956, p. 3.
3. No. 1518, July 15, 1957, p. 16.
4. See Chapter Seven for a discussion of Egypt's policy in the Sudan.

The fate of the Arab people in Egypt and the fate of the Arab nationalist movement, which binds together all Arab nations, is physically tied to the African continent's struggle and destiny.[5]

As relations with the West deteriorated, Egypt feared Western retaliation against the vital Nile water resources such as Britain threatened in 1924. Thus, the increasing support given to the nationalist movements from the time of the Bandung Conference derived primarily from strategic purposes. Accordingly, *Rose El-Youssief* at that time stated:

We should watch . . . Britain in Central Africa. She might try to create difficulties for our projects on the Nile. This puts forward our duty to support all nationalist movements anywhere. They are behind the enemy lines. Let's make them our bases there.[6]

Egypt's involvement with the nationalist movements, then, was actually regarded as a strategic necessity. "The field of our nationalist movement," wrote Fathi Khalil, "is being enlarged, and the enemies of our nationalist movement will be met on a broader front."[7] In 1965, Muhammad Hassanein Heikal emphasized the concept that Egypt's fate is tied to the African continent and that its security lies in a broad front of anti-imperialist movement. "In Africa itself this existing and necessary association is not only a matter of principle but is a matter of security and protection." He saw a danger to Egypt in the Rhodesian problem because as another racist African country, South Africa, had brought the problem closer to the Portuguese colonies of Angola and Mozambique, so might the Rhodesian problem affect Malawi and Zambia and perhaps even Tanzania, where the origins of the Nile exist. "As a result," wrote Heikal, "the southern portions of Africa will lose their Africanism." He saw a similar threat in the Congo problem

5. *Al-Ahram,* October 12, 1962, p. 1.
6. No. 1490, December 31, 1956, p. 3.
7. "Mashakil Ifriquia wa Asiya" [The problems of Asia and Africa], *Rose El-Youssief,* no. 1544, January 13, 1958, p. 8.

113

because, as he suggested, the "imperialists" might attempt to intervene in the southern part of the Sudan.[8]

Prior to 1957, while the greater part of Africa was still under colonial rule, Egypt's policy was aimed at establishing bases through the nationalist movements in order to combat the West, which Egypt considered the main source of threat to its self-preservation. That its policy was dictated by geopolitical factors is made clear from a statement in a textbook used by Cairo University:

> We are not exaggerating if we state that Egypt's . . . foreign policy is very much influenced by its geographic location. It is an African state, closely connected with the continent through the Nile River whose origins are situated in the heart of the continent.[9]

THE INTERMEDIATE OBJECTIVE

Egypt's intermediate objective can be broadly described as "Africa for Africans," or an African adaptation of America's Monroe Doctrine. After colonialism declined and the major blocs began competing for influence in Africa, Egypt sought to safeguard herself against any state achieving substantial influence and thereby constituting a threat. To that end, Egypt attempted to utilize the concepts of anti-imperialism, nonalignment, positive neutrality, African will, African unity, and African personality. Commenting on the principle of Africa for Africans, a suggested African program for Egypt published in 1956 stated:

> Egypt's declaration of this principle at a suitable time, its endeavours to stabilize this principle and not to deviate from it or go against it resembles the Monroe Doctrine (America for Americans). The reaffirmation by Egypt of this principle, keeping staunchly to it and defending it, will enable her to win a high position in the hearts of the peoples of Africa. This

8. *Al-Ahram,* December 24, 1965, p. 1.
9. Butrus Butrus Ghali and Mahmud Khairi Isa, *Mabadi al-'ulum al-siyasiya* [An introduction to political science] (Cairo: Anglo-Egyptian Bookshop, 1962–63), p. 564.

114

will make all these countries direct their gaze towards Egypt and gather around her.[10]

Nasser considered that the West posed the greater threat of dominating Africa because through colonial rule it had acquired economic, political, and cultural influence. To combat African dependence on the West, Egypt allied herself with the Soviet Union, which had no base of influence and which was regarded suspiciously by the Western-oriented African countries. That the policy was aimed directly against the West was made clear by a 1959 government publication:

> The U.A.R. should clearly announce that its policy is centered around the principle of Africa for Africans. This is very similar to the "Monroe Doctrine" which was declared by the American President Monroe to stop Western imperialism.
>
> The U.A.R.'s role in the African continent is similar to the U.S.'s role on the American continent . . . announcing this principle, we negate the accusation of the Western imperialists . . . that we are seeking to establish an African empire.[11]

Thus, Egypt introduced a "Monroe Doctrine" for Africa. This was very clearly manifested in Nasser's meeting with President Eisenhower in September, 1960. Summarizing that meeting, Nasser stated:

> I explained to him that the United Arab Republic was endeavoring to contribute to the purpose of securing the independence of the African countries. I also explained that the African continent should remain aloof from the Cold War and that we would resist any imperialist influence in Africa.[12]

Nasser's major effort in this direction was directed through the Casablanca Group. The Casablanca Charter emphasized the main

10. "An African Policy for Egypt," *Egyptian Economic and Political Review,* II (August, 1956), 22–23; see Appendix I for the full text of this article.

11. Muhammad Fathi Al-Tobji, *Al-Tayyarat al-siyasiya fi Ifriqiya'* [The political trends in Africa], Political Books Series, no. 112 (Cairo: Political Books Committee, 1959), pp. 94–95.

12. *Al-Ahram,* October 13, 1960, p. 1.

concepts of his African "Monroe Doctrine," that is, noninterference by foreign powers, nonalignment, positive neutrality, African unity, African will, and African personality. On his return from the 1961 Casablanca Conference, Nasser's statements indicated his strategic motives: "The Arab struggle is being extended . . . from Bandung to Casablanca. Time and experience prove that this . . . is the line of Arab security and the line of peace."[13] In his speech to the National Assembly summarizing his position at the Casablanca Conference, Nasser further declared that "the success of the aims of the African struggle cannot be achieved by pushing Africa into the Cold War among the blocs." In the same speech he made his objectives even clearer by stating that Egypt would protect "the unity of the African march and will never allow imperialism to drag them into branch fights with reactionaries in these countries."[14]

Egypt regarded Israel's involvements in Africa to be another major threat to its strategic position. "No doubt our interests in Africa will remain in danger as long as Israel continues to penetrate the heart of Africa" stated an Egyptian writer.[15] Abdul Malik Audah, an Egyptian African specialist, considered Israeli activities in Africa an attempt to attack "the Arab revolution from the back and . . . an alliance between imperialism and Israel for the destruction of the Arab revolution."[16] Audah considered that Israel has been successful in Africa in part because it provided an excellent example for African nations that aspire to modernize along Western lines.

To combat this threat, Egypt attempted to identify Israel as a base of imperialism through which the West was trying to regain a foothold on the continent. This was clearly expressed in the National Charter.[17] Egypt has emphasized that European imperialism is behind Israeli activities in Africa, that Israel is not a humanitarian

13. *Al-Ahram,* January 21, 1961, p. 1.

14. *Majmu'at khutab wa tasrihat wa bayanat al-Rais Gamal Abdel Nasser* [Collection of speeches, statements, and remarks of President Gamal Abdel Nasser], Part III, *February, 1960–January, 1962,* comp. U.A.R. Information Department (Cairo, n.d.), p. 365.

15. Abdul Mun'im al-Khudari, "Taghalghul Israil fi Ifriqiya" [The Israeli penetration in Africa], *Nahdhat Ifriqiya,* no. 50, January, 1962, p. 15.

16. *Israil wa Ifriqiya* [Israel and Africa] (Cairo: League of Arab States, Institute of Higher Arabic Studies, 1964), pp. 40–41.

17. *The Charter* (Cairo: U.A.R. Information Department, 1962), p. 100.

state but an expression of imperialism, that in the future Israel will serve as the middleman between Africa and the European Common Market, and that the European Common Market is nothing but a facade of neocolonialism.[18]

In mid-1964, in an attempt to combat Israel's success, the Egyptian ambassadors to Africa held a conference dealing exclusively with this subject. This was viewed by Israel as a challenge to its interests in Africa. Ahud Avriel, the assistant chief of the Israeli Foreign Ministry, warned, "If the Egyptians carry out their decisions to harm the friendly relations existing between Israel and the countries of Africa we shall sharpen our means to defeat their work of incitement and undermining."[19]

THE MAXIMUM OBJECTIVE

The maximum objective of Egypt's policy is to return Egypt to the glories of its past and to re-establish the ancient boundaries that at times reached deep into Ethiopia. A political-science textbook used by Cairo University states:

> The first to lay the foundations of Egypt's foreign policy toward Africa were the Egyptian Pharaohs. . . . Their aim was to extend Egyptian influence over the Sudan and some regions that today are called Somalia and Ethiopia. They succeeded at times and failed at others.[20]

Like their pharaonic forefathers it is the aspiration of some Egyptians to establish a greater state of the Nile Valley that will be the leading nation of the continent. Unlike the ancient Pharaonic empire, however, this state would not result from imperialist adventures. Rather, Egyptian intellectuals consider that such a state will be the logical result of the Pan-African movement. A text-

18. Al-Khudhari, "Taghalghul Israil fi Ifriqiya" [The Israeli peneration in Africa], p. 15.

19. *Davar* (Tel Aviv), August 30, 1964, p. 2.

20. Ghali and Isa, *Mabadi al-'ulum al-siyasiya* (An introduction to political science), p. 565.

book written by the chairman and another faculty member of the
political science department of Alexandria University states that
Egypt must carry the burden of responsibility in this movement
because it is "the forerunner of the African states in civilization,
culture, wealth, and power." The book further states:

> There is no doubt that all the probabilities point out that the
> situation of this state will be in the northern part of the con-
> tinent because the nations in this part have been more progres-
> sive technologically throughout . . . history and have all the
> contemporary consciousness which will enable them to achieve
> this role.[21]

Prior to the revolution, there were demands for a more aggressive African policy which would prepare for "our natural and
legitimate growth. . . . We have directed a portion of our concern
to our Asian sisters but neglected the African regions where we
are justified in desiring that our influence reach them without any
ambitions to control their affairs."[22] An African policy was considered essential because Egypt and the Sudan are "a nation that
possesses the Nile and the Nile possesses Africa."[23] After the revolution, Egypt hoped to establish a greater state of the Nile Valley
through a union with the Sudan. In 1953, General Nagib, speaking
of the inherent unity of the Nile Valley, spoke of the potential of
such a union for Egypt's position in the world:

> Egypt should be transformed into a great state. This is not an
> illusion. We do not depend on dreams. Our dependence is only
> on proven fact. Egypt possesses all of the means of greatness.
> In its strategic position it is at the head of Africa. . . . We are
> not an insignificant people and we should not remain a small
> state. We have in our history, in our location, in our natural
> and human resources, that which enables us to create a great
> state with weight in the international balance. The past proves
> our point, and history mentions that the Egyptian nation is a
> great nation and that each time it was provided with honest

21. Muhammad Badawi and Muhammad al-Ghanami, *Dirasat siyasiya wa
qawmiya* [Political and national studies] (Cairo: Dar Al-Ma'arif, 1963), p. 574.
22. *Al-Ahram*, February 8, 1948, p. 3.
23. *Al-Ahram*, February 18, 1948, p. 3.

and faithful leadership it accomplished the impossible and achieved miracles. History mentions too that the Egyptian soldier is patient, brave, efficient, and hard working. . . . We do not want to conquer or colonize. We don't want anything but our freedom and our complete independence. We want to have a place suitable to the greatness of our history, the greatness of our nation and the greatness of our resources.[24]

Similarly, Fathi Radhwan, at various times a minister of communications, minister of state, and minister of culture and guidance, noted that "Egypt never lived for herself. . . . Her history testifies that any time she became strong and liberated she became a source of great power, leading nations and teaching them."[25]

Upon the failure of the Sudan policy, Egypt attempted to form a military pact wih Ethiopia and the Sudan. Muhammad Kamil Abdul-Hamid, a general and later a member of Parliament, considered that the pact represented the nucleus of a "Cairo–Khartoum–Addis Ababa axis" that would result in the establishment of a northeastern state in the Nile Basin.[26] This pact also failed, and Egypt adjusted its policy to deal more realistically with the aggressively independent and proud African states and liberation movements.[27]

A belief that a greater state of the Nile Valley will be the first tangible expression of the Pan-African movement is a dominant theme in Egyptian intellectual and academic circles today. That the government itself considers this thesis valid can be gleaned from the prevalence of the concept in textbooks and in the strictly censored Egyptian press. For example, a textbook written by a professor of international law at 'Ain Shams University Law School states that imperialism created barriers between Arab North Africa

24. Republic of Egypt, Armed Forces, *Mithaq al-Thawra min aqwal rais wa naib rais wa a'adha majlis qiyda al-thawra* [The charter of the revolution from the speeches of the president, vice-president, and members of the Revolutionary Command Council] (Cairo: Egyptian Armed Forces, Public Relations Department, 1953), p. 17.

25. *Al-Ahram,* May 2, 1955, p. 8.

26. *Al-Sharq al-Awsat fi al-mizan al-istiratiji* [The Middle East in the strategic balance] (Cairo: Modern Publishing House, n.d.), pp. 321–26.

27. See Chapter Two, above, for a discussion of Egypt's policy toward nationalist movements.

119

and Central and South Africa in order "to limit the spread of Arab civilization into Africa and to stop cooperation between the Arab nationalist movement and the struggling African peoples against European imperialism." The book further states that this was done because "the imperialist powers feared that the U.A.R.'s contact with Africa would result in strengthening its economic and political power."[28]

Abdul Ghany Abdallah Khalaf Allah, in his book *Mustaqbal Ifriqiya al-syassiya* [The political future of Africa], treats this concept thoroughly. He considers the creation of a united states of Africa, with the U.A.R. possibly acting as its nucleus, to be one of the most urgent needs today. He calls for a Monroe Doctrine for the continent and believes that Nasser could play the role of the Monroe of Africa. It is his contention that a greater state of the Nile Valley would be the future state to lead Africa and that it is the duty of Egypt to start this state, which should include Egypt, Sudan, Ethiopia, Somalia, Uganda, Kenya, and Tanganyika because they have "the historic, religious and linguistic ties between them . . . also the ties of race." According to this book, the imperialist powers have attempted to destroy the historic, economic, religious, cultural and racial ties existing between these states because they fear the establishment of a greater state of the Nile Basin.[29]

Khalaf Allah wrote with two objects in mind: to demonstrate Egypt's concern with Africa and to denounce the Western powers opposition to Egypt's role in that region. He traces Western opposition back to the early 1820s when the European states forced the fleet Muhammad Ali had built to remain in Egypt. It should be noted in this connection that the concern of the Western powers at this time was not so much the rising power of Egypt. Rather, their concern was with the weakness of the Ottoman Empire, which served as the West's bulwark against Russian ambitions in the Middle East, and with the threat posed to the Ottomans by Muhammad Ali's Syrian adventures. The Western powers in fact encouraged Egyptian ambitions in the Sudan as a means of distract-

28. Muhammad Hafiz Ghanim, *Al-alaqat al-dawliya al-'Arabiya* [Arab international relations] (Cairo: Nahdhat Misr, 1965), p. 367.

29. (Cairo: Muassasat al-Matbu'at al-Haditha, 1957), pp. 364–68.

ing Egypt from further incursions into Syria. In the latter part of the nineteenth century the manner in which the British directed Egyptian policy left the appearance, if not the substance, of power with the Egyptians, and thus the Egyptians were able to maintain prestige in the Nile Valley. The view of the West's perpetual opposition to Egypt's African ambitions which Khalaf Allah presents may be overdrawn, but it is both evidential and supportive of Egyptian government policy under Nasser.

Khalaf Allah concludes that during Ismail's era the West appointed Gordon as the governor of the Sudan, an area which was "the only link between Egypt and the middle of the continent," as "a security to smother any African policy that might be born in Egypt."[30] In addition, he considers the Suez War to have been the latest of the imperialist attempts to destroy the Egyptian state:

> It was very clear from the military action in the Suez Canal War that Britain and France felt they were being threatened by the establishment of a great state in Egypt under the leadership of a great, strong leader who has clear aims and objectives.[31]

Khalaf Allah also maintains that the objective of the Suez War was to destroy Nasser because he was "the first Egyptian head of state who mentioned Africa in his political program as a circle for future Egyptian activities."[32] Khalaf Allah described Egypt's duty in Africa to be "the establishment of a great state in the whole Nile basin, the mandate over the rest of the oppressed nations of the continent, and the unlocking of their shackles."[33]

It is significant to note that Khalaf Allah outlined a program for Egypt which closely approximates Egypt's actual policy during the early 1960s. The ultimate goal of this policy, according to Khalaf Allah's book, is the establishment of the greater state of the Nile Basin. The program outlined calls for the industrialization of the Nile Valley to meet the rising population problem. This indus-

30. *Ibid.,* p. 369.
31. *Ibid.,* p. 377.
32. *Ibid.,* p. 378.
33. *Ibid.,* pp. 390–91.

trialization is expected to result in the grouping together of all the societies from southern Sudan, Kenya, Uganda, and Tanganyika and is expected to help raise the standards of living and to aid the spread of education. Also, greater communication between the parts of the state should ensue. Further, the program recommended that Egypt should aid the liberation movements in Africa, should establish diplomatic relations with the independent African states, and should help those states achieve their goals for the future of Africa. This, it is thought, will "expel the oppressor and will be the first stone in the building of the future united states of Africa, and will pave the way to the union of the Nile Valley in order to achieve its mission . . . on the continent."[34] In addition, the program called for a campaign for the awakening of Africa and for Egypt to send missions to the various independent African countries. Khalaf Allah asserted that the united nations of the Nile Valley are to be the nucleus for the future united states of Africa and that this political entity will be among the big powers of the world, as the U.S.S.R. and the U.S. are today.

In an article published in 1964 in a government-supervised journal, Khalaf Allah again advocated the same idea. He surmised that "the cultural, economic, political and social development on the African Continent since the end of World War II had proven beyond a doubt the need for an African great power." He stated that what he calls "the continuity of African freedom" cannot survive without the creation of this great power because the world itself is composed of super powers.[35] Here, too, he indirectly indicated the U.A.R. should be the nucleus of this greater state of the Nile Valley.

ECONOMIC OBJECTIVES

Although the U.A.R.'s maximum African policy objective is to create a greater state of the Nile Valley, its attempt to gain influ-

34. *Ibid.,* p. 428.

35. "Active Factors in Future African Development," *Egyptian Political Science Review,* no. 35, February, 1964, English Section, pp. 15–17.

122

ence in Africa and to reduce the influence of other powers, especially the European powers, has been more directly influenced by the need to solve certain internal economic problems by external means. The U.A.R. is faced today with two critical economic problems. The first is the problem of overpopulation and a concomitant shortage of food. The second, and perhaps the more immediate, problem is the U.A.R.'s need to create new markets and find new sources of raw materials for its industrial establishment. It is believed by a number of Egypt's leaders that the application of an African Monroe Doctrine would solve these two pressing economic problems.

The United Nations estimation of the U.A.R.'s 1965 population was 29,600,000.[36] The annual increase of population is 800,000. At this rate it was estimated that the U.A.R.'s population would reach 34,000,000 by 1970. It was also estimated that Cairo would have a population of 5,000,000 and Alexandria, 2,300,000.[37] It is estimated that by 1985 the U.A.R.'s population will reach 52,000,-000.[38] The enormity of the population problem is demonstrated by the density of population per unit of cultivated land. In these terms Egypt is the most densely populated country in the world.[39] The average rate of population growth in the U.A.R. is the highest in the world after Brazil, the Philippines, Mexico, Thailand, and Turkey.[40]

Nasser himself has for some time emphasized the urgency of Egypt's population problem. He has pointed out that food and agrarian production have not increased correspondingly with the population increase.[41] In 1966 he declared, "The national action

36. United Nations, Department of Economic and Social Affairs, *Demographic Yearbook, 1965,* 17th issue (New York: U.N. Statistical Office, 1966), p. 131.

37. U.A.R. General Agency for Public Mobilization and Statistics, *Al-Ta'bia al-'amma wa al-ihsaa* [Public mobilization and statistics], IX (April, 1966), 26.

38. *Arab Observer,* September 3, 1962, p. 12.

39. Charles Issawi, *Egypt in Revolution: An Economic Analysis* (London: Oxford University Press, 1963), p. 85.

40. U.A.R. General Agency for Public Mobilization and Statistics, *Al-Ta'bia Al-'Amma wa al-ihsaa* [Public mobilization and statistics], IX (May, 1966), 5.

41. *Khutab al-Rais Gamal Abdel Nasser fi Mutamar al-itthad al-ishtiraki al-'Arabi,* [Speeches of President Gamal Abdel Nasser in the convention of the Arab Socialist Union], *March, 1965,* comp. U.A.R. Information Department (Cairo, n.d.), p. 45.

is exposed to internal explosion because of the effects of two problems: the increase in population and the increase in consumption."[42] Between 1937 and 1960 the population increased by approximately 64 per cent, while crop production increased by only 33 per cent, animal production by 45 per cent, and food production by 43 per cent. The total agricultural production increased by 36 per cent.[43] In 1966 Nasser announced that the annual rate of population increase in the U.A.R. was 3 per cent.[44] He also noted in 1966 that since he took office in 1952 the population had risen by 10 million. He declared:

> The increase in the population in our country has reached astronomical figures. The population since the revolution has grown by ten million, at a rate of 750,000 a year. These people need clothing, food, education, medical and social care; they also claim their right to employment. All this takes place in a limited area of land to which Nature has given nothing except human capabilities. We should take for granted that as a part of this problem we pay the tax of success scored in the social aspects.[45]

That Egypt regards Africa as a likely outlet for its population overflow is apparent. The African program for Egypt published in the *Egyptian Economic and Political Review* recommended that Egypt should "encourage the emigration of Egyptians to many African countries, such as Sudan and East Africa, facilitate their journeys and grant them subsidies."[46] In his book Abdul Ghany Abdallah Khalaf Allah recommended the creation of a Ministry of Emigration whose duties should include (1) searching out African countries that need technical and cultural assistance; (2) establishing priorities for the most overpopulated areas in Egypt and extending assistance to aid the migrants to Africa; and (3) preparing

42. *Al-Jumhuriya,* February 3, 1966, p. 3.
43. *Arab Observer,* September 3, 1962, p. 11.
44. *Al-Muharrir* (Beirut), June 16, 1966, p. 6.
45. *Egyptian Gazette* (Cairo), November 25, 1966, p. 5.
46. "An African Policy for Egypt," 23–24.

the population for emigration to Africa and granting assistance to help them settle.[47]

A number of Egyptian writers have suggested that the Sudan, because of its underpopulation, could be an outlet for Egypt's overpopulation.[48] The Ministry of Labor has established a section dealing with the emigration operation. Projects for growing wheat for the U.A.R. in large areas of Mali and Somalia have also been reported.[49]

Egypt is also looking to Africa in search of solutions to its second major economic problem. Africa offers not only one of the most promising markets for Egypt's manufactured goods but also a source of raw materials for Egypt's expanding industrial establishment. A report issued by U.A.R. economic authorities in 1962 stressed the importance of Africa "for the disposal of U.A.R. goods and products" and the need "to ensure a continuous flow of raw materials from Africa to feed U.A.R. industries."[50] As early as 1956 Egypt's economic objectives in Africa were clearly identified. Suggested activities to pursue these objectives appeared in the proposed program for an African policy.[51] The same objectives were emphasized again in 1959;[52] these included sending trade missions to Africa, concluding agreements, and granting export-promotion loans in an attempt to expand the potentialities of this vast market.[53] In 1962 the U.A.R. exported products to the Sudan, Somalia, Libya, Ghana, Ethiopia, Nigeria, Algeria, Sierra Leone, Morocco, and Guinea.[54]

47. *Mustaqbal Ifriqiya al-siyassiya* [The political future of Africa], pp. 407–8.

48. See Dawlat Ahmad Sadiq, "Mushkilat al-sukkan fi Misr" [The problem of population in Egypt], *Hawliyat kulliyat al-adab* [Annals of the faculty of arts], ed. 'Ain Shams University, IV (January, 1957); also see Ahmad al-Khashab, *Dirasat dimoghrafiyya fi sukkan al-alam al-'Arabi* [Demographic studies in the population of the Arab world] (Cairo: Contemporary Cairo Bookshop, n.d.).

49. *Rose El-Youssief,* no. 1938, August 2, 1965, p. 8.

50. *Arab Observer,* September 3, 1962, p. 41.

51. "An African Policy for Egypt," p. 23.

52. A government publication outlined a program for economic activities (Al-Tobji, *Al-tayyarat al-siyasiya fi Ifriqiya* [The political treds in Africa]).

53. Issawi, *Egypt in Revolution,* p. 307.

54. U.A.R. Ministry of Industries, *Al-Thawra al-sina'iyya fi ahada 'ashara 'aman* [The industrial revolution in eleven years], *1952–1963* (Cairo: General Organization for Governmental Presses, 1963), p. 147.

Substance of the Policy

In the early sixties, the U.A.R.'s foreign trade with African states greatly expanded. Between June, 1962, and June, 1963, the value of trade was LE 15,000,000—LE 6,000,000 more than in previous years. Between January and December, 1963, exports to West African states (which provide the major market for U.A.R. goods) through the U.A.R. General Trade Organization (Nasr Company for Import and Export) were estimated to value LE 4,330,651. The chief items of export were textiles, cement, tires, leather goods, perfumes, canned food, and rice. The company's imports, consisting chiefly of coffee, cocoa, aluminum alloys, and pineapples, added up to LE 1,064,713 for the same period. The table below indicates the chief customers for U.A.R. goods in 1963 and the value of goods the U.A.R. exported to them.

VALUE OF U.A.R. EXPORTS (IN LE) TO
MAJOR AFRICAN IMPORTERS, 1963

Guinea	1,511,004	Dahomey	88,507
Ghana	754,863	Niger	86,990
Mali	570,583	Sierra Leone	31,181
Nigeria	548,137	Congo	15,481
Senegal	321,679	Liberia	1,826

By 1967 the Nasr Company for Import and Export had established nineteen branches in the following African states: Nigeria, Guinea, Sierra Leone, Ghana, Mali, Senegal, Congo (Kinshasa), Congo (Brazzaville), Cameroon, Dahomey, Niger, Ivory Coast, Kenya, Zambia, Tanzania, Uganda, Togo, Mauritania, and Liberia. In addition to these states, the U.A.R. had contracted commercial agreements with Ethiopia, Somalia, and Burundi.[55] From 1960 to 1964 alone, the value of U.A.R. trade with non-Arab African countries jumped from LE 1,700,000 to LE 7,600,000—a more than fourfold increase. Also in the period from 1960–61 to 1964–65, Africa's share of U.A.R. trade rose from 1.7 per cent to 6 per

55. See Appendix III.

cent.[56] The table below indicates the distribution of this significant expansion.

VALUE OF U.A.R. EXPORTS (IN LE) TO
SELECTED AFRICAN COUNTRIES, 1960 AND 1964

	1960	1964
Somalia	96,000	2,191,000
Nigeria	—	1,083,000
Ghana	25,000	630,000
Guinea	—	565,000
Liberia	—	565,000
Congo (Leopoldville)	—	498,000
Southern Rhodesia	—	412,000
Cameroon	—	391,000
Angola	—	260,000
Kenya	—	69,000
Tanganyika	—	59,000

SOURCE: *Al-Ahram al-Iqtisadi,* no. 242, September 15, 1965.

In August, 1970, it was announced that the volume of U.A.R. trade with African countries increased over the previous fiscal year to LE 12,000,000. Furthermore, the value of international trade which the United Arab Republic conducted by marketing African products in Europe amounted to LE 15,000,000. Mr. Muhammad Ghanim, president of the Nasr Export-Import Company, stated that many significant indications characterized Egypt's economic relations with African countries during this period, chief among which were increased exports to these countries amounting to LE 8,135,000, while imports dropped to LE 3,894,000. Furthermore, new markets were opened in certain countries, including Upper Volta and Central African Republic. Egypt exported industrial products to them for the first time, along with increased rice

56. U.A.R. Ministry of National Guidance, *Al-kitab al-sanawi* [The yearbook], *1966* (Cairo, 1966), p. 111.

exports. The international marketing which Nasr Export-Import Company conducted amounted to LE 15,000,000, of which LE 11,500,000 were transacted by the Egyptian trade branch in Nigeria through which Nigerian products were exported to West European countries. Mr. Ghanim added, "It has been decided to expand the scope of international trade this year and a treaty of cooperation has recently been signed in this respect with foreign trade companies in Japan for the purpose of exporting African products to Far Eastern markets."[57]

However, there is keen competition from the West, the Soviet bloc, Japan, and Israel for the African markets. In order to limit this competition, Nasser has attempted to utilize his political tools —anti-imperialism, positive neutrality, Africa for Africans, and African unity—to insulate Africa economically. He has indicated that without this policy Egypt could not establish relations with African states.[58]

The U.A.R. made a clear attempt at the 1961 Casablanca Conference to reduce foreign competition in Africa. The participating nations signed seven economic agreements that provided for the establishment of an African Common Market, the creation of an African Development Bank, the establishment of an African Payments Union, the institution of an African Aviation Organization and of a Navigation and Naval Transport Pact, the establishment of an African Economic Unity Council, and the creation of an African Federation of International Air Transport Companies.[59] Regarding the African Common Market, Nasser stated:

> The struggle against imperialism is a struggle for the sake of the African land and for the sake of the mines. . . . We cannot understand African independence as carrying the flag and leaving the lands and the mines in the hands of imperialism.[60]

57. Faruq Juwaydah, "Volume of our Trade with Africa Increased," *Al-Ahram,* August 21, 1970, p. 8.

58. U.A.R. Documentation Research Center, *Dairat al-ma'arif al-siyasiya al-'Arabiya: Nashrat al-wathaiq* [The Arab political encyclopedia: bulletin of documents], XIII (September–December, 1964), Section of the President, p. 15.

59. *Arab Observer,* April 9, 1962, p. 25.

The U.A.R. also participated in and sponsored many economic conferences that were aimed at improving African and Afro-Asian economic cooperation. These included the Afro-Asian Economic Conference in 1958, the second Afro-Asian Economic Conference at New Delhi in 1961, the African Economic Conference in 1962, the Conference on Economic Development Problems in 1962, the African Economic Committee of the U.N. at Leopoldville in 1963, and the First Industrial Conference for African States in 1966. The U.A.R.'s purpose at these conferences was described as "strengthening our political and economic affairs in the framework of . . . the liberation movements . . . and the independence of the continent."[61]

In pursuing an economic Monroe Doctrine in Africa, Egypt condemned the participation of African countries in foreign economic blocs and identified the European Common Market as a tool of new imperialism in Africa. The possibility that the African states might be integrated into the European Economic Community was considered a major threat to the U.A.R.'s objectives. An official report stated that "the U.A.R.'s concern over this possible development stems from the fact that it is only through export that the U.A.R. industrialization drive can achieve its objectives once a state of self-sufficiency has been attained."[62]

Commenting on the O.A.U. summit conference at Cairo in 1964, a government publication stated that one of the major reasons for holding the conference was "to establish an African Common Market so that the wealth of the continent may remain in the hands of its own people. Europe must be stopped from pursuing its trade activities in Africa through the European Common Market."[63] In 1963, Dr. Abdul Mun'im al-Qaisuni, the minister of economics, declared that the U.A.R. "works to strengthen economic ties with

60. *Ifriqiya wa al-istaqlal al-iqtisadi* [Africa and economic independence], Political Books Series, no. 350 (Cairo: Political Books Committee, n.d.), p. 100.

61. Abdul Ariz Rifai, "Thawrat 23 Yuliyo sanat 1952 wa harakat al-taharrur fi Ifriqiya" [The 23rd of July, 1952, revolution and the revolutionary movements of Economics], *Al-Ahram al-Iqtisadi,* no. 190, July 15, 1963, p. 3.

62. *Arab Observer,* September 3, 1962, p. 41.

63. U.A.R. Information Department, *Towards the Second African Summit Assembly* (Cairo, 1964), p. 5.

the African states and cooperates with them in the liberation of the African continent from all manifestations of economic imperialism . . . and works to increase cooperation with them and supply the states with . . . technical economic assistance."[64]

64. Ahmad Zando, "Nashrat wizarat al-iqtisad," [The activities of the Ministry of Economics], *Al-Ahram al-Iqtisadi,* no. 190, July 15, 1963, p. 3.

Chapter Six

Instruments
of the Policy

The principles of U.A.R. foreign policy are expressed and implemented through various instruments. The use of these instruments has been determined not only by the nature of U.A.R. policy but also by the world situation at a given time. The African Bureaus in Cairo, for example, were a natural outgrowth of Egypt's support for anticolonialism, but the form they took was determined by the environment in which they were formed. That is, they were possible only because the facilities available in Cairo were useful to nationalist leaders who had been exiled from their homelands. Cairo's use of the radio is a second example. The fact that many Africans are illiterate may be said to make the radio essential in reaching the masses, but it is only because of Egyptian attitudes about political action that the masses are regarded as being of such importance. Another case is the use of Islam. It may be seen as simple opportunism to turn the African need for education and respect for Islam, as well as the reputation of Al-Azhar, to political uses. However, the fact that the curriculum of Al-Azhar under Nasser has been adapted to modern needs indicates something more than opportunism. In part, the revival of Islam in a modern form for a modern world is a major factor in Arab nationalism. Modernized Islam is a method of equipping the people, by way of respected symbols, with a means of reacting to modernization.

The instruments of Egyptian foreign policy then are shaped by two forces: the principles of the Egyptian policy makers and the goals of Egyptian foreign policy, and the limitations and modifications of these preferences imposed by the environment in which policy is made. The first limitation is in Egypt's capacity to use or develop effective instruments; it is most apparent in the field of technical and economic aid. The second factor limiting and modifying the utility of the policy instruments is the set of conditions external to Egypt. There may be variations in the acceptability of instruments in the several states; Richard Cottam has spoken of this as tolerance levels for types of interference.[1] Other conditions may make one instrument more useful than another: conference diplomacy, for example, is most useful in providing contacts between states that have few opportunities for contact in ordinary relations. Thus, the goals of Egyptian policy and the attitudes of her policy makers lead to the creation of instruments by which that policy can be expressed. The effectiveness of the instruments is demonstrated in the course of state-to-state relations, when limiting and modifying factors appear. The instruments are modified and given priorities for use in particular countries and in a given set of international circumstances. Changes in the attitudes and positions of other countries, changes in Egyptian policy, and changes in Egyptian capabilities tend to further modify the use of instruments over a period of time.

To summarize, the instruments of the policy are the point of contact between Egypt and other states—the point at which policies formed in an Egyptian context by Egyptian ideas adjust themselves to a non-Egyptian world. In large part, the success of these instruments in fulfilling this function determines the success or failure of the foreign policy of the United Arab Republic. The variety of instruments the U.A.R. has utilized in pursuit of its

1. *Competitive Interference in Twentieth Century Diplomacy* (Pittsburgh: University of Pittsburgh Press, 1967).

African objectives may be broadly categorized here as diplomacy, culture, religion, propaganda, and economic aid and technical assistance.

DIPLOMACY

Diplomacy is one instrument used by all states to implement their foreign policies. Diplomatic relations are primarily state-to-state relations, that is, relations between legal governments, although diplomacy may operate bilaterally, in conferences, or in international institutions. Aside from the state-to-state character of diplomacy, which excludes appeals to the people of a state or to interest groups, the primary distinguishing characteristic of diplomatic relations is their legal nature. That is, diplomatic relations are operative in a certain legal environment and are governed by a legal order. Because of their official, legal, and discreet nature, these relations are useful for states which may not be friendly or may not maintain other contacts. At the same time, diplomatic relations may greatly facilitate the reaching of mutual agreements between states.

The U.A.R. has made every effort to open up diplomatic channels and to utilize fully diplomatic tactics to achieve closer relations with the African states. In 1956 a proposed African policy for Egypt clearly outlined Egypt's subsequent diplomatic drive in Africa. It suggested that Egypt first establish a net of consular services in Africa. Then,

> When positions in Africa are changed and the system of government is altered, the government of Egypt must be quite ready to establish diplomatic representation. The Egyptian diplomatic envoys must have received the necessary preliminary studies made by those consuls or those acting for them so that it may be possible to start at once calmly to execute the new African policy.[2]

As the African countries gained independence, Egypt hurried

2. "An African Policy for Egypt," *Egyptian Economic and Political Review,* II (August, 1956), 21; see Appendix I for full text of this article.

133

to recognize them. Nasser usually sent his top diplomatic aids and advisers in African affairs to participate in independence celebrations and to offer Egypt's assistance. A typical example of such interest occurred during Kenya's independence celebration in 1963. Vice-President Zakaria Mohieddin attended the celebrations. He immediately made arrangements to exchange ambassadorial representation and concluded Kenya's first trade and technical co-operation agreement as an independent state. The *Arab Observer* reported that "every detail of the agreement had been discussed between the two countries prior to Kenya's independence."[3]

Egypt's diplomatic drive into Africa began after the 1955 Bandung Conference. At that time there were only four independent African states: Egypt, Ethiopia, Liberia, and Libya. The *Arab Observer* noted that "between 1956 and the great emergence of Africa in 1960 a great deal of work had been put into the formation of the 'African personality'."[4] The way had been pointed out at Bandung. During this period Egypt concentrated on the liberation movements. The African nationalist leaders set up African Bureaus in Cairo to facilitate their activities. Egypt provided the heads of the nationalist groups with facilities to open an office, a salary of LE 100 a month, and free tickets to travel anywhere. Felix Mumie of Cameroon and John Kale of the Uganda National Congress were among the many who established bureaus in Cairo.[5] The African Association, subsidized by Egypt, was established in 1957 to coordinate and expand the activities of the Bureaus.[6] By 1962 fifteen countries had "made their appeal for freedom [through] . . . the African Association." The nature of the Association activities is made evident by the following statements, reported in the *Arab Observer*. Amani Thani of the Zanzibar office noted: "One is able to contact both East and West from here, give press conferences that make propaganda for party activities, get scholarships from the U.A.R. and through the U.A.R. from other countries." Vusumzi Make, the head of the African National Congress

3. No. 186, January 13, 1964, p. 37.
4. No. 265, July 19, 1965, p. 39.
5. Peter Mansfield, *Nasser's Egypt* (Baltimore: Penguin Books, 1965), p. 100.
6. See Chapter Two, above, for a discussion of the African Bureaus.

of South Africa, praised "the African Association's generous facilities which enable him [Make] to publish and distribute memoranda, make broadcasts to South Africa, contact friendly governments, get scholarships for many . . . students."[7]

By 1960 the U.A.R. had ambassadorial representation in ten African countries. The African Department of the Ministry of Foreign Affairs maintained close contact with the U.A.R. Embassies in Africa. It received "at least 40 reports a week dealing with the many phases of situations in different parts of Africa."[8] New instructions were sent to the embassies daily, and messengers left daily from the foreign office to the African states. By 1965 the U.A.R. had exchanged ambassadorial representation with Algeria, Cameroon, Ethiopia, Ghana, Guinea, Ivory Coast, Kenya, Liberia, Libya, Mali, Morocco, Nigeria, Senegal, Sierra Leone, Somalia, Sudan, Tanzania, Togo, Tunisia, Uganda, and Zambia.[9]

Nasser also attempted to strengthen Egypt's relations with Africa by maintaining personal contact and friendships with the African leaders. At one time or another, either prior to attaining office or as official representatives of their governments, most African heads of state had visited Cairo at least twice.

Another facet of the U.A.R.'s diplomatic drive into Africa was marked by the numerous African and Afro-Asian conferences that it participated in and sponsored.[10] These conferences gave the U.A.R. the opportunity to establish important contacts at all levels of African society. At the O.A.U. Summit conference of 1964, for example, several African leaders were so favorably impressed with their reception in Cairo and with the economic progress Egypt had made that they "expressed thanks to their hosts with a warmth which went far beyond the normal requirements of protocol."[11] This conference, in fact, paved the way for

7. *Arab Observer,* July 23, 1962, p. 33.

8. *Arab Observer,* July 10, 1960, pp. 19–20.

9. U.A.R. Central Agency for Mobilization and Statistics, *Statistical Handbook of the United Arab Republic, 1952–1965* (Cairo, 1966), pp. 322, 328.

10. See "Al-Qahira al-haditha markaz li al-way al-Ifriqi al-mustanir" [Modern Cairo is the center of African enlightened consciousness], *Egyptian Political Science Review,* no. 41, August, 1964, p. 7.

11. Mansfield, *Nasser's Egypt,* p. 105.

closer relations with East Africa. After a visit to the High Dam, President Nyerere of Tanganyika said "There are many and unlimited opportunities for joint effort and fruitful cooperation between the United Arab Republic and the sons of East Africa in carrying out numerous schemes to benefit from the Nile and its sources."[12] Egypt sponsored conferences that covered every facet and level of society, including economic conferences, industrial conferences, writers' conferences, women's conferences, labor conferences, rural-development conferences, youth conferences, medical conferences, and the first conference for African Socialist parties. Mahmud Fawzi's activities at the 17th Session of the U.N. General Assembly are typical of the U.A.R.'s eagerness to participate in conferences. At that session alone he was ordered to attend the following meetings: the meetings of the Afro-Asian states foreign ministers and economic ministers; the meetings of the independent African states foreign ministers and economic ministers; the meetings of the Casablanca bloc foreign ministers and economic ministers; and the meetings of the nonaligned nations foreign ministers and economic ministers.[13]

In a two-month period alone, March–April, 1963, one Afro-Asian and four all-African conferences were held in Cairo. Those conferences dealt with a variety of subjects such as improving Africa's railway system, postal services, and broadcasting and television networks. Three more conferences were held in Cairo in December of the same year: a meeting of the Preparatory Committee of the African Students Conference, an Afro-Asian Housing Conference, and an African Labor Conference. A government publication declared, "If the African freedom-seekers find in our capital the most favourable meeting place and the best medium for publicizing their cause, our government and people are merely doing their duty."[14]

Another diplomatic measure has been U.A.R. encouragement of closer links between the Arab world and sub-Saharan Africa to be

12. *Ibid.*

13. *Rose El-Youssief,* no. 1789, September 24, 1962, p. 9.

14. Shawqi Iqladius, *Yagadhat Ifriqiya* [The awakening of Africa], Africa for Africans Series, no. 1 (Cairo: Middle East Research Center, n.d.), p. 12.

established through the Arab League. In 1958 the League encouraged member states to grant scholarships to African students.[15] At the Arab Foreign Ministers Conference of February, 1961, the U.A.R. was successful in pushing the adoption of a resolution calling for the Arab heads of state to adopt the resolutions of the January, 1961, Casblanca Conference.[16] It was announced in 1964 that Arab League missions would be established in West African countries; the League also called for cooperation between the missions and the Arab minorities in Africa,[17] and the second Arab summit conference supported the resolutions of the 1964 O.A.U. summit conference.[18]

CULTURE

In attempting to win support among the emerging African nations, the U.A.R. utilized cultural relations aimed to familiarize the new generations with Egyptian ideas and political doctrines. These cultural instruments included (1) admitting large numbers of African students to Egypt's universities and granting them scholarships and (2) sending teachers into Africa. The former was by far the more extensive and comprehensive program. An official of the Ministry of Higher Education described the nature and objectives of this program:

> The state realized that the encouragement of foreign students is one of the most important methods which the civilized nations depend on to spread culture. . . . The position of our republic between the Afro-Asian states and its great responsibility . . . in the international sphere forced us to give great attention to the thousands of foreign students who come to

15. Salah Sabri, *Ifriqiya waraa al-Sahra* [Africa beyond the Sahara], Thousand Books Series, no. 303 (Cairo: Ministry of Education, 1960), pp. 376–77.

16. *Al-Ahram,* February 7, 1961, p. 5

17. Muhammad Ismail Muhammad, "Sierra Leon wa al-dual al-Arabiya" [Sierra Leone and the Arab States] *Nahdhat Ifriqiya,* no. 60, November, 1962, pp. 30–31.

18. League of Arab States, *Jami'at al-duwal al-Arabiya fi 'amiha al-ishrin* [The League of Arab States in its twentieth year] (Cairo: General Secretariat, 1965), p. 41.

our universities every year. . . . Hence, the state saw that the attraction of cultural missions . . . is one of the most effective ways which exposes in a practical way the wicked propaganda and helps to win a number of friends who often play an important role in their countries after their graduation from our universities.[19]

The proposed African policy outlined in 1956 considered African students an important element in Egypt's policy. It stated that "Egypt must accept the largest possible number of natives from African countries to be educated in Egypt and must care for their social and financial problems and help to settle them."[20] To facilitate the expansion of the foreign-students' program, the U.A.R. relaxed admission requirements and also reduced the requirements in certain subjects. Comfortable dormitories were created, televisions and radios provided, and the cost of living minimized to make the students' sojourn in Egypt a pleasant experience. African students were also given priority treatment on tours designed to exhibit Egypt's history, industrial progress, and modernization. These tours were supplemented with films on the U.A.R.'s industrial projects, plays from Egyptian literature, and stories about Egypt's traditional heritage.[21] The Ministry of Education closely supervises the foreign students by channeling their activities through clubs and various associations. A government publication, describing the assistance given to foreign students, stated:

The Republic tries its best to provide the means to meet these students and help them to join different institutions, colleges, and schools in the U.A.R., to guide them culturally and solve their social problems through assistance and aid. . . . The ministry also tries its best to house them in the university cities, dormitories, and students' housing.[22]

19. Muhammad Saqar Khafaja, "Al-Ta'lim al-'ali" [Higher education] in 'Ashar sanawat majida [Ten glorious years], Political Books Series, no. 277 (Cairo: Political Books Committee, n.d.), p. 123.

20. "An African Policy for Egypt," p. 22.

21. Muhammad Saqar Khafaja, "Jami'atuna fi ahada 'ashara 'aam" [Our universities in eleven years], Egyptian Political Science Review, no. 28, July, 1963, pp. 146–48.

In 1960 there were 4,000 African students in Cairo alone. In that same year 1,000 scholarships were granted to African students: 490 to Sudan; 160 to Somalia; and the remainder allocated to Algeria, Eritrea, Ethiopia, and Zanzibar. The Higher Committee for Cultural Relations awarded an additional 31 scholarships: Togoland, 3; Cameroon, 15; and Nigeria, 13. Scholarship students receive free education plus a monthly allowance from the government — LE 15 per month for university students studying in theoretical faculties and LE 20 per month for students in practical faculties.[23]

In the period 1953–54 there were 5,500 foreign students in Egypt. By 1963–64 this had increased to 27,975.[24] In 1952–53 Egypt awarded 332 scholarships to foreign students. By 1962–63 these had increased to 3,000.[25] The U.A.R. vice-president announced that a total of 14,500 cultural scholarships had been awarded to Afro-Asian students in 1963.[26] Although the exact number of African students in Egypt in 1962–63 is not known, the following states had students studying there: Somalia, Ethiopia, Eritrea, Ghana, Chad, Zanzibar, Guinea, Nigeria, Uganda, Senegal, Mauritania, Mali, Liberia, South Africa, Kenya, Northern Rhodesia, Tanganyika, Congo (Leopoldville), Sierra Leone, Ivory Coast, and Niger.[27] In 1963–64 a total of 979 African students were admitted to universities and higher institutions: 635 in general and technical education, 102 in higher institutions, and 242 in universities.[28] In 1964–65, 1,250 students were admitted: 233 in higher

---

22. U.A.R. Information Department, *Al-Ta'lim al-'ali fi al-'aam al-hadi 'ashar li al-thawra* [Higher education in the eleventh year of the revolution] (Cairo, 1963), p. 25.

23. *Arab Observer,* July 10, 1960, p. 17.

24. U.A.R. Information Department, *Al-Ta'lim* [Education] (Cairo, 1965), p. 8.

25. U.A.R. Information Department, *Al-Ta'lim al-'ali* [Higher education], p. 25.

26. U.A.R. Documentation Research Center, *Dairat al-ma'arif al-siyasiya al-'Arabiya: nashrat al-wathaiq* [The Arab political encyclopedia: bulletin of documents], XI (March–June, 1963), Section of African Affairs, 63; hereafter referred to as *Nashrat al-wathaiq.*

27. U.A.R. Information Department, *Al-Ta'lim al-'ali* [Higher Education], p. 26.

28. U.A.R. Central Agency for Mobilization and Statistics, *Statistical Handbook of the United Arab Republic, 1952–1964,* p. 141.

institutions, 720 in general education, and 297 in technical institutions. (These figures do not include high schools and grammar schools.) By 1964 there were 30,000 African students in Egypt, studying at all levels of education.[29] In 1966, 1,860 foreign students from 26 Afro-Asian and Latin American states graduated from U.A.R. universities.[30] In 1967 there were 3,087 African students with scholarships for university, Islamic, agricultural, and nursing studies.[31]

Language presented one of the major obstacles for foreign students studying in Egypt. For this reason, the Ministry of Education established an institute to teach Arabic. However, this caused an interruption in their education. To breach this problem, an Egyptian writer suggested that the first two years be taught in English and French. Simultaneously, the foreign students should receive instruction in Arabic, it being expected that by the third year they would be able to grasp the language. He also suggested that evening classes in Arabic be instituted in African countries to serve potential students going to the U.A.R.[32]

The U.A.R.'s program of sending teachers into Africa is the second front of its cultural instrument. A government publication noted that "outside the Casablanca Group, the U.A.R.'s strongest link with her sister African countries is, in fact, through educational and technical cooperation."[33] Although this program is not extensive, it is increasing steadily. To facilitate the expansion of the program, Egyptian universities have established a section to coordinate and study the need for teachers and experts in Africa. In 1952 Egypt had only two teachers in sub-Saharan Africa; by 1962 there were 254.[34] In 1963–64 the U.A.R. had a total of 4,500 teachers in

29. *Arab Observer,* January 13, 1964, p. 36.

30. *Al-Jumhuriya,* June 24, 1966, p. 6.

31. "U.A.R. Technical and Cultural Aid to African Countries," *Remarques Africaines,* Brussels, no. 299, 19 October 1967, pp. 511–20; see Appendix III.

32. Rashid al-Barawi, "Al-Jumhuriya al-Arabiya al-muttahida wa tanmiat al-iqtisad al-Ifriqi" [The U.A.R. and African economic development], *Nahdat Ifriqiya,* no. 67, June, 1963, p. 16.

33. *Arab Observer,* July 23, 1962, p. 32.

34. Abdul Fattah Ismail, "Al-Ta'lim al-'ali fi ashar sanawat" [Higher Education in Ten Years], *Egyptian Political Science Review,* no. 16, July, 1962, p. 201.

Africa.[35] However, the great majority of these went to Arab League states. This is evident from the figures below, which show the total number of Egyptian teachers in foreign countries, excluding the Arab League states. Approximately 90 per cent of these went to sub-Saharan Africa.[36]

EGYPTIAN TEACHERS IN
FOREIGN COUNTRIES

1953–54	44
1959–60	700
1960–61	751
1961–62	556
1962–63	335
1963–64	293
1964–65	1,041

SOURCE: U.A.R., *Statistical Handbook,*
1952–1965

Most of the teachers sent into Africa are at the grammar- and high-school levels. In 1962–63 the U.A.R. had teachers in the following African countries and all, except two professors, taught at the grammar- and high-school levels: Sudan, Somalia, Libya, Algeria, Congo (Leopoldville), Sierra Leone, Nigeria, Zanzibar, Mali, and Guinea.[37] By 1967, Tanzania, Uganda, Ethiopia, Togo, and Niger had been added to the program.[38]

The U.A.R. is very selective in choosing teachers to send abroad. They must pass qualifying examinations and go through extensive training before undertaking their assignments. Describing the program, a government publication stated:

---

35. Abdul Mun'im Shmayis, *Sanawat al-majd: ithna 'ashara 'aaman min al-thawara* [Years of glory: twelve years of the revolution], National Books Series, no. 286 (Cairo: National Books Committee, n.d.), p. 52.

36. U.A.R. Central Agency for Mobilization and Statistics, *Statistical Handbook of the United Arab Republic, 1952–1965*, p. 180.

37. U.A.R. Information Department, *Al-Ta'lim al-'ali* [Higher education], p. 31.

38. "U.A.R. Technical and Cultural Aid to African Countries," pp. 517–20.

The Ministry [of Education] prepares training seminars for the teachers who will be delegated to different countries to acquaint them with the countries that they will serve in and to enlighten them with their message . . . in order to make their duties easier and achieve the desired success in their work.[39]

The U.A.R. has also established sixteen schools and institutions in different African states. Cairo University has a branch in Khartoum that in 1963–64 had 1,600 students.[40]

The U.A.R. has also attempted to reach the new generations by associating with the youth movements in Africa. The U.A.R. youth organization has connections with seventy-one African organizations. The coordinated activities of these organizations include "conferences, visits, and exchange of information and experience."[41] The U.A.R. proposed the reorganization of the General African Students Union "to tie all activities and associations active in the African youth field and protect them from any external international influence."[42]

RELIGION

The existence of a large Muslim community in Black Africa has given Egypt an important cultural link with Africa. This linkage has appeared to Nasser to be a potential source of great political influence, and Egypt has made considerable efforts since 1952 to utilize these religious connections. It is estimated that there are 123 million Muslims in Africa. Islam is most prominent in the north, and the ratio of Muslims to total population decreases as one moves in a southerly direction, but Islam does constitute the majority religion in many of the West African countries. In others it makes up a significant minority. Approximately 50 per cent of Africa is Muslim, and Africans account for about 20 per cent of

39. U.A.R. Information Department, *Al-Ta'lim al-'ali* [Higher Education], p. 31.

40. Shmayis, *Sanawat al-majd* [Years of glory], p. 52.

41. U.A.R. Information Department, *Ri'ayat al-shabab* [Youth Care] (Cairo, 1965), p. 7.

42. *Akhbar Al-Yawm* (Cairo), January 23, 1965, p. 11.

142

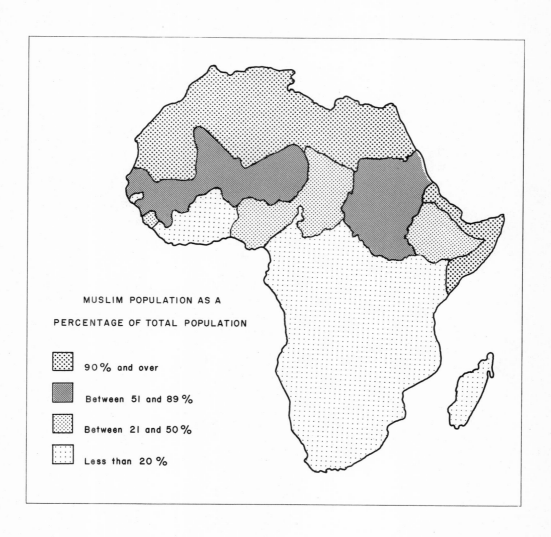

Distribution of Muslims in Africa

Muslims worldwide.[43] Even in countries in which Islam is a minority religion, the Muslim community may have made a considerable impact upon the society. The heads of state being the most important decision makers in Africa, it is significant to note that in 1965 nine presidents, two kings, and one prime minister were of the Islamic faith.[44]

The concepts of universality and brotherhood in Islam, in conjunction with the rituals of faith such as the hadj, the prayers, and the Koran readings, bridge ethnic and national differences to bind all Muslims together in a common faith and fraternity. Although there are divisions in the Islamic community, especially between the orthodox Sunnites and the Shiites, the potential power of such a community, if it could be unified, solidified, and organized for social and/or political purposes on a regional, continental, or international basis, is obvious. That Nasser, as early as 1953, envisaged the development of this power on an international level under the tutelage of Egypt is apparent in *The Philosophy of the Revolution:*

> As I ponder over these hundreds of millions of Muslims, all welded into a homogeneous whole by the same Faith, I come out increasingly conscious of the potential achievements co-operation among all these millions can accomplish—co-operation naturally not going beyond their loyalty to their original countries, but which will ensure for them and their brethren-in-Islam unlimited power.[45]

In this context, Nasser discussed the use of religious ritual as a factor to bind Muslims together. In explaining this concept in 1966 he stated:

> I said we should change our attitude towards pilgrimage, that pilgrimage should become a great political power, and that

43. Mahmud Brelvi, *Islam in Africa* (Lahore: Institute of Islamic Culture, 1964), p. 574.

44. Vernon McKay, "The Impact of Islam on Relations Among the New African States," in *Islam and International Relations,* ed. J. Harris Proctor (New York: Praeger, 1965), p. 159.

45. (Cairo: National Publication House [1954]), p. 72.

144

pilgrimage should become a political conference. I called for regular meetings among leaders of Islamic countries during pilgrimage. I called for such leaders to meet, weak before Almighty God but strong before their problems and enemies, dreaming of another life, and with strong faith in their par-·ticular place under the sun which they should occupy. We advocated this idea, but on a political basis.[46]

Between 1953 and 1955 Egypt undertook to create an Islamic ideological front. The first Arab Islamic Conference of the Liberation Organization was held at Cairo in August, 1953. More than one thousand Muslims who resided in Cairo and who represented many different countries "discussed the means to liberate the Islamic world from imperialism." In his address to that conference, Nasser stated: "We should know that the Arab world and the Islamic world are facing today one enemy and are cooperating against one disease —the enemy is imperialism and the disease is disunity and abandonment of the fight for the cause of God."[47]

Egypt attempted to use the first East African Islamic Conference held at Nairobi, Kenya, in December, 1953, to achieve the same aim. Egyptian newspapers stated that the purpose of the conference was to "discuss the creation of a third political Islamic power in East Africa."[48] Salah Salem, then minister of guidance, dramatized this in his letter to the conference which was read at the opening session:

> Oh, free Muslims, allow me on this great day to talk to you about your country, Egypt. I'm not exaggerating when I say your country, Egypt. One of the greatnesses of Islam is that it considers all Muslim lands a home for each Muslim. Brethren, may God be my witness. . . . Egypt today truly believes that God is just and victory is from him and greatness is for him, his messenger and his follower. Egypt . . . promises to extend its hand to each brother nation and each friendly peo-

46. *Address by President Gamal Abdel Nasser at the Great Popular Rally Held by the Arab Socialist Union in Celebration of the Anniversary of Unity Party: Cairo, 2 February 1966,* trans. U.A.R. Information Department (Cairo, 1966), p. 37.

47. *Al-Ahram,* August 27, 1963, p. 4.

48. *Al-Ahram,* December 27, 1953, p. 7.

ple for the sake of freedom and liberation, for the sake of world peace and the benefit of all humanity. Oh, free people; oh, the sons of free Africa; oh, the sons of all Islamic nations; oh, the sons of every Arab state, wake up and fight for God . . . seek death and you gain life. Stand up and fight for your freedom, you gain dignity and integrity. Stand up and fight for your nations, you will win happiness and sovereignty.[49]

Meanwhile, Nasser was also turning his attention to the role Islamic missions might play in building an Islamic community, and the Council of Ministers resolved that such missions should be sent to Afro-Asian rather than European countries. Commenting on this resolution, *Al-Ahram* stated: "It is much better to have a mission in China, Japan, Nigeria, Eritrea, Somalia, or Kenya than in London or Washington."[50] The Council of Ministers also established an Institute where the members of Islamic missions could study the social organization, culture, and environment of the countries where they would work. At the same time, it was decided to relax the traditional methods of teaching the Koran through memorizing the Arabic verse accompanied by literal translations. Instead, short, simple pamphlets would expound the main principles of the Koran. Dr. Abdul Rahman Taj, the imam of Al-Azhar, the Muslim university, explained the new role of missionaries:

> We saw that these nations are [easily] molded . . . because they are still virgin. . . . The new direction is to train the delegates with special cultural training in order to enable them to achieve their mission.[51]

In 1954 Nasser attempted to institute "the policy of the revolution toward the Islamic world . . . by making the *Hadj* a means for the establishment of an international Islamic organization which supervises the affairs of the Islamic people."[52] At a meeting in August, 1954, Nasser, King Saud, and Ghulan Muhammad, the

49. *Al-Ahram,* December 30, 1953, p. 1.
50. *Al-Ahram,* December 22, 1953, p. 6.
51. *Al-Ahram,* February 14, 1954, p. 4.
52. Butrus Butrus Ghali and Mahmud Khairi Isa, *Mabadi al-'ulum al-siyasiya risalatahu wa ahdafahu—nashatahu wa a'malahu* [An introduction to political science] (Cairo: Anglo-Egyptian Bookshop, 1962–63), pp. 568–69.

146

prime minister of Pakistan, established the Islamic Congress. The new general secretariat later explained its "noble aims" as follows:

> To strengthen the ties of confidence and Islamic brotherhood, raise the standards of the Muslims culturally and economically, create new bonds and strengthen existing bonds between them, and coordinate their efforts to achieve cooperation and unity.[53]

The Congress was designated an agency of the Presidency of the Republic and as such came under Nasser's direct supervision. Anwar al-Sadat was appointed the general secretary, and the activities of the Congress were considered so important that he devoted nine hours a day to its affairs.[54] The aims of the Congress included:

1. Study the affairs of Muslims and the conditions they live in, in their different countries . . . religiously, historically, and socially.
2. Offer technical assistance. . . .
3. Strengthen economic and financial ties, which include commercial, agrarian and industrial development.
4. Coordinate Islamic religious and legal affairs. . . .
5. Create and strengthen cultural relations and cooperate in educational matters. . . .[55]

The Congress awarded scholarships to students from the Islamic world to study at either Al-Azhar or Egyptian secular institutions, and three cultural centers were established, two in Nigeria (one in the north and one in the south) and one in Madagascar.[56]

There is a striking parallel between the nature, scope, methods, and organization of Nasser's Islamic movement and those of the later African and Afro-Asian movements. The similarity between the Islamic Congress and the Afro-Asian Solidarity Council is one illustration; another example might be the Islamic Conference held

---

53. Islamic Congress, General Secretariat, *Al-Mutamar al-Islami* [The Islamic Congress] (Cairo, n.d.), p. 11.

54. *Rose El-Youssief,* February 6, 1956, p. 9.

55. *Al-Mutamar al-Islami* [The Islamic Congress], p. 11.

56. *Ibid.,* pp. 16, 27.

at Nairobi in December, 1954, the resolutions of which were analogous in nature to those of the Afro-Asian Solidarity Conference of 1957. The Nairobi conference called for the creation of an Islamic bank (as suggested by the Egyptian delegation), the establishment of Islamic chambers of commerce, exchange of technical aid and assistance, cultural and educational cooperation, and the creation of Islamic schools and institutions to teach Arabic. There were also resolutions calling for Islam to be taught in all schools and for the creation of regional student unions that would be tied to a general Islamic student union. The most significant parallel, however, is the resolution calling for Islamic and African unity to fight imperialism.[57]

Egypt's desire to mobilize Islamic political forces was such that the duties of the Ministry of Endowments were not confined to Egypt, but included the whole Muslim world. In early 1956, Ahmad Hassan al-Baquri, the minister of endowments, made a trip to Senegal and Liberia with the following mission:

> To watch over Muslim affairs there and to continue a message carried by Egypt since the beginning of the nineteenth century, which was interrupted for a while and should be revived—it is Egypt's concern for the affairs of the black continent and its guardianship over the welfare of the Muslims there.[58]

By 1956 the attempt to establish an Islamic ideological front at the governmental level had failed. Nasser attributed the failure to the Baghdad Pact and revised his approach, as he explained in a later speech:

> After the creation of the Baghdad Pact and the joining of Turkey, Iran, Pakistan and Iraq, it became difficult for the Islamic conference to meet on a political basis. We therefore pursued the idea on a popular level.[59]

57. *Al-Ahram,* January 4, 1955, p. 4.

58. *Rose El-Youssief,* January 9, 1956, p. 17.

59. *Address by President Gamal Abdel Nasser at the Great Popular Union of the Anniversary of Unity Party: Cairo, February 22, 1966,* trans, U.A.R. Information Department (Cairo, n.d.), p. 38.

148

Subsequent to the failure of the policy at the governmental level, Egypt's interest in a pan-Islamic movement diminished. However, religion continued to be an important instrument in local and regional affairs.

Al-Azhar's role as the intellectual center of Islam provided Egypt with an effective tool. To maximize this advantage, Al-Azhar was completely reorganized in July, 1961, and divided into five administrations: (1) the Supreme Council of Al-Azhar; (2) the Islamic Research Council; (3) the Cultural Administration and Islamic Missions; (4) Al-Azhar University; (5) Al-Azhar Institutions. Article 2 of Law 103, which instituted the reorganization, placed Al-Azhar directly under the Presidency of the Republic, and Article 3 created a ministry for its affairs. It is in Article 2 that Al-Azhar's role in Islamic society is described:

> Al-Azhar carries the burden of the Islamic missions to all nations and works to expose the truth of Islam and the influence of it on the progress of man . . . and civilization and the renaissance of the scientific and cultural heritage of the the Islamic people . . . and expose the influence of the Arabs in the development and progress of humanity.[60]

Sheik Muhammad Chaltout, rector of the University of Al-Azhar, defined the roles of this program in a revealing order: the fight against Israel's political and economic action; the admission of Egypt as the natural representative of all Africa on the international scale; development of Egypt's cultural and political influence over East African and Upper Nile countries; ousting the West in order to improve Egyptian positions; neutralizing the advance of Christianity by showing that the latter is a Western religion linked to imperialism, while Islam is an emancipating religion whose teaching coincides with the requirements of African nationalism.[61]

Al-Azhar's political function came into full focus at the first Afro-Asian Islamic Conference in March, 1964, sponsored by the Congress of Al-Azhar Academy of Islamic Research. Delegations

60. *Nashrat al-wathaiq,* XX (August, 1961), p. 45.

61. Drawn from an article by Jean-Claude Froelich in *Le Mois en Afrique,* January, 1966, pp. 54–70.

149

from forty-two Afro-Asian countries and fifty members of the Islamic Research Council attended. The U.A.R. vice-president, Husain al-Shafai, in outlining the aims of the convention in his opening statement, clearly indicated the political direction of the meeting: "Imperialism as yet bears the Islamic world a grudge; seeking to dissipate and fragment its powers in order to make it an easy target for exploitation and domination."[62] Subsequently, the conference announced its support for the Palestinian people against Israel, which it considered "a permanent threat to all Muslims," and "stressed the need to consolidate the Islamic cause, to defend it against any external challenge, to guide the lives of Muslims everywhere. . . . [and] to strengthen the relations between Muslim countries."[63]

The second Afro-Asian Islamic Conference, held at Cairo in May, 1965, also suggests an attempt by the U.A.R. to use religion as a vehicle for its foreign policy. Here, too, the parallel with Egypt's African policy is evident. The conference actually dealt extensively with the political organization of Islamic people. This is apparent in the items on the agenda, which included: (1) discussion on methods to consolidate the "Islamic personality on Islamic principles, so that Muslims will be able to throw back any aggression on a Muslim country" (this is analogous to the concept of an "African personality" which was a prominent element in Egypt's African policy); (2) discussion of means of meeting the challenges facing Islam and the problems facing Islamic society; (3) the formulation of laws based on Islam to meet the problems of modern society, with the Koran as a guide to the organization of Islamic society; (4) consideration of the religious aspects of the struggle against imperialism; and (5) the consolidation of relations between all Muslims.

The first sessions of the conference were dominated by the Palestine problem. Egypt was much more successful here in gaining a favorable response than it had been at most of the African political conferences.[64]

62. *Arab Observer,* March 16, 1964, p. 8.
63. *Arab Observer,* March 30, 1964, p. 35.
64. *Arab Observer,* May 24, 1965, p. 34.

Al-Azhar is a cultural instrument of the same nature as the U.A.R.'s secular institutions. A government publication declared: "Along with the U.A.R. universities, Al-Azhar will also offer its students Islamic culture of an ideological nature."[65] The Supreme Council for Islamic Affairs emphasized this function when it explained that Al-Azhar had been reorganized so that it could supply the urgently needed qualified leadership for the Islamic world.[66] Also, Sheik Hassan Ma'amun, appointed rector of Al-Azhar in August, 1964, in describing the role of the institution, stated: "The most prominent role of Al-Azhar is the international call to Islam, its propagation of the Holy Koran, the Arabic language, and religious jurisprudence among people who do not speak the language of the Holy Book."[67]

By 1964 Al-Azhar had placed more than two hundred *ulamas* (religious scholars) all over the world, with the greatest number of them concentrated in Africa, and had established cultural centers in Morocco, Libya, Ghana, Liberia, Nigeria, Zanzibar, and the Tanzania mainland.[68] As of 1967, further cultural centers had been established in Somalia, Mauritania, and Sierra Leone. In addition to this, foreign students make up a large portion of its university body. In 1963–64 Al-Azhar had students from thirty-two African countries. Of the 3,087 scholarships held by African students in the U.A.R. in 1967, an unknown but substantial proportion were for Islamic studies.[69] In 1952–53, the government had appropriated only LE 15,000 for foreign students to attend Al-Azhar, but by 1963–64 this allotment had increased to LE 375,000 a year. Similarly the scholarship, which provided a stipend of LE 3 per month in 1952–53, had increased by 1963–64 to LE 10 for grammar- and high-school students and to LE 12 and LE 15 for students in higher education.[70]

65. *Arab Observer,* September 3, 1962, p. 44.

66. *Manbar Al-Islam* (Cairo), September 26, 1965, pp. 87–110.

67. *Arab Observer,* August 10, 1964, p. 16.

68. "Al-Azhar al Sharif: the Mosque and the University," *Scribe* (Cairo), (November 4, 1964), p. 99.

69. "U.A.R. Technical and Cultural Aid to African Countries," pp. 517–20; see Appendix III.

70. Al-Azhar, *Al-Azhar fi ithnay 'ashara 'aaman* [Al-Azhar in twelve years]

Substance of the Policy

In November, 1963, Muhammad al-Bahai, the minister of endowments, announced that Al-Azhar was establishing Islamic Arab missions in Africa. These missions would include grammar and high schools, a mosque, and a small infirmary. Each would be headed by highly qualified *ulama,* well equipped with a knowledge of foreign languages and Islamic history and culture including "Arabic philosophy, the history of civilization, and nationalist movements against imperialism in the Arab world and Africa." The missions' political implications were quite clear. *Al-Ahram* described them as "the callers for Islam who will meet the enemy of Islam and the Arab revolution."[71] Elaborating on the role of Al-Azhar, the sheik of Al-Azhar announced that the university had greatly expanded both the number of people it was sending abroad and the number of scholarships it was granting to students from foreign countries. He stated that the responsibilities of the missionaries included "protecting Islam from the distortions of its enemies" and that it was part of their mission to fight Zionist propaganda. He also noted that they were being aided by a large number of pamphlets written in many foreign languages.[72]

In 1964 Al-Azhar instituted a daily thirteen-hour radio program, the "Voice of Islam," solely for the chanting of the Koran. By 1965 the program had expanded its services throughout sub-Saharan Africa and included broadcasts in many of the indigenous languages. In 1966 the National Assembly passed resolutions to enlarge the "Voice of Islam" to include broadcasts propagating Islamic culture and missions.

The Supreme Council for Islamic Affairs publishes a monthly magazine in various languages, *Manbar al-Islam* [The Forum of Islam]. This magazine is largely devoted to justifying Egypt's internal and foreign policies on the basis of Koranic verses and Islamic tradition. The Council also puts out two pamphlet series, *Kutub Islamiyah* [Islami Books] and *Derasat fi Islam* [Studies in Islam].

(Cairo: National Publishing and Printing House, 1964), p. 211.
   71. November 18, 1963, p. 6.
   72. *Al-Jumhuriya,* November 21, 1964, p. 5.

152

Butrus Butrus Ghali was quite explicit in stating that political indoctrination is an important factor motivating the U.A.R.'s missionary work:

> While Egypt's policy originally aimed at spreading Islam among the heathens of Africa, as well as spreading the Arabic language, it now aims, besides these two objectives, at spreading the principle of positive neutrality regarding the European cold war, and spreading socialism for the sake of economic development.[73]

Two major problems confront Egypt's use of religion as an instrument of foreign policy. The first, which becomes evident in the attempts to link Islamic countries on an interstate basis, is that religious affinities do not dominate political decisions, and that common membership in the Islamic community may have no further implication for many governments and/or their citizens. The other is that the nature of African Islam limits its usefulness to Egypt. There are divisions in the Muslim community in Africa—Sunnites and Shiites; Arab, Indian, Berber, and indigenous traditions—which, together with the fact that the adoption of the Islamic faith is often a matter of convenience rather than of conviction, and many Africans are only superficially Muslim, restrict the impact of appeals to a common faith. It may be said that while the potential for power that Egypt discerned is actually there, the problems of unifying African Muslims have prevented that potential from being realized. However, as J. Spencer Trimingham has written, "even though the power of religion to shape and change societies has declined, there is no reason to minimize the degree of influence it still has."[74] Thus, while it appears that Egypt's use of religion as an instrument of foreign policy has not been as productive of results as had once been hoped, through the use of this instrument affinities between Egyptians and Black Africans have been reinforced.

73. "The U.A.R.'s Foreign Policy," *Egyptian Political Science Review,* no. 21, December, 1962, p. 5.

74. "Islam—A Force in Africa," *L'Observateur du moyen-orient et de l'Afrique* (Paris), IX (August 13, 1965), p. 10.

Substance of the Policy

PROPAGANDA

Propaganda is perhaps the U.A.R.'s single most important vehicle for disseminating and popularizing its policies at all levels of African society. As early as 1953, Fathi Radhwan, then the minister of state, was given the task of studying propaganda. He drew up two principles to guide Egypt's propaganda policy: (1) propaganda should be continuous and contain a unity of purpose, and (2) propaganda should be geared to the audience and be colorful, interesting, and entertaining. He called for the creation of a Ministry of Guidance, the enlistment of capable propagandists, and an increase in the budget allocated for propaganda.[75]

In 1956 the proposed African policy for Egypt specifically called for greater attention to be given to propaganda in Africa as "an effective weapon calling for support for Egypt and its policy." Three media for propaganda were identified and outlined:

1. Egyptian Broadcasting

   Greater attention must be paid to strengthening it so that it shall reach all parts of the con [sic] directed to natives of the various zones and to broadcasting in the African languages and dialects.

2. The Cinema

   To allocate documentary and cultural films and others with useful subjects and to distribute them regularly. Such films open the mind and enable people to grasp the extent of Egypt's civilization. They would induce African peoples not to delay joining the caravan that marches in the path of civilization and that Egypt has prepared for them.

3. Press, Printed Matter, and Publications

   The Press must adopt the policy of supporting Africa and the Africans and follow the instructions of all organizations concerning their importance. As for printed matter and publications, they must be written in Arabic, English, and French, possess simplicity of style and good printing,

75. *Al-Ahram,* October 21, 1953, p. 4.

and call for Egypt and its African policy. All this printed matter should bear the impression of realism and be remote from exaggeration and artificiality.[76]

There is little information available on the nature, extent of circulation, or impact of Egyptian films in Africa. However, newspapers, printed matter, and publications are widely circulated throughout the continent. But the radio represents the most important of the mass media in nonliterate societies. In 1958 Nasser himself commented on its role in Africa:

> The world today is completely different from what it was 10 or 15 years ago. The peoples of Africa, for example, have undergone very great changes; they are now totally different from what they were in the past. I feel the world now is much smaller than it was 10 years ago. The African peoples now own wireless sets and broadcasts from all parts of the world are now regularly listened to by these people and they know that wars are being launched for liberation. They also realize that there are different standards of living and that theirs is not like that of the people in the U.S.A. They know a great deal about the modern principles of freedom and peace as well as the struggle of people in different places for freedom.[77]

It is through radio broadcasts that the U.A.R. channels the major portion of its propaganda to Africa. A daily half-hour program in Swahili to East, Central, and Southern Africa was inaugurated in July, 1954. The program included readings of the Koran, daily news, two commentaries a week, and a cultural program that heavily emphasized the history, culture, economics, and politics of Egypt. In July, 1955, the program was increased to three-quarters of an hour; in 1958, to a full hour; and in 1961, to an hour and a half.[78] The nature of these broadcasts is made evident by Britain's complaint to the Egyptian government in 1956 about "the incendiary character of Cairo Radio's East African serv-

76. "An African Policy for Egypt," p. 21.
77. Speech delivered on November 27, 1958 ("President Gamal Abdel Nasser on Africa," comp. and trans. U.A.R. Information Department [Cairo, n.d.], p. 8).
78. U.A.R. Information Department, *Al-Idha'a fi ashar sanawat* [Broadcasting in ten years] (Cairo, 1962), pp. 208–10.

ices."[79] Indeed, Egypt's attacks on the European colonizers have been at times vehement and provocative. But the African nationalist movements that Cairo Radio supported and encouraged have succeeded, and Egypt may well consider that its sponsorship of anti-imperialism was justified.

Egypt also initiated a half-hour program in Amharic in December, 1955. This was increased to three-quarters of an hour in 1961. Broadcasts in Somali began in March, 1957, and increased to a full hour in 1961. Broadcasts in Lingala, Nyanji, and English were inaugurated in 1961. Egypt instituted broadcasts to West Africa in English, French, and Hausa in December, 1959, and broadcasts in Fulani began in July, 1961. These programs are assembled on the basis of requests received from the listeners, requests which come in at the average of 140 letters per month. The programs also include political news of, and commentaries on, the national movements.[80] The *Arab Observer* declared that "the least that could be said about the effect of these commentaries and news bulletins is that they are inflaming national sentiment and encouraging revolutionary activities. The programs have led to positive reaction there."[81]

The dramatic increase in budget and transmission hours reflects the importance that the U.A.R. gives to this instrument. The 1963 budget for broadcasting was less than LE one million. In 1964 it was increased to LE seven million. In that year the U.A.R.'s total transmission time reached 766 hours per week and occupied second place afer the United States.[82] The U.A.R. opened the largest broadcasing station in the world in March, 1965, and its transmissions are more powerful than those from America, London, or Moscow.

79. *Arab Observer,* July 22, 1963, p. 45. Britain began transmitting in Swahili in 1958 and was followed by Russia, Israel, Ghana, and Nigeria (U.A.R. Information Department, *Al-Idha'a fi ashar sanawat* [Broadcasting in ten years], p. 10.

80. U.A.R. Information Department, *Al-Idha'a fi ashar sanawat* [Broadcasting in ten years], p. 211–19.

81. July 10, 1960, p. 19.

82. U.A.R. Information Department, *Al-Jumhuriya Al-Arabiya al-muttahida fi ithray 'ashara 'aaman* [The United Arab Republic in twelve years] (Cairo, 1964), Section of Culture and Guidance, p. 1.

AID AND TECHNICAL ASSISTANCE

The U.A.R.'s aid and technical-assistance program to Africa is circumscribed by its limited financial resources. The program was undertaken to combat Israeli and Western ecnomic penetration into the area. Dr. Al-Qaisuni, the minister of economics, asserted in 1961 that the West attempts to regain control over African economies through two methods:

> The first is to create economic blocs, such as the Commonwealth and the European Common Market, and include new nations in them. The second is to offer economic aid and technical assistance through other states such as Israel. Since the U.A.R. passed through bitter experiences, President Nasser decided to extend the hands of help to these nations in order to aid them in achieving . . . freedom of their economies and to support them in opposing this trend.[83]

The U.A.R.'s technical assistance program consists primarily of training technicians in the U.A.R. and providing teachers, doctors, and technical experts for the African states. In 1966 the U.A.R. had technical experts in the following African countries: Congo (Brazzaville), Congo (Leopoldville), Algeria, Sierra Leone, Upper Volta, South Africa, Zambia, Senegal, Liberia, Central African Republic, Cameroon, Ghana, Tanzania, Mali, Guinea, Gabon, Uganda, Tunisia, Mauritania, Kenya, Malawi, Morocco, Eritrea, Burundi, Ivory Coast, Dahomey, Chad, Niger, Madagascar, Nigeria, and Somalia.[84]

The U.A.R. has also participated in many projects in Africa, some of which are reviewed here to indicate their nature and extent. Outside the Casablanca Charter states, the U.A.R. has close links with Somalia, Sierra Leone, Libya, Dahomey, Senegal, Liberia, Niger, and Tunisia. Most, if not all, of these countries have trade, payment, and cultural alliances with the U.A.R. The U.A.R. had concluded, by 1967, some twenty commercial agree-

83. *Al-Ahram,* February 4, 1961, p. 6.
84. *Al-Jumhuriya,* March 10, 1966, p. 9.

ments with sub-Saharan states.[85] Somalia received a loan of LE five million and signed trade, industrial cooperation, and cultural agreements with the U.A.R. in 1962.[86] An expert delegation was sent to Somalia in 1963 to study the country's First Five-Year Development Plan and "to see where the U.A.R. could help in its implementation." Dahomey had a trade agreement, and in 1962 the U.A.R. promised to build a hotel and a bridge at Cotonou. Also in 1962 the U.A.R. concluded an agreement with Sierra Leone to build a resettlement house at Freetown.[87] Experts in civil aviation were sent to Ghana, and a dredger was dispatched to Conakry to take part in the work of extending the port.[88] An agreement was concluded with Mali in 1962 under which the U.A.R. undertook to build a hotel and a road. Both projects were financed under a U.A.R. LE six million low-interest loan.[89] Agrarian specialists have been sent to Niger to assist in agricultural extension projects, and delegations have been sent to Tanzania to help in irrigation and drainage plans.[90] The U.A.R. has built factories in Kenya, Tanzania, and Uganda and has provided technical assistance and management for the factories.[91] Nigeria and Congo (Brazzaville) have received loans of LE 3,000,000 and LE 1,500,-000 from the U.A.R.[92]

Although the U.A.R.'s technical-assistance program is relatively small, as compared to that of the United States, for example, it has been of significant aid to some of the new African states. It may be noted from the discussion that the countries which receive this aid most generously are those which have other ties with the U.A.R.[93] It thus seems that the U.A.R., rather

85. "U.A.R. Technical and Cultural Aid to African Countries," pp. 517–20; see Appendix III.

86. *Arab Observer,* July 23, 1962, p. 32.

87. *Arab Observer,* January 13, 1964, p. 37.

88. *Scribe* (Cairo), July–August, 1963, p. 55.

89. *Arab Observer,* January 13, 1964, p. 37.

90. *Middle East News: Economic Weekly* (Cairo), V (March 26, 1966), 42.

91. *Rose El-Youssief,* no. 1945, September 20, 1964, p. 6.

92. "U.A.R. Technical and Cultural Aid to African Countries," 517–20; see Appendix III.

93. See Appendix III.

158

than spending these funds in broadcast fashion, is directing its efforts where it is felt they will be most productive. Since the 1967 June War, loans and grants have significantly diminished due to the priority of the war situation.

Part III

Case
Studies

Chapter Seven

Egypt and the Sudan

Egypt's policy in the Sudan represents a continuum of traditional interests, and protecting these interests constitutes the minimum objective of its African policy. As such, the policy has been formulated to achieve certain specific fixed goals. The primary objective of the policy is to safeguard Egypt's strategic interests in the Sudan, the most vital concern by far being the Nile River. The importance of this as a consideration in Egypt's foreign policy was graphically expressed by an Egyptian army colonel in 1948:

> No politican can ignore Egypt's interest in the Sudan. Its permanent and vital interest concerns Egypt's life. Egypt gets its waters from the Nile, which flows in the heart of the Sudan. The Nile to Egypt is a matter of life or death. If the waters of this river were discontinued or were controlled by a hostile state or a state that could become hostile, Egypt's life is over. Of course, whoever controls the Sudan naturally controls the northern Nile Valley. Egypt in this era of conflicting political doctrines cannot trust the neigh-

bors of the Sudan. Today's friends may become tomorrow's enemies. For this reason, all of Egypt's efforts are to insure for herself a secure life in the future.[1]

Egyptian strategists have dealt in great detail with the importance of the Sudan. The primary consideration is that the Sudan controls the sources of the Nile River. It is the place where all the branches of the Nile meet to form the so-called Great Nile. The salient point is that "any aggressive power that controls the Nile sources will govern the waters coming north." Another important strategic consideration is the location of the Sudan. It has "an excellent position" in the heart of the continent and is "considered a base controlling the regions surrounding it," and conceivably it could control the vital lines of communication that run to and from Africa.[2] Explaining Egypt's interest in Africa, Nasser in *The Philosophy of the Revolution* emphasized the location of the Sudan, noting that the Sudan's "boundaries extend to the heart of the Continent, where it is bounded by neighborly relations, being the sensitive center."[3] Therefore, concludes a prominent Egyptian strategist, in view of the struggle of the big powers for spheres of influence in Africa, Egypt considers it especially vital to keep the Sudan neutral.[4]

Besides the geopolitical factors, there are economic and commercial considerations influencing Egypt's policy in the Sudan. The underpopulation of the Sudan, its mineral and agricultural richness, and the potential market for Egyptian products have all been cited as strategically important factors for Egypt.[5] These factors are becoming increasingly dominant as Egypt seeks solutions to the problem of overpopulation. When the census of 1927 made the extent of its population problem apparent, Egypt, in

1. Abdul Rahman Zaki, *Al-Sharq Al-Awsat* [The Middle East] (Cairo: Egyptian Renaissance Bookshop, 1948), pp. 63–64.

2. Abdul Salam Badawi, *Al-Tatawurat al-siyasiya wa al-iqtisadiya fi al-'alam al-'Arabi* [Political and economic developments in the Arab world] (Cairo: United Publishers and Distributors, 1959), pp. 262–63.

3. (Cairo: National Publication House [1954]), p. 69.

4. Badawi, *Al-Tatawurat al-siyasiya* [Political development], p. 263.

5. *Ibid.,* pp. 385–86.

negotiations with the British, brought up the question of emigration to the Sudan. In 1936 Nahas Pasha, then prime minister, succeeded in obtaining an agreement for unrestricted emigration; however, no large-scale emigration plan was ever instituted under this agreement.[6] As Egypt's population has continued to expand rapidly, emigration to the underpopulated Sudan remains a tantalizing possibility.

As Egypt turns increasingly toward industrialization to relieve the pressures of overpopulation, the need to create new outlets for its manufactured products becomes vital. The Sudan, consisting largely of a rural population with little industrialization, presents a potential market. However, the sale of Egyptian products has been seriously affected by foreign competition. A good illustration of this is the cotton-textile industry, on which Egypt is heavily dependent. Because a majority of the Sudanese wear cotton goods year round, there is a big demand in the Sudan for cheap cotton goods, but prior to World War II most of these were imported from Japan. Another example is the sugar industry. Before World War II sugar was imported from Egypt. After a dispute over prices in 1941 Sudan went elsewhere for its supply. Egypt subsequently regained the Sudanese sugar market, and by 1960 cane sugar was Egypt's chief export to the Sudan. In that year Egypt exported 44,303 tons of cane sugar to the Sudan at a value of LE 1,517,031.[7]

There are also political objectives affecting Egypt's policy in the Sudan. Many Egyptian writers emphasize that the Sudan can be the nucleus of the greater state of the Nile Valley. In the words of one authority, Egypt, united with the Sudan, "will create a great power for the Nile Valley in all respects which will enable her [to gain] sovereignty and real leadership, not for the continent alone but for the whole Middle East group, giving her a very special position in the Afro-Asian bloc."[8]

6. Mekki Abbas, *The Sudan Question: The Dispute over the Anglo-Egyptian Condominium, 1884–1951*. (London: Faber and Faber, 1952), pp. 91–92.

7. *Arab Observer,* May 21, 1962, p. 26.

8. Muhammad Kamal Abdul-Hamid, *Al-sharq Al-Awsat fi al-mizan al-istiratiji* [The Middle East in the strategic balance] (Cairo: The Modern Publishing House, n.d.), p. 385.

165

Case Studies

The above points indicate that the Sudan is very important to Egypt, and Egypt's policy has always been to maintain influence there. This is evident in a study of the policy in practice, which can be divided into six phases: Unity of the Nile Valley: 1947–1952; rationalization of the policy: 1952–1955; relations in crisis: 1956–1958; military rule: 1958–1964; return to civilian government: 1965–1969; and the new military regime: 1969.

UNITY OF THE NILE VALLEY: 1947-1952

The attempt to achieve complete domination over the Sudan was manifested in the Unity of the Nile Valley movement. This became a dominant factor in Egyptian-Sudanese relations after World War II and remained a strong influence after the revolution. The origins of this doctrine, however, can be traced far back into Egypt's history.

Egypt's relations with the Sudan began during the time of the Pharaohs when Egypt entered Nubia to establish control over the prosperous trade routes and gold mines of the Eastern Desert. By the Eighteenth Dynasty (1580–1350 B.C.), Nubia was an Egyptian province administered by two governors, one in the north and one in the south, and at this time large numbers of Egyptians migrated to the new colony. Through the process of intermarriage and assimilation, Nubia was Egyptianized. When Egypt fell to foreign conquerors, beginning with the Persians in 525 B.C., the influence of those conquerors also penetrated from Egypt into Nubia, and in the same manner Christianity and Islam passed from Egypt into the Sudan. Thus, there developed through this historic relationship ethnic and cultural similarities between the two countries.

The basis of Egypt's claim to sovereignty over the Sudan rests on this ancient unity and on Muhammad Ali's conquest of the Sudan in 1820, which resulted in its complete integration into the Egyptian "empire."[9] Muhammad Ali's success was later reversed

9. See Muhammad Fuad Shukri, *Misr wa al-siyada 'ala al-Sudan* [Egypt and sovereignty over the Sudan] (Cairo: Arab Thoughts Publishing House, 1946); the entire book deals with this subject.

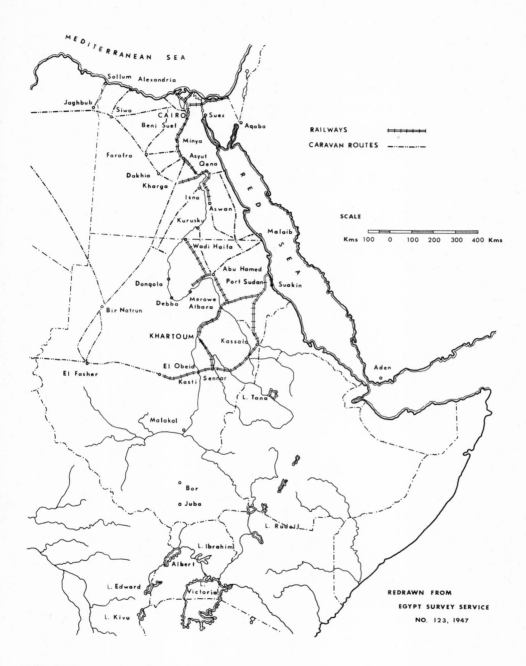

Nile Basin: Communications

by the Mahdi rebellion in 1884, and Egypt was forced to withdraw. From that time, it became the dominant aspiration of the Egyptian government to regain its lost dominion. In 1899 after the reconquest of the Sudan and the conclusion of the Anglo-Egyptian Agreement, Egypt did secure some voice in the Sudan's affairs, but this was nominal in view of Britain's domination of both countries. The Sudan question, therefore, has long been a source of dispute between Egypt and Britain. Egypt's demands for complete sovereignty over the Sudan gained momentum after World War I but did not reach their peak until after World War II. Then in 1947 an Egyptian government publication asserted that

> The history of the Sudan is an integral part of that of Egypt. Since the Sudan became known and its remote regions explored, it has always been linked with Egypt by political, racial and economic ties. If Egypt is a gift of the Nile, it is also a fact that Egypt has uninterruptedly participated in the formation of the Sudan and integrated the two countries into one unit.[10]

After World War II the doctrine of the Unity of the Nile Valley became an integral part of Egypt's demands for complete independence. The justification of this doctrine was based on topographic, ethnic, cultural, and economic factors.[11]

RATIONALIZATION OF THE POLICY: 1952-1955

Prior to the July, 1952, revolution, the issue of the Unity of the Nile Valley had reached such dramatic proportions that Egypt in 1951 abrogated the Condominium Agreement.[12] Thus, the im-

10. Egyptian Government, Presidency of the Council of Ministers, *Committee of Experts: Status of the Sudan* (Cairo: Government Press, 1947), p. 1.

11. See Egyptian Government, Presidency of the Council of Ministers, *Wahdat Wadi al-Nil: usuluha al-jughrafiya wa madhahiruha fi al-tarikh* [The Unity of the Nile Valley: its geographic basis and historic phenomenon] (Cairo: Government Press, 1947), pp. 1–6.

12. For a detailed analysis of the history of the condominium, and its provisions, see Abdul Fattah Ibrahim al-Sayid Baddur, *Sudanese-Egyptian Relations: A Chronological and Analytical Study* (The Hague: Martinus Nijhoff, 1960), pp. 84–139.

mediate goal of the new Egyptian regime was to adjust Egypt's policy toward the Sudan in the light of the political realities in both countries. However, Egypt's own internal situation made the carrying out of the abrogation through forceful means entirely unfeasible. Also, it was doubtful whether the Sudan, in fact, favored unity. The situation in the Sudan was already complicated by the multiplicity of parties, some in favor of unification and others opposed. Egypt's unilateral action served only to undermine her position and to create more Sudanese factions. The Umma Party, led by Sayid Abdul Rahman al-Mahdi, called for complete independence from both Egypt and Britain; the Socialist Republican Party, which was composed largely of tribal chiefs, called for independence but with strong ties to Britain; the Ashiqqa, the National Front, and the Unity of the Nile Valley group were the unionist parties.

After the Egyptian revolution the idea of self-determination for the Sudan was accepted for the first time by the new Egyptian military elite. President Nagib was himself an intimate friend of Sayid al-Mahdi (the head of the anti-Egyptian Ansar). In October, 1952, Al-Mahdi arrived in Cairo to discuss the draft constitution for the Sudan proposed by Britain. These meetings resulted in the following statement by the Egyptian government:

> Egypt, who believes in freedom and who considered sovereignty over the Nile Valley with its existing boundaries a right to both Sudanese and Egyptians without discrimination, and who believes in the unity of the Sudan, welcomes full home rule for the Sudanese people and declares that she preserves the right of the Sudanese to sovereignty in their country until the day they determine their future. If they determine their future in complete freedom, we shall respect this decision. Egypt always welcomes the friendship of the brotherly Sudanese in any form they may choose, and will cooperate with them in the political, economic, and social fields.[13]

Shortly after this meeting the unionist parties of the Sudan also

---

13. Rashid al-Barawy, *The Military Coup in Egypt: An Analytical Study* (Cairo: Renaissance Bookshop, 1952), Appendix 4.

met with Nagib in Cairo. Their meetings resulted in the amalgamation of the unionist parties to form the National Unionist Party with Ismael Al-Azhari as president. The new party comprised the following parties and bodies: Ashiqqa, Sudan Congress and Graduates Conference, Unionists, National Front, Unity of the Nile Valley, and Liberal Constitutional. The agreement they reached stipulated that the party would stand for

(a) Liquidating the status quo and evacuation of British troops and the establishment of a Sudanese Democratic Government united with Egypt. Bases of this unity are to be decided, however, after the exercise of self-determination.

(b) Developing the Sudan with its integral boundaries economically, socially, with a special view to the South and the rural areas, developing the country's resources to bring prosperity to its peoples, and safeguarding the human rights and realization of social justice among the people regardless of race, color or sect.[14]

The reason behind Egypt's change in policy regarding the self-determination of the Sudan was the new regime's goal to rid both countries of British occupation. Therefore it was decided that Egypt's interests could best be served with a compromise on the issue that had been the major source of dispute in Anglo-Egyptian negotiations. Furthermore, the amalgamation of the Sudanese unionist parties greatly increased the prospect that union could be achieved through popular choice. And even if complete independence were chosen, once Britain evacuated the Sudan, the country would be free of foreign influence that could threaten the Nile. Also, once the evacuation was achieved, Egypt could exercise more influence through political means.

On November 2, 1952, about four months after the revolution, the Egyptian government delivered to the British government a note concerning the Sudan and self-determination. For the first time in its negotiations with Britain Egypt declared that "The Egyptian government believes firmly in the right of the Sudanese

14. *Ibid.*, pp. 263–67.

to decide their destiny." The note consisted of sixteen articles, dealing mostly with the internal organization of the Sudanese government. It suggested the reduction of the power of the British governor general, and it dealt with the evacuation of the Sudan and with the creation of the Constituent Assembly which was to decide the destiny of the country, write a constitution, and prepare election laws for the Sudanese Parliament. The note emphasized that the Constituent Assembly would choose either "to bind the Sudan and Egypt in some form, or . . . [for] complete independence from Egypt, the United Kingdom, and any other country."[15]

In 1953, Salah Salem and Zulficar Sabri went to Khartoum to discuss negotiations. On January 10 the Sudanese parties signed an agreement accepting the following recommendations regarding Egyptian-British negotiations: (1) the Egyptian proposal regarding the maintenance of unity between North and South Sudan; (2) the Egyptian proposal regarding the establishment of a committee to aid the governor general; (3) the concept of Sudanization, which stipulated that Egyptian and British officials holding posts in the Sudan should be replaced by Sudanese wherever possible; (4) the Egyptian recommendations regarding the elections; and (5) the complete evacuation of foreign armies prior to the elections for the Constituent Assembly. The agreement was signed by representatives of the Umma Party, the Socialist Republican Party, the National Unionist Party, and the National Party, with Salah Salem as a witness.[16]

On February 12, 1953, Britain and Egypt signed an agreement regarding the self-determination of the Sudan. That agreement embodied most of the suggestions incorporated in the Egyptian note of November 2, 1952. On the same day British Prime Minister Eden expressed his government's opinion in the House of Commons that the Sudan could freely join the British Commonwealth if it so desired. In a vigorous reaction to this proposal, on February 16, 1953, President Nagib replied:

15. Republic of Egypt, Presidency of the Council of Ministers, *Al-Sudan thala-that 'ashara Febrayir 1841 ila ithnay 'ashara Febrayir 1953* [The Sudan from 13 February 1841 to 12 February 1953] (Cairo: Government Press, 1953), p. 296.
16. *Ibid.*, pp. 297–99.

> Self-determination will be on the foundation of balancing
> and choosing between one of two things, not a third. . . .
> First is the unity of the Sudan with its brother Egypt in any
> form of union and the second is the independence of the
> Sudan, complete independence without any hated foreign in-
> fluence. . . . Anything other than that . . . is nothing but some
> kind of dream and has no foundation of truth in it. The
> agreement did not include anything but these two things. No
> dominion, no commonwealth . . . Any attempt of this kind
> will contradict completely the agreement of 12 February 1953.
> This will result in the abrogation of the agreement.[17]

After the signing of the Anglo-Egyptian Agreement, Egypt immediately began preparing for the new phase in relations that the
Sudan's self-determination would bring about. In April, 1953, a
decree was issued reorganizing and strengthening the department
of the Undersecretary of Sudanese Affairs and two additional
bureaus were established: the Bureau of Economic Affairs and
Public Relations and the Bureau of Cultural and Social Affairs.
The main objective of the Bureau of Economic Affairs and Public
Relations was to concentrate on the study of the factors influencing the economic relations between Egypt and the Sudan, and for
this purpose a Department of Statistics was created. In describing
the duties of this department, a government publication stated:

> The statistical studies will be like a faithful mirror to show the
> extent of economic relations between Egypt and the Sudan
> and direct the attention to the weaknesses in order to correct
> them. Then the agency will be able to draw up an economic
> policy which aims to strengthen the economic exchange be-
> tween Egypt and the Sudan.[18]

The Bureau of Economic Affairs and Public Relations immedi-

17. Republic of Egypt, Armed Forces Public Relations Department, *Mithaq
Al-thawra min aqwal Rais wa Naib Rais wa a'adtha Majlis qiydada al-
thawra* (The Charter of the Revolution from the speeches of the president, vice-
president, and members of the Revolutionary Command Council), (Cairo, 1953),
pp. 172–73.
18. Republic of Egypt, *Jumhuriyat Misr fi a'amiha al-awwal* [The Egyptian
Republic in its first year] (Cairo: Armed Forces Public Relations Department,
1954), p. 596.

ately instituted programs to achieve its purpose. One of the primary duties was to investigate methods to expand the Sudanese market for Egyptian products and to protect these products from foreign competition. Economic missions were sent to the Sudan, and Egyptian industrial exhibits were sponsored. The agency also supervised economic and commercial exchanges between the two countries and aided Egyptians migrating to, or traveling in, the south. In addition, it established an office for propaganda to aid the textile industries in developing interest in their products in the Sudan. Egyptian companies were directed to the Sudanese markets

> to explore the mineral, agricultural, and animal riches of the Sudan and increase the effectiveness of Egyptian exports by designing products that would fulfill the demands of Sudanese climate, taste, and buying power in order to create self-sufficiency between Egypt and her southern neighbor.[19]

The agency also aided the Egyptian agricultural and cooperative loan banks and industrial banks to establish branches in the Sudan. In addition, it watched over the actions of the governor general to assure his compliance with the Sudanese agreements.

Upon its establishment, the Bureau of Cultural and Social Affairs took over supervision of Sudanese living in Egypt. It helped Sudanese who wanted to travel to Egypt to find jobs and extended aid to the Sudan. The exchange of visits between cultural and scientific missions of students and teachers was organized and regulated. In addition, the agency supervised Sudanese students in Egypt and organized trips to demonstrate "the scientific, social, and economic life of Egypt." It also supervised the welfare of the Sudanese students and expressed a paternal concern for "their . . . scholastic, moral, health, and social affairs. . . . It is the guardian of the Sudanese student in Egypt as far as his [relations with his] institution are concerned."[20]

The Bureau of Cultural and Social Affairs also supervised the Sudanese students in Al-Azhar, allocating to them monthly sub-

19. *Ibid.*, p. 598.
20. *Ibid.*, pp. 596–99.

sidies of LE 8 and locating housing for them. Their number was reported to be 3,000 in Al-Azhar schools alone in 1953–54. There were 1,200 Sudanese students studying in other Egyptian universities and higher institutions in that year. The agency paid tuition for 600 and gave them LE 6.5 a month for food and LE 3 for housing. The agency also paid 200 of the above 600 students an additional LE 5 a month. It encouraged the students to specialize and take graduate studies in Egyptian universities. In addition, there were 1,000 Sudanese students in high school, of whom about 600 received a stipend of LE 4 a month. The agency also organized trips and entertainment for them, and in 1954 the government allocated LE 200,000 for establishing dormitories especially for high-school students.[21]

The Sudanese elections which took place in November, 1953, resulted in an absolute majority for the pro-Egyptian National Unionist Party. In the lower house, or the House of Representatives, they won 50 out of 97 seats; the Umma Party won 23. In the upper house, or Senate, the National Unionist Party won 21 out of 30 electoral seats. These results were considered a victory for Egypt. In a speech commenting on the elections, President Nagib declared:

> Egyptian-Sudanese close ties and good relations . . . are not the creation of one man and are not the fruit of a political plan. . . . It is God's will that drove the Nile between us, united our language and religion, and gathered us into one belt of history, memories, pains, and hopes. When imperialism came, it strengthened these relations. . . . We experienced disaster together under occupation. Henceforth, we had a common fight aiming for a mutual objective. . . . The Sudanese elections and what they reflect of political facts and spiritual facts about the Sudanese people are a true and transitional point not in the life of the Sudanese only but in the life of the whole Nile Valley if not the life of Africa and in turn the life of the oppressed nations.[22]

21. *Ibid.,* pp. 599–60.
22. *Al-Ahram,* February 13, 1954, p. 1.

It is apparent that Egypt considered the success of the National Unionist Party in the Sudanese elections to be a guarantee of unity. In early 1954 Egypt moved rapidly to further consolidate relations with the Sudan. The Egyptian government established religious grammar and high schools in the Sudan, whose graduates would be sent directly to Al-Azhar. Salah Salem suggested that arrangements be made to accommodate 4,000 Sudanese students in Egyptian summer camps by 1955.[23] In February, 1954, he and Abdul Hakim Amir arrived in the Sudan for a four-day trip. The trip was extended to twenty-five days, and they traveled ten thousand miles through the country promoting Egyptian-Sudanese relations. Also in February the minister of works and a number of Egyptian technical experts arrived in the Sudan to discuss future projects. Emphasizing the importance of the Sudanese question to the Egyptian government, Salah Salem stated:

> The duty of Egypt toward the Sudan . . . was given the first place of priority by the revolution's leadership and the policy of its government, and Egypt is ready to do everything in order to reach the goal.[24]

On the occasion of the opening of the Sudanese Parliament, the Egyptian government sent gifts to the Sudan, including a number of arms. Egypt stated that these were sent to celebrate

> this happy occasion as a practical token of her love and to strengthen the Sudan . . . by giving her [Egypt's] citizens in the south [Sudan] arms that are sufficient to equip 1,000 Sudanese soldiers and five new training airplanes to train the sons of the south . . . because power is the sign of success in this materialistic age.[25]

The Bank Misr (Bank of Egypt) also became very active in the Sudan, and Salah Salem emphasized how important it was to strengthen "economic ties between Egypt and the Sudan in order

23. *Al-Ahram,* February 4, 1954, p. 7.
24. *Al-Ahram,* February 13, 1954, p. 11.
25. *Al-Ahram,* February 17, 1954, p. 1.

175

to bind the Valley in a strong tie to achieve its true freedom, not an artificial one."[26]

There were many other indications of an attempt to consolidate relations between the two countries. For example, both Egyptian government and religious associations aided the Sudanese religious associations.[27] Ismail al-Azhari, who became the prime minister of the Sudan, made a visit to Egypt for the second anniversary of the revolution celebration and brought with him his secretary to be trained in Egypt in the affairs of the prime minister's council secretariat.[28]

The intensity of Egypt's conviction that unity was guaranteed, and her drive to integrate the two countries, is demonstrated by this statement of the commander of the Staff College after a class visit to the Sudan:

> If a visit to the Sudan is a duty of each Egyptian, it is in the opinion of the War Staff College that it is the most urgent of the obligations, and these visits are included in the academic program of the college that created the revolution for the sake of liberating the Nile Valley.[29]

RELATIONS IN CRISIS: 1956-1958

In May, 1955, Ismail al-Azhuri told Egyptian leaders in Cairo, including Nasser, that "unity was no longer contemplated by any of the major Sudanese political parties." Of even greater consequence to Egypt was Al-Azhari's threat against its most vital interest. He declared: "The Nile flows through the Sudan first and we can no longer be content to receive our share last."[30] Several observations can be made with regard to the cause of this change in attitude. The fear that union with Egypt would precipitate a civil war was very likely a major factor. The Umma Party had

26. *Al-Ahram,* April 30, 1954, p. 1.
27. *Al-Ahram,* April 17, 1954, p. 9.
28. *Al-Ahram,* July 10, 1954, p. 6.
29. *Al-Ahram,* February 17, 1954, p. 8.
30. *New York Times,* June 2, 1955, p. 8.

effectively demonstrated its ability to mobilize support for its political cause, and the clashes it created delayed the opening of Parliament. The National Unionist Party's victory in the 1953 elections had been close, and Al-Azhari did not desire a test of strength.[31] Then there were also developments that resulted in a loss by the Egyptian regime of its popularity with the Sudanese public. Nagib's disputes with Nasser and his subsequent removal from power created an adverse reaction among the Sudanese because of his personal popularity; Nasser had also lost the support of the Muslim Brotherhood, the Communists, and the leftists in the Sudan when he suppressed these groups in Egypt. Quite aside from the rifts in the Arab political community, there was the North-South division. The Negro South (pagan and Christian) and the Arab North (Muslim) had been in conflict for years, a conflict which broke into serious and long-lasting guerrilla warfare after independence. Union with Egypt would have exacerbated this situation, which was partially generated by southern fears of Arab domination.

In August, 1955, Egypt began a radio and press campaign against Al-Azhari in an apparent effort to discredit his government among the Sudanese people. On August 11 Radio Cairo announced that Al-Azhari had refused Salah Salem's offer to supply the Sudan with Egyptian arms and military advisers and had refused Egypt's offer to train Sudanese soldiers and officers.[32] The campaign was heavily directed toward Southern Sudan, where it attempted to win support for union with Egypt.[33] The broadcasts accused Al-Azhari of discriminating against the South by not accepting Egyptian aid for that less-developed region. The Egyptian government claimed that its offer to establish cultural and health projects in the South—an offer that would cost Egypt LE 3.5 million annually—had been refused.[34]

31. See L. A. Fabunmi, *The Sudan in Anglo-Egyptian Relations, 1800–1956* (London: Longmans, Green & Co., 1960), pp. 349–52.

32. *Al-Ahram,* August 12, 1955, p. 1.

33. *New York Times,* August 23, 1955, p. 3.

34. *Al-Ahram,* August 13, 1955, p. 6. The offer included the establishment of an institution to train Southern Sudanese in agrarian sciences and the establish-

But by the end of August, 1955, it was apparent that there was also division over the Sudan within the Egyptian government. Salah Salem resigned his posts of minister of national guidance and minister of Sudanese affairs, and Nasser himself took over the direction of Egypt's Sudanese policy. On the day of Salem's resignation the campaign against Al-Azhari was dropped, and Egypt's policy toward the Sudan became conciliatory.[35] When the Sudanese Parliament declared independence in December, 1955, Egypt was the first country to extend formal recognition and immediately appointed Lt. General Muhammad Saif al-Yazal Khalifah as ambassador to the Sudan, where he became dean of the diplomatic corps.

The Sudan's emergence into the community of independent nations opened a new phase in Egyptian-Sudanese relations. It was of immediate concern to Egypt to reach agreement over the Nile-waters division and to facilitate the commencement of the Aswan High Dam project; and there remained Egypt's traditional strategic and economic interests in the Sudan. Since Sudan's independence, Egypt has aimed at maintaining amicable relations with all Sudanese governments. At times the policies of the two governments have taken diametrically opposed courses, but even then Egypt has attempted to assume at the very least a semblance of friendship, utilizing indirect influences.

Protection of its interests in the Sudan was one of the causes of the expansion of Egypt's African policy. In January, 1956, Nasser formed the "Supreme Committee to Supervise African Affairs" to formulate an African policy for Egypt. That the Sudan was an important consideration in the new plan can be gleaned from the fact that the Egyptian ambassador to the Sudan, the Egyptian director of Sudanese irrigation works, and the economic chancellor of the Egyptian Embassy in Khartoum were all members of the committee. Africanism became a potent force in Sudanese politics;

---

ment of a hospital. Both institutions would be secular. Egypt claimed that under terms of the agreement it had proposed to pay teachers' salaries and the Sudanese government would have the right to appoint all personnel.

35. *New York Times,* August 31, 1955, p. 7.

Egypt also had greatly expanded its support of the African national liberation movements;[36] thus by the time of the Sudan's admission to the Arab League in January, 1956, Egypt's policy was already being formulated within an Afro-Arab framework. An Egyptian political-science textbook explains:

> This admission had a very important political significance . . . the relationship between the Sudan and Egypt was moved from the African circle to the Arab circle. As a result of this new direction, Egyptian policy toward Africa expanded beyond the belt of the Nile Valley . . . to a wider belt extending to the heart of the African continent. One of the results of that is the charter of the Casablanca bloc.[37]

For its part, the new Sudanese government could not afford to ignore public demands for independence nor could it afford open hostility toward the north. Therefore, when the Sudan received its independence, all of the Sudanese political leaders affirmed their desire to maintain close ties with Egypt. Al-Azhari declared in the Sudanese Parliament: "The Sudan will always remain the closest, most sincere and fraternal country in its relations with Egypt."[38]

Egypt's shift in policy led to the development of cordial relations between the two countries. In April, 1956, Egypt made a gift of 1.5 million dollars worth of arms to the Al-Azhari government, and when Abdullah Khalil, head of the fiercely anti-Egyptian Umma Party, became premier in July, 1956, the mutual accord continued. In Khalil's first month in office, Egypt offered his government military aid and offered to send two professors from the War Staff College to train Sudanese officers. In addition, the Sudan sent 11 officers and 25 soldiers to be trained in Egyptian military institutions. After his visit with Nasser in late July, 1956, Khalil stated that the Sudan had no desire to unite with Egypt. However,

36. See Chapter Two, above, for a discussion of this support.

37. Butrus Butrus Ghali and Muhammad K. Isa, *Mabadi al-'ulum al-siyasiya* [An introduction to political science] (Cairo: Anglo-Egyptian Bookshop, 1962–63), pp. 566–67.

38. *Scribe* (Cairo), January, 1956, p. 10.

he added, "I returned to the Sudan with a new idea. Now I can feel free to put my hand in Egypt's."[39]

During the Suez crisis, Egypt accused Britain of using pressure in the Sudan in an effort to obstruct Sudanese support for Egypt. Egyptian newspapers charged that Britain had threatened to withdraw £20 million invested in the Sudanese market and had attempted to influence public opinion by claiming that British goods scheduled for shipment to the Sudan would be delayed because of the Canal problem.[40] Whether this is a fact or whether Egypt was merely attempting to inflame Sudanese sentiment against the British cannot be determined. However, it is clear that the Suez crisis created a new bond between the Sudanese and Egyptians. The Sudan offered its unqualified support: the Sudanese people donated LE 96,000 and the government donated LE 20,000 to aid Egypt.[41] The Sudanese Council of Ministers expressed the extent of this sentiment:

> In accordance with the strong will of the Sudanese people in general to actively assist our sister Egypt in its present disaster by volunteering to participate in stopping this unjust and wicked war . . . [we will] organize the efforts of parties, organizations, and factions into one national united movement that will be responsible to organize, train, and send these volunteers to Egypt.[42]

In late 1956 Egypt attempted to form a defense alliance with Ethiopia and the Sudan, perhaps hoping to utilize the emotions aroused by the Suez crisis. It was reported that the Sudanese government had taken the matter under serious consideration and was negotiating with Ethiopia. The Egyptian ambassador was reportedly given all the details of the meetings, and Nasser discussed the subject with Khalil during the latter's visit to Cairo in December, 1956.[43] During this visit Khalil stated:

39. *New York Times,* July 26, 1956.
40. *Rose El-Youssief,* no. 1447, October 1, 1956, p. 4.
41. *Rose El-Youssief,* no. 1489, December 24, 1956, p. 5.
42. Ali Ibrahim Abda, *Misr wa Ifriqiya fi al-'asr al-hadith* [Egypt and Africa in modern times] (Cairo: Dar Al-Qalam, 1962), pp. 93–95.

Our ties with Egypt will always remain strong. It is the closest state in the world to us. The policy of our government is
close, strong cooperation with Egypt in all vital matters between the two brotherly countries.[44]

Egypt apparently hoped to forestall by means of a pact the
threat of American penetration into the Sudan through economic
and technical assistance. As early as mid-1956 Egyptian newspapers accused America of attempting to assume through aid
Britain's former hegemony in the Sudan. There was also the threat
that Uganda and Ethiopia would attempt to participate in the Nile-
waters negotiations, and in April, 1956, the Sudanese government
announced that Britain had in fact requested that Uganda be included in the discussions. In late 1957 Ethiopia also attempted to
participate in the negotiations.[45]

However, the alliance never materialized, and in February,
1957, the Sudan officially requested economic and military assistance from the United States. The *New York Times* noted that
"the trend of the Khalil government is definitely pro-Western and
in the Arab League alignment, the government now leans toward
Iraq rather than Egypt. The Premier will visit Baghdad . . . as a
guest of the Iraqi Premier Nuri al-Sayid. There was even talk
of the Sudan joining Iraq in an alliance.[46]

---

43. *Rose El-Youssief,* no. 1497, February 18, 1957, p. 4.

44. *Rose El-Youssief,* no. 1449, March 19, 1956, p. 18.

45. *Rose El-Youssief,* no. 1536, November 18, 1957, p. 7. Ethiopia controls
the source of the Blue Nile, which provides 84 per cent of the floodwaters to the
Lower Nile. Thus, Ethiopia has a strategic importance for Egypt. Relations between the two states have not always been cordial. Egypt has utilized the large
Muslim minority and dissident non-Muslim tribes in Ethiopia to bring pressure to
bear on the Addis Ababa government. This was evidenced prior to Egypt's nationalization of the Suez Canal. Because Haile Selassie felt that Ethiopia should
be consulted on the Aswan Dam project, Egypt broadcast an intense propaganda
campaign against him. The *New York Times* reported that after the nationalization there was evidence of an agreement between the two countries whereby
Egypt abated her propaganda campaign and Ethiopia refrained from participation
in the Suez Canal Users Association (an association to which Egypt strongly
objected). The truce continued until 1957 when Haile Selassie requested a large
increase in American military aid, and Egypt resumed her propaganda activities
(*New York Times,* February 16, 1957, p. 1; see also *ibid.,* April 2, 1957, p. 2).

46. February 19, 1957, p. 1.

181

Case Studies

By early 1957, as a result of the Baghdad Pact, the Suez War, and other factors, Egypt regarded America as its principal rival in Africa and the Middle East. Thus, the threat of American influence in the Sudan had the same implications as the Baghdad Pact. Egypt considered that any

> assistance to the countries that are outside of the aggressive pacts is the price which America offers to build new pacts in these countries. America is aiming to create a Central African Pact which is called the African Belt. From this we see that the Sudan's acceptance of American economic assistance is the first step to its entrance into military pacts.[47]

Egypt viewed the extension of American aid into Africa as an attempt to create "obstacles in the face of the liberation movements" on the continent.[48] Vice President Nixon's visit to the Sudan and Ethiopia in March, 1957, "aroused deep anxiety and suspicion . . . [as] it was seen as a new campaign to isolate Egypt."[49] The cool reception he received in the Sudan indicated the reservoir of influence that Egypt could still command there. Egypt's alliance with the Communists was also very clear. Neither the Egyptian ambassador nor the Russian ambassador was at the airport to greet Nixon. During this period, in response to the threat of American penetration into the Sudan, Egypt supported the Sudanese Communist Party in an anti-American campaign. For example, Abdul Khaliq Magub, a well-known Communist and secretary of the Sudanese Anti-Imperialist Front, wrote an introduction to a book published in Cairo in which he accused the American Embassy in Khartoum of bribing Sudanese officials. He stated that America's aim requires "the isolation of the Sudan from the Arab progressive area and depends on Sudanese friends

47. Maamun Muhammad al-Amin, *Al-Sudan wa muamarat al-isti'mar* [The Sudan and the imperialist conspiracies] (Cairo: Dar Al-Fikir, 1957), p. 34.

48. *Al-Sudan . . . haqaiq wa wathaiq* [The Sudan . . . facts and documents], Political Books Series, no. 85 (Cairo: Political Books Committee, 1958), pp. 18–19.

49. *New York Times,* April 2, 1957, Section M, p. 4.

of the West and strengthens them in order to disassociate the idea of Arab freedom from Africa."[50]

Egypt also accused America of attempting to threaten Egypt's most vital interest, the Nile, at its origins by penetrating and influencing the Nile Valley. It considered this was the purpose of America's invitations to the Sudan, Ethiopia, Uganda, and Tanganyika to discuss the possibility of projects on the Nile.[51] The great expansion of Egypt's aid to the liberation movements in 1957 was in part an attempt to strengthen its bases of influence and nurture anti-Western sentiment in order to hinder the extension of America's influence.

Ismail al-Azhari, perhaps hoping to utilize an upsurge of pro-Egyptian sentiment in a return to power, attempted to regain Egypt's confidence. He also boycotted Nixon during the vice president's visit to the Sudan, declining a government invitation to greet Nixon at the airport and attend a palace reception. He declared his support for the creation of a mutual-defense pact with Egypt, stating, "We must stand with Egypt in defense." He also declared that the Sudan's foreign policy should be closely linked with the U.A.R.'s.[52]

Even during this tense period in Egyptian-Sudanese relations, both countries attempted to maintain a degree of cordiality. Egypt's campaign was directed against Western influence, not against the government directly. For its part, the Sudanese government was not stable enough to withstand an intense effort by pro-Egyptian and anti-Western factions if they should mobilize their efforts. Abdullah Khalil expressed this when he declared, "I want to develop this country and raise the standard of living of the people. I cannot face intrigue. I cannot fight on two fronts. I have to be on peaceful terms with Egypt."[53]

50. In Gayli Abdul-Rahman, *Al-Ma'una al-Amrikiya tuhaddid* [American aid threatens Sudan's independence] (Cairo: Dar Al-Fiker, 1958), p. 4.

51. *Al-Sudan . . . haqaiq wa wathaiq* [The Sudan . . . facts and documents], pp. 18–19.

52. *New York Times,* February 22, 1957, p. 3.

53. *New York Times,* February 19, 1957, p. 13.

Case Studies

Even though Egyptian-Sudanese relations were cool, there was no open hostility between the two countries until 1958. In that year two issues strained the relations between Egypt and the Sudan to the point of crisis: the Sudanese-Egyptian border issue in February and the Nile-waters problem in July and August. The border dispute arose when the Sudanese government announced the delineation of constituencies for the Sudanese parliamentary elections which were to take place on February 27, 1958, and included areas that Egypt claimed to be Egyptian territory. Egypt complained that while a Sudanese delegation was in Cairo working on the dispute, suddenly, and without consulting the Egyptian government, the Sudanese government made the conflict public a half-hour prior to the last meeting of the two parties and issued a statement on the results of the meeting. Egypt considered this to be an attempt by the Sudanese government to create an artificial disturbance in the relations between the two countries. It contended that if the Sudanese government had been serious about the negotiations, it would have waited until after the final meeting before issuing a statement.[54]

On February 20, 1958, the Sudan brought the issue before the U.N. Security Council and claimed that Egypt was massing troops on the disputed border to aggress against the Sudan. The pro-Egyptian factions in the Sudan urged the Egyptian government to solve the problem without disturbing the relationship between the two countries. Nasser personally promised ex-Prime Minister Al-Azhari and Al-Merghani, the leader of the Khatmia sect, to do so. On February 21 the Egyptian government issued the following communiqúe:

> Egypt, who supported the Sudan on its way to freedom and independence, takes this decision with the aim of stopping . . . those who took this opportunity to disturb the permanent relationship between the two brotherly nations. Egypt did not react to these attempts . . . to picture the situation . . . in the form of armed intervention against the Sudanese land. At the time, Egypt had nothing on the southern border but

54. *Al-Ahram,* February 20, 1958, p. 1.

184

the normal border patrols. The Egyptian government will announce again that the Egyptian armed forces are not created to invade the Sudan but always support the Sudan against the common enemy.[55]

On February 21, 1958, the United Nations Security Council met to consider the issue. Both the Egyptian and Sudanese representatives expressed their desire that the issue be negotiated after the Sudanese elections and emphasized each country's desire to maintain friendship with the other. Consequently, the Security Council took no action and ended the meeting. The heated intensity of the border dispute subsequently subsided.

The second problem arose in July, 1958, when the Sudanese government opened the Gezira Canal at an earlier date than that provided by the 1929 Nile-Waters Agreement. In reply to an Egyptian memorandum regarding the violation, the Sudan declared that it did not recognize the 1929 agreement. Relations between the two states deteriorated as negotiations on the issue failed. In September, 1958, it was reported that the Sudanese government had enjoined Sudanese merchants from importing U.A.R. goods and had encouraged that European goods be imported instead.[56] Egyptian newspapers considered that the aims of the Sudanese government were "to isolate the Sudan from its natural atmosphere, the Arab world, and to direct it toward . . . the West and imperialism."[57]

With the problem of the Nile waters, and for the first time since the Sudan's independence, Egypt attempted to intervene directly in the Sudan's internal politics through the Sudanese National Liberation Party. This party, which was founded in 1958 after the first Sudanese post-independence parliamentary election, called for close cooperation with the National Unionist Party, the Democratic Peoples' Party, the Southern Liberal Party, and the Anti-Imperialist Front. The National Liberation Party also claimed to have the

---

55. *Al-Ahram,* February 22, 1958, p. 1.

56. *Rose El-Youssief,* no. 1577, September 1, 1958, p. 5.

57. Ihsan Abdul Quddus, "Ma'rakat al-shi'arat fi al-Sudan" [The battle of slogans in the Sudan], *Rose El-Youssief,* no. 1577, September 1, 1958, p. 6.

support of the religious faction, Al-Khalifah al-Ma'aishi, whose aim was "the liberation of the Islamic world and its unity."[58]

In September, 1958, the National Liberation Party leaders met in Cairo. One of them declared: "We believe that the only security against the maneuvers of the imperialists are close ties with the U.A.R. and coordination of our relations to the fullest extent." He also explained:

> Politically, we believe in the necessity of following the policy of nonalignment and positive neutrality and adherence to the resolutions of the Bandung and Cairo conferences. Economically, we believe that our interest requires abolishing all existing restrictions of commerce between the U.A.R. and the Sudan. Culturally, we believe in the necessity of unifying school programs in the two countries. Militarily, we strongly believe in the coordination of all military affairs between the two countries.[59]

The party called for the problems between Egypt and the Sudan to be resolved in a peaceful and friendly manner, especially the Nile-waters dispute, and it condemned the Sudanese government for its attempt to disturb relations between the two countries. The party also asked for the transformation of the Sudan into a socialist democratic society. The leaders stated:

> We see that the call for an African government is a reactionary movement supported by Anglo-American imperialism. Its aim is to separate the Sudan from Arab nationalism in order to achieve the imperialist project of the African Belt. We will fight this call with all our power.[60]

The visit of the party leaders to Cairo and their absolute support for Egypt indicate the degree of Egyptian influence. That the problem of the Nile waters was a major cause of Egypt's support

58. *Rose El-Youssief,* no. 1578, September 8, 1958, p. 10.
59. *Rose El-Youssief,* no. 1578, September 8, 1958, p. 10.
60. *Rose El-Youssief,* no. 1578, September 8, 1958, p. 10.

for the party is demonstrated by Ihsan Abdul Quddus' statement:

> Imperialism attempts to create a strong front to block us from the south, from the Sudan and Ethiopia supported by the British colonies in Africa. The role of this front is to divert the Nile waters from the Egyptian region until Egypt is forced to its knees. . . . Its role also is to stop the influence of Arab nationalism in the Sudan.[61]

On November 17, 1958, it was reported that Sudanese mediators in Cairo had reached a basis for negotiations over the Nile-waters problem. Khalil's postponement of the opening of Parliament from November 17 to December 8 was reported to be an attempt to resolve the dispute prior to the legislature's reassembly.[62] Khalil proposed to travel to Cairo to reach a settlement on all issues. The degree to which Egyptian pressure was responsible for bringing about this development can only be conjectured; however, it would seem that Khalil was anxious to reach an agreement prior to the convening of Parliament in order to save his government, which was faced with a united pro-Egyptian front led by the National Liberation Party. The military coup of November 18, 1958, superseded Khalil's trip to Cairo. Discussing the proposed trip, Nasser described the nature of Egyptian-Sudanese relations:

> Of course, it's our intention to solve all the problems. . . . We do not want to create problems. I sent an invitation to Abdullah Khalil. We did not fix the time of his arrival, and unexpectedly the Sudanese nationalist army staged its revolution and declared that this revolution is to destroy corruption and exploitation. We were the first who supported this revolution.[63]

61. *Rose El-Youssief*, no. 1587, November 10, 1958, p. 3.

62. *Al-Ahram*, November 16, 1958, p. 1, and November 17, 1958, p. 1; see also the *Times* (London), November 18, 1958, p. 11.

63. *Majmu'at khutab wa tasrihat wa bayanat al-Rais Gamal Abdel Nasser.* [Collection of speeches, statements, and remarks of President Gamal Abdel Nasser] *Part II, February 1958–January 1960*, comp. U.A.R. Information Department (Cairo: n.d.), p. 228; hereafter referred to as *Nasser's Speeches, February, 1958–January, 1960.*

Case Studies

MILITARY RULE: 1958-1964

The coup was considered advantageous for Egypt. The first statement by the new prime minister, Abboud, clearly indicated his desire for friendship with the U.A.R.

> It is my pleasure to affirm here that the free independent Sudan will build its relations with all states . . . and the brother Arab states especially, on the basis of respect, sincerity, and mutual benefit. With our brother, the U.A.R., we will work very hard to improve relations, to solve all the unsettled questions between us and to end the artificially cool relations that have been between the two brother countries.[64]

All the leaders of the new regime immediately affirmed the government's good will and friendship toward Egypt. The foreign minister declared:

> The Sudan has a special position which makes it feel that it has certain commitments toward the Arab countries and the African countries. This is in accordance with the Sudan's historic and geographic position. The Sudan as a nation feels it is a part of the Arab entity. What strengthens this belief and this feeling is our common history and common thinking. We will work on our side to strengthen these relations that bind us to the Arab fate, especially the U.A.R. Our determination, the honesty of our feeling, and our belief in solving all the problems between our two countries let us look at the future of the relationship between our countries with assured optimism.[65]

General Abdul Wahab, the deputy prime minister, stated:

> Our brothers in Cairo will find out when they negotiate with us that we are a government that is working to solve its problems with its neighbors and brothers. I am optimistic about solving all the problems . . . with the U.A.R.[66]

64. *Khutab al-thawra* [The speeches of the revolution], comp. Republic of the Sudan, Central Information Bureau (Khartoum, n.d.), p. 2.
65. *Ibid.,* p. 6.
66. *Al-Ahram,* November 23, 1958, p. 1.

188

And General Abboud, the leader of the coup, emphasized the desire for friendship with the U.A.R. when he said:

> Our policy is to have better relations and cooperation with all states . . . we have a special policy with the Arab states, especially the U.A.R. The Egyptian region and the Sudan are brothers from old times, and the bonds of love between us are strong and continuous.[67]

The most striking aspect of the official declarations is the desire to solve all unsettled questions. Of course, the outstanding issue at the time was the Nile-waters problem, and Egypt feared the intervention of other states, particularly of Ethiopia (a close friend of the United States) and Uganda (a British colony), in the negotiations. This fear was quietly allayed when Muhammad Talaat Farid, the new Sudanese minister of information, said, "The problem of the Nile waters will be solved between the two governments of Cairo and Khartoum only."[68] The new government also declared that it welcomed the establishment of the High Dam. Nasser, in turn, expressed his personal pleasure with the new regime's desire to solve the unsettled issues and its intention to allow the resumption of Egyptian imports.[69]

The U.A.R. was the first state to recognize the new Sudanese government. As soon as the government was formed, the Egyptian ambassador to Khartoum was instructed to extend to it Egypt's formal recognition and offer Nasser's congratulations.[70] On the second day after the coup Nasser sent a personal message to Abboud.

General Muhammad Talaat Farid declared that the reasons behind the coup were American influence and interference in the internal affairs of the Sudan and the problems between Egypt and the Sudan, especially the Nile-waters issue and the stoppage of commercial exchange between the two countries.[71] And the new

67. *Al-Ahram*, November 27, 1958, p. 1.
68. *Al-Ahram*, November 29, 1958, p. 1.
69. *Nasser's Speeches, February, 1958–January, 1960*, p. 228.
70. *Rose El-Youssief*, no. 1589, November 24, 1958, p. 5.
71. *Rose El-Youssief*, no. 1590, December 1, 1958, p. 8.

regime declared its adherence to the policy of nonalignment and neutrality. Commenting on the government's first full year in office, *Al-Ahram* stated: "The aims of the Sudanese revolution are very similar to the aims that were achieved by the 23rd of July revolution for the nation of the U.A.R."[72]

In November, 1959, Egypt and the Sudan signed the Nile-Waters Agreement. Eight months later, *Al-Ahram* reported that both the U.A.R. and the Sudan instructed their delegations to the negotiations to accept all conditions specified by the other country.[73] The agreement provides that when the High Dam is completed, the Sudan will be entitled to one-third of the total annual flow instead of the one-twelfth share provided under the 1929 agreement. This would provide the Sudan with 18.5 million cubic meters of water instead of 4 million and Egypt with 55.5 million compared with the 48 million it had been receiving. It was also agreed that Egypt would pay LE 15 million to meet the costs of providing homes and lands for the 70,000 Sudanese living in Wadi Halfa who would be displaced and that the two states would share the costs of other Nile projects designed to increase the total annual flow of the Nile.[74] The agreement was generally hailed as "a welcome sign that the leaders of both countries are determined to end polemical bickering which has hitherto made nonsense of their fervent protestations of good will . . . [in] negotiations over the Nile."[75] U.A.R. Vice-President Zakaria Mohieddin, the head of the Egyptian delegation to the Nile-waters negotiations, stated: "We hope that this will pave the road to more agreement to coordinate the two countries in the economic, cultural, and military fields." He also discussed the possibility of unifying the cotton policy between them.[76]

The agreement did, in fact, mark the beginning of expanded cooperation. Trade, payments, and custom-dues agreements were

72. November 18, 1959, p. 6.
73. July 22, 1960, p. 2.
74. *Scribe* (Cairo), November 30, 1959, pp. 11–12.
75. *Times* (London), November 9, 1959, p. 11.
76. *Al-Ahram,* November 21, 1959, p. 4.

190

signed in 1959. In May, 1961, an Egyptian commercial mission arrived in Khartoum to explore the possibility of an economic and commercial alliance between the two countries, and in August of the same year, another group appeared that represented the most productive companies of the U.A.R. This latter mission concluded a L.E. half-million agreement of commercial exchange between U.A.R. and Sudanese businesses and established the Arab-Sudanese petroleum company.[77] The members also expressed their interest in building a LE one million hotel in Khartoum. Their spokesman declared: "I assure you here that the U.A.R. is in need of more cattle from the Sudan but this increase should be accompanied by a corresponding increase in the Sudan's purchases."[78] A third U.A.R. commercial probe, following closely upon the heels of the second, discussed the creation of a commercial fleet designed to operate between Egypt and the Sudan on the Lake of the High Dam and to transfer 100,000 passengers, 80,000 tons of goods, and 60,000 head of cattle between the two countries annually.[79] In September, 1961, the U.A.R. and Sudanese governments were reported to be investigating the possibilities of creating telephone and telegraph communications between the two states.[80]

There also appeared to be cooperation in foreign-policy matters external to both nations. During an eight-day visit to Egypt in July, 1961, Abboud declared his adherence to a policy of non-alignment. In the final joint communiqué issued by Abboud and Nasser both parties pledged their full support to the Congo, called for Afro-Asian support for the Congolese people, denounced Israel and French actions in Algeria, and assured increasing cooperation between the two countries.[81]

77. *Al-Raiy Al-'Aam* (Khartoum), August 18, 1961, p. 1. The secretary of the Khartoum Chamber of Commerce hailed this agreement, stating that it resulted from the reduction of prices on U.A.R. goods to compete with world-market prices. He considered this to be the beginning of greater commercial exchange between the two states (*Al-Raiy Al-'Aam* Khartoum, August 23, 1961, p. 3).

78. *Al-Raiy al 'Aam* (Khartoum), August 18, 1961, p. 3.

79. *Al-Raiy al-'Aam* (Khartoum), August 25, 1961, p. 1.

80. *Al-Raiy al-'Aam* (Khartoum), September 26, 1961, p. 4.

81. *Al-Ahram,* July 29, 1961, p. 11.

Case Studies

Two months later, Nasser made an eleven-day visit to the Sudan to participate in the celebrations of the third anniversary of the revolution. In welcoming Nasser, Abboud declared: "The principles that you established the foundations for and are working for in the Arab sphere or the international sphere . . . These principles we adhere to in the Sudan and work for them."[82] On the basis of Abboud's statements, the Sudan's foreign policy appeared to be compatible with the U.A.R.'s, and Abboud seemed prepared to take action in cooperation with Nasser, especially with regard to the Congo crisis. For example, Abboud also stated:

> I see with great concern the attempt of imperialism to penetrate Africa either directly as in the case of the Congo, or indirectly, and during your visit we should exchange opinions and take serious steps to destroy imperialism in all its shapes and forms.[83]

However, the Sudanese government apparently was merely paying lip service to these foreign-policy principles, perhaps only to mollify Nasser, as its actual policy turned out to be quite moderate compared with Egypt's. The disparity between Abboud's statements to Nasser and the Sudan's actual stand was very evident during the Congo crisis. The Sudan regarded the Congo issue as an internal Congolese problem, took a neutral position with regard to the U.N. action, and refused to allow any country to assist the Congo through Sudanese territory.[84] That Abboud desired to appease Nasser on this issue and at the same time pursue a moderate policy himself is clearly manifest in the telegram he sent to Dag Hammarskjold upon Lumumba's assassination. In an obviously empty threat, he warned the secretary-general that unless he received assurances that the U.N.'s aims in entering the Congo were to safeguard the "independence, unity and security" of the country, he would "be forced to request the withdrawal of the Sudanese forces if their presence proved not to be in the interests of the

82. *Al-Ahram,* November 16, 1961, p. 1.
83. *Al-Ahram,* November 16, 1961, p. 1.
84. *Al-Raiy al-'Aam* (Khartoum), February 1, 1961, p. 1.

Congolese people as defined by the U.N. resolutions."[85] Copies of
the telegram were sent to the U.A.R., the African Arab states,
and the sub-Saharan African states.

The Congo issue, the Sudan's identification with the Monrovia
Group rather than the rival Casablanca Group, and the continued
acceptance of large-scale American aid and technical assistance
(which amounted to 82 million dollars between 1958 and 1964)
resulted in a cooling of U.A.R.–Sudanese relations.

RETURN TO CIVILIAN GOVERNMENT: 1965

By the end of 1964, anti-government demonstrations against Abboud's military regime created an internal crisis in the Sudan.
A general strike called on October 24 virtually immobilized the
government. Cairo informants reported scores killed and hundreds
injured during the ensuing riots. In an attempt to quell the civil
unrest, Abboud dissolved the ruling Armed Forces Supreme Council and the Cabinet. Beirut newspapers reported that Abboud took
this action upon an ultimatum issued by a group of "Free Officers."
A transitional government was formed preparatory to the drafting
of a constitution, but the unrest continued. At the end of October
a coalition government was formed by Serr al-Khatm Khalifa,
and Abboud remained as head of state. However, anti-government demonstrations, led by Communists, students, and white-
collar workers, continued. These demonstrations were apparently
directed against the American aid program, which was considered
to have helped maintain the military regime, and the demonstrators
chanted: "No United States aid after today."[86] In mid-November,
Abboud was forced out of power.

The U.A.R. immediately recognized the new Sudanese government. Egypt considered it to be an ally, and Cairo news media
describing the attitude of the new regime declared: "The Sudanese National Government, which assumed power last October, has

85. *Al-Raiy al-'Aam* (Khartoum), February 16, 1961, p. 1.
86. *New York Times,* November 9, 1964, p. 5.

been eager to dissolve all differences between the Sudan and the Egyptian people, and to consolidate the age-long ties which bind them together."[87] The Sudanese government affirmed its friendship with the U.A.R., and Dr. Mubarak Shaddad, chairman of the Sudanese Sovereignty Council, in a statement broadcast from Radio Omdurman maintained that "the friendship of the two peoples and the two countries grows stronger every day, and the will to live happy and dignified lives has made our states an invincible wall against colonialism."[88]

On January 6, 1965, the new Sudanese prime minister, Serr al-Khatm Khalifa, visited Nasser in Cairo. Egyptian news media gave the following description of their meeting:

> President Nasser's first meeting gave them the impression that there was no need to discuss new bases because all [that] is necessary is to organize the already existing understanding in the interest of the two nations. The Sudanese Prime Minister said that the result of these relations would shortly show their practical nature particularly in the fields of trade and economic cooperation.[89]

In late January, 1965, an Egyptian economic delegation headed by the minister of economics and foreign trade, and including the minister of communications and twelve other members, visited the Sudan to negotiate economic questions and to "lay the strong foundation . . . for the continuation and the growth of economic and commercial exchange between the two countries. . . ." New commercial agreements were also discussed.[90] On July 26, 1965, it was announced that the Sudan and the U.A.R. had agreed to coordinate their cotton-marketing arrangements. The trade agreement reached in January of 1965 was renewed upon its expiration in January of 1966.

Return to civilian rule, however, did not resolve the instability of Sudanese politics. Prime Minister Serr al-Kathm Khalifa held

87. *Arab Observer,* January 18, 1965, p. 10.
88. *Arab Observer,* January 18, 1965, p. 10.
89. *Arab Observer,* January 18, 1965, p. 50.
90. *Al-Jumhuriya,* January 25, 1965, p. 6.

office only until June of 1965. During his term of office the political situation in the Sudan deteriorated into one of continual crisis. The government's plan to hold elections in April was opposed by the Southern rebels, and considerable violence attended the elections themselves. Muhammad Ahmad Magub became prime minister in June, 1965, after a prolonged cabinet crisis. Mahgub remained in office little more than a year. In July, 1966, the Parliament voted no-confidence in his government, and he was replaced by Sadiq al-Mahdi. A split within Al-Mahdi's Umma Party, generated by the defection of his uncle, the conservative Imam al-Hadi al-Mahdi, led to the fall of his government in May, 1967. Thus when the government of Prime Minister Magub returned to office it was faced with the Arab-Israeli crisis and, after only three weeks in power, the June, 1967, war in the Middle East.

Further evidence of the internal instability of the Sudanese government is the fact that elections to Parliament, scheduled to be held by April, 1965, were not held until April, 1967, in the three Southern provinces of Bahr el Ghazal, Upper Nile, and Equatoria. Even then, they were attended by violence and disruptive activities.

During Magub's first term of office the Sudan remained in a position of pro-Western neutrality. Major loans were obtained from the Agency for International Development and the Import-Export Bank of Washington. For example, on March 11, 1966, AID granted a loan of 5.9 million dollars for road and airport equipment and services, and on April 22, 1966, the U.S. agreed to supply 2.3 million bushels of wheat under the Food-for-Peace program. On March 15, 1966, the Sudanese government urged reconsideration of the action taken by the Arab states in breaking relations with West Germany upon that country's recognition of Israel. On April 17, 1966, Sudanese diplomatic relations with Britain, broken over the issue of Rhodesian independence, were resumed.

Friendly relations were also maintained with the Communist states during this period. On March 18, 1966, the sale of 70,000 bales of cotton to Red China was arranged. On May 27 the Sudan concluded economic agreements with Czechoslovakia and the U.S.S.R., and on July 27 a trade agreement was concluded between Sudan and the Chinese People's Republic. This even-handed attitude on the part of the Sudan continued up to the June, 1967, war.

The impact of the Arab-Israeli war on Sudanese attitudes toward the Arab world was decisive in determining the course of Sudan's policy to date. In fact, the June, 1967, war may have been of considerable importance in providing a favorable environment for the coup of May 25, 1969. Sudanese policy underwent a decisive shift at this point, and its new policy seemed to have few roots in past policy as it had developed since independence.

However, the new direction in Sudanese policy was the expression of old and well-developed trends in the Sudan, trends which had long been frustrated by domestic factors. While there had been a strong pro-Egyptian, somewhat Arab-nationalist, element in the Sudan for a number of years (as expressed by the Unionist Party before independence and by the National Liberation Party during 1958), the supporters of close union with Egypt had never reached a position of dominance. The power of the large landowners and the entrenched political parties with their quasi-religious bases was exerted against the Egyptian connection. This opposition was based on the threat of the Egyptians to various established interests, both political and economic. In addition, a strongly Arabist outlook at Khartoum would have aggravated the possibility of a violent revolt in the South Sudan. Much of the rebel program and popular support for it was based on a fear of assimilation to the Arabs and the consequent destruction of the native culture. The Arab-Israeli war involved the supporters of Egypt and the Arab world and stimulated them to overlook their domestic constraints, at least temporarily. The personnel who were involved at this point were perhaps crucial in the course of events. Both Prime Minister Magub and Ismail al-Azhari, president of the Supreme Council of State, were favorably inclined toward Egypt (Al-Azhari had been head of the Unionist Party during the 1950s) and neither was strongly bound to the old, traditional parties.

One result of the June, 1967, war was a break with the West. When war broke out, the Sudan mobilized her forces, gave full (moral) support to the Arab states, and severed diplomatic relations with both the United States and Great Britain. Although there was for some time hope of a restoration of relations with the U.S., by October, 1967, these hopes faded and the Sudanese shift from the West appeared permanent.

After the June War the Sudan found other sources of arms to replace the former major suppliers—West Germany and Great Britain. In August, 1967, the Sudan reached agreement with Yugoslavia for the construction of a Red Sea naval base, and a Sudanese arms-buying mission to the Communist states was successful in replacing Western sources. This obvious turn from the West was sealed by the termination of a program in which twelve Sudanese military officers were receiving training in the U.S. Since that time, the growth of Soviet influence has been rapid, and the Russians have gained an apparently permanent position in the Sudan. Soviet arms and technicians are the chief and most effective tools of U.S.S.R. policy in the Sudan.

The Sudan's shift to the East brought it into greater agreement with the U.A.R. on foreign policy, and after the June War the Sudan seemed prepared to assume a greater role in Arab affairs than it had performed previously. Thus, in the months following the war the Sudan moved into the mainstream of Arab politics. Prime Minister Muhammad Ahmad Magub played a key role in this emergence. He sent a force of Sudanese troops to join the U.A.R. forces near the Suez Canal and was active in arranging the Arab summit conference held at Khartoum in August, 1967.

Magub not only arranged the conference, which was first proposed in June, but played a key part in the preliminary negotiations that ensured its success. On July 13, 1967, a number of Arab statesmen (Nasser of the U.A.R., Atassi of Syria, Aref of Iraq, and Boumediene of Algeria) commenced a meeting in Cairo to determine a course of action to be taken in eliminating the "consequences of Israeli aggression."[91] On the 14th they were joined by

91. *New York Times,* July 14, 1967, p. 3.

Prime Minister Magub, who participated in the issuance of a joint commnniqué on July 16. (On August 1 Magub visited President Nasser in Cairo, and on August 24 he visited King Faisal in Riyadh. In these meetings he laid the basis for the settlement of the Yemen question which was then reached at Khartoum.) The government of the Sudan spared no effort to make the Khartoum conference successful, even arranging for crowds of demonstrators to greet the visiting heads of state. The success of the conference, embodied in the agreements reached on Israel, renewal of oil shipments to the West, and Yemen, was a major diplomatic success for the Sudan. Syria boycotted the meetings, and the settlements reached were not fully acceptable to the Iraqi government; but the willingness of the U.A.R. to moderate its stance allowed the efforts at compromise to succeed.

After the conference the Sudanese government continued to consolidate its position in the Arab world. Extensive trade agreements were arranged with Egypt. The Sudan also joined the Arab common market and announced that all Arabs would be allowed free entry to the Sudan. While the former measure may have little immediate effect, freer commerce with the Arab world will have considerable impact on economic relations with Egypt, Sudan's closest Arab neighbor.

The Magub regime laid the basis for U.A.R.—Sudan cooperation in foreign policy, and the new regime that took power in May, 1969, has continued and extended that policy. But Mahgub's government would not, or could not, take the steps in domestic policy necessary to provide the basis for close Egyptian-Sudanese relations. Differing domestic situations left too many areas capable of generating friction. Under the Sudanese party system, with power centers acting to constrain Magub in important policy areas, permanent closeness to the U.A.R. was unlikely.

THE NEW MILITARY REGIME: 1969

A junta of colonels and majors overthrew the civilian regime on the morning of May 25, 1969, and installed former Chief Justice

Abubakar Awadallah as prime minister. (Awadallah had left office in 1967 after the Constituent Assembly reversed the Supreme Court's decision to admit eight Communists to membership in the Assembly.) Actual control appeared to be in the hands of Jaafa al-Numeiri head of the Revolutionary Command Council, although Prime Minister Awadallah became the chief spokesman for the regime. On the day of the coup, Awadallah stated that the U.A.R., "which is part of us, . . . will occupy a special and marked position in our relations with the Arab world consolidated by its revolutionary regime which is taking a leading role in the Arab nation and which represents the centre of the Arabs struggle against the plots of neo-colonialism and Zionism."[92] At his first official press conference, Colonel (later Major-General) Al-Numeri made a point of praising President Nasser "as a great revolutionary with whom he hoped to cooperate in full."[93] Al-Numeri's subsequent close relations with Nasser have led a correspondent of the London *Times* to regard him as a protégé of the Egyptian president.[94] The first delegation sent to a foreign government to explain the new regime's policies was dispatched to Cairo the first week in June. The regime also developed a social-democratic domestic policy line which would bring it into closer agreement with the political system of the U.A.R. and other Arab revolutionary states. On May 25, the new regime announced its "leftist, socialist" character.[95]

In addition to greater cooperation with the Arab world, the new regime sought closer ties with the Soviet bloc. On May 27 the Sudan recognized East Germany because of the European nation's opposition to Israel. In the announcement the Sudan's support of the Arab position on Israeli-occupied territory was emphasized.[96] Although the importance of this action, which had been contem-

---

92. The Democratic Republic of the Sudan, The Cultural Section, Ministry of National Guidance, *The 25th May Revolution* (Khartoum: Government Printing Press [June, 1969]), p. 18.

93. *Baghdad Observer,* June 2, 1969, p. 1.

94. November 3, 1969, p. 5.

95. *New York Times,* May 27, 1969, p. 11.

96. *New York Times,* May 28, 1969, p. 16.

199

plated by the former regime, should not be overestimated, it does indicate the orientation of the new government.[97] On May 31 the Sudanese government requested a long-term credit from the U.S.S.R. After a visit to Moscow by General Al-Numeri in early November, the credit was granted. It thus appears that Sudan is moving closer to the U.A.R.'s position in Cold War politics.

In general, the new regime has identified itself more closely with Egypt than did the Magub government. Prior to and during the Arab summit conference in Rabat, Morocco, from December 20 to 24, 1969, Egypt, Sudan, and Libya were engaged in talks "to explore possibilities of new rear base areas in Sudan and Libya for Egyptian forces in wartime."[98] After the conference, President Nasser and General Al-Numeri flew together to Tripoli, Libya, to confer with Colonel Muamar Qaddafi, head of Libya's Revolutionary Council, on military and economic coordination. President Nasser and U.A.R. Foreign Minister Mahmud Riadh visited Khartoum on January 1 and 2 for celebration of Sudan's fourteenth independence anniversary and for talks with the Sudanese regime. Nasser chose the occasion to announce a major arms deal. On January 14, 1970, it was announced that "Egypt, the Sudan, and Libya moved a step closer to a regional alliance . . . with agreement to organize a series of ministerial commissions to study coordination of economic, cultural, military and political affairs."[99]

Soon after the 1969 coup, Joseph Garang, a Catholic from a Southern tribe, and a member of the Communist Party, became minister of Southern affairs, a new position indicating the interest of the government in the Southern region. At the same time, the government promised a large measure of autonomy to the South, thus alleviating Southern fears of Arabization and removing one constraint on cooperation with the U.A.R. The large landholdings of the Mahdi and Mirghani families were expropriated, and politi-

97. See Lawrence Fellows, "Sudan's Leaders Plan Socialist State," *New York Times,* June 8, 1969, p. 24.

98. John K. Cooley, "Possible French Presence in Libya Cheers Arab Summit Conferences," *Christian Science Monitor,* December 22, 1969, p. 5.

99. Raymond H. Anderson, "Three Arab States Closer to Pact," *New York Times,* January 14, 1970, p. 4.

cal parties were banned. This removed from the scene independent power centers and rivals for the army's claim to legitimacy. The new regime took a radical ideological stance, and included a number of Communists in the cabinet. A massive program for social change has been instituted, which, if it succeeds, is likely to bring Sudanese practice into line with the socialist development of the U.A.R. The programed line of development in the Sudan seems certain to make economic cooperation with Egypt more feasible, just as the political line should make cultural and political cooperation easier.

Overt foreign-policy collaboration and cooperation with Egypt is evidently a keystone of the Al-Numeri regime's policy. But, more importantly, the new regime has neutralized or removed the constraints which had hampered Magub. The unity of viewpoint, however, extends beyond cooperation in foreign affairs to the coordination of certain domestic services, and has included the young Libyan regime which replaced King Idris on September 1, 1969. Prior to the Rabat conference, discussions were begun among Libya, Sudan, and the U.A.R.; these were brought to an apparently satisfactory conclusion during talks in Tripoli, on December 25, 1969. On January 14, 1970, it was announced that Egypt, the Sudan, and Libya were delegating ministerial commissions to study various aspects of the coordination of transportation, communications, and economic affairs. It appeared that by early 1970 Sudan had become a member of a tripartite alliance with the United Arab Republic and Libya. On November 9, 1970, a formal federation was agreed upon among the three nations. Syria expressed its interest in joining.

While it is still too early to predict the viability of the federation, the potential of such a revolutionary alliance cannot be ignored. Its effects upon all three countries, its impact on Africa, the Middle East, and international politics, could be profound, altering the balance of regional politics, displaying the potency of Arab natonalism in the Sudan, and breathing new life into the old slogan—"Unity of the Nile Valley."

Chapter Eight

The U.A.R.
and the Congo

The U.A.R.'s involvement in the Congo was a ramification of its overall African policy. As such, the Congo policy exhibited the U.A.R.'s ideological commitment to the cause of African liberation and anti-imperialism, and its *de facto* foreign-policy alliance with the Soviet Union.

Not only was the U.A.R.'s Congo policy a result of its African aspirations but the Congo issue also presented a challenge to Nasser's African policy, which was at that time mainly directed at his intermediate objective of "Africa for Africans." To Nasser, the Congo issue represented the West's attempts to maintain a sphere of influence which threatened the U.A.R.'s geopolitical position. On February 21, 1961, Nasser explained the reasons for the U.A.R.'s involvement in the Congo:

> The imperialists aim at suppressing the freedom of the Congo and at placing it within their spheres of influence. We have to comply with our duties towards the Congo and towards Africa. The more independent countries there are, the more secure will be our freedom. . . . We cannot remain idle while

the nationalist elements are being liquidated there by the imperialists and imperialist stooges.[1]

Five years later, in 1965, Nasser disclosed the geopolitical nature of the U.A.R.'s involvement in the Congo when he stated:

We are concerned . . . with what is happening in the Congo. . . . This [concern] is not only because of our sympathy for the struggle of the brave Congo nation . . . but also because of the realization of geographic fact . . . that the Congo's borders are close to the borders of the Sudan. And another fact is that the independent Congo is situated in the heart of the African continent. We refuse to allow the transformation of its lands into a base to threaten the nations of the whole continent.[2]

In late 1965 Muhammad Heikal, chief editor of *Al-Ahram* and a confidant of Nasser, also stressed this view. He declared that Egypt's involvement in Africa and its close connection with the anti-imperialist movement was not only a matter of principle but also a matter of security and protection. He asserted that the unsettled situation in the Congo could create a crisis in the Southern Sudan by forces "aiming to carve it from the Northern Sudan in order to tie it to the swamp of frightening exploitation in which they [imperialists] are preparing to sink the Congolese people."[3]

Heikal's statement implied that extension of the Congo conflict into Sudan was a direct threat to the U.A.R. and that whoever succeeded in controlling the Congo would eventually attempt to move eastward. This, he declared, was a direct threat because Egypt's only opportunities for future Nile projects, which are a life or death matter for Egypt, are in the Southern Sudan.

U.A.R. RELATIONS WITH THE LUMUMBA GOVERNMENT

U.A.R.–Congolese relations began in a routine manner. A strong

1. *President Gamal Abdel Nasser on Africa,* comp. and trans. U.A.R. Information Department (Cairo, n.d.), p. 29.

2. *Al-Akhbar,* January 2, 1965, p. 5.

3. *Mulhaq al-Ahram,* December 24, 1965, p. 1.

U.A.R. delegation, headed by Nagib al-Sadir, the U.A.R. Ambassador to Cameroon, arrived in the Congo on June 25, 1960, to participate in the independence celebrations and to offer aid in an attempt to establish cooperation between the two countries. Upon his return to Cairo, after a week in the Congo, Al-Sadir announced that he was the first diplomat received in Lumumba's private home. He considered that the Congolese people had the greatest admiration and respect for the U.A.R.[4]

The clash between Belgian and Congolese troops at Leopoldville airport alarmed Lumumba, and as the situation deteriorated, he looked to Ghana for military aid. On July 11, 1960, Moise Tshombe, premier of Katanga Province, the mainstay of the Congolese economy, declared Katanga independent of the Congo government. The following day the U.A.R. announced its support of Patrice Lumumba's government. When, on July 14, Nasser received a letter from Nkrumah requesting the use of U.A.R. aircraft to transport the Ghanaian army to the Congo, he replied, "The U.A.R. supports all the measures that will be taken by Ghana to protect the independence of the Congo. We are ready to put the necessary aircraft under the disposal of Nkrumah in order to allow the Ghanaian forces to reach the Congo as soon as possible."[5] Four transport planes were subsequently sent to Ghana for this purpose.

It may be noted that Nasser did not commit the U.A.R. to any direct action until the Soviet Union's position was clarified. On July 15, Khrushchev warned that he would intervene "against any state that aggresses against the Congo."[6] Then, on July 17, Nasser pledged his support and promised military aid and arms at the Congolese government's request, commenting, "When I hear what is happening in the Congo, I remember what happened in Egypt in 1956. . . . We support the question of freedom in the Congo because we consider it a matter that concerns us. If the Congolese issue is lost, freedom everywhere in the world will be threatened."[7] Cairo's silence up to this time and the subsequent consultations be-

4. *Al-Ahram,* July 9, 1960, p. 5.
5. *Al-Ahram,* July 16, 1960, p. 1.
6. *Al-Ahram,* July 17, 1960, p. 6.
7. *Al-Ahram,* July 17, 1960, p. 6.

tween the U.A.R. and the U.S.S.R. suggests that Nasser waited for Soviet assurances before becoming directly involved. In mid-July a spokesman of the U.A.R. Foreign Office declared that the government was studying the situation developing in the Congo "with concern."[8] It was reported that on July 19 the U.S.S.R. ambassador to the U.A.R. called the assistant undersecretary of foreign affairs, Dr. Farid Zain al-Din, at his home and requested a meeting, which took place in the Ministry of Foreign Affairs the same evening.[9] The next day Omar Lutfi, the head of the U.A.R. delegation to the U.N., met with U.S.S.R. Deputy Foreign Minister Kuznetsov in the U.N. to discuss the Congo problem.

Radio Moscow's Arabic broadcast announced that Lumumba had requested Soviet aid and that Russia was ready to support the Congo "with action."[10] The next day a Soviet delegation visited Lumumba. By the end of July it was reported that the U.S.S.R. had agreed to send aid to the Congo and had requested the use of U.A.R. and Sudanese airports for refueling. (It was then reported that they had decided to use Rome instead.)[11]

During his visit to the U.N. Security Council at the end of July, Lumumba had a forty-five minute meeting with Dr. Mustafa Kamil, the U.A.R. ambassador to Washington. The ambassador was said to have written a detailed report to his government regarding this meeting.[12] It was also announced that Lumumba would stop in Cairo on his return to the Congo.[13] At the end of July Nasser affirmed the U.A.R.'s commitment to Lumumba, stating:

> Congolese government requests them. We support the Congo in its struggle for independence and look around us to see the We . . . support the Congolese people in their struggle for freedom. . . . We are ready to help the Congolese people in any way they want and we are ready to send them arms if the killing in Kenya, Rhodesia, and Africa. . . . We tell all these

8. *Rose El-Youssief*, no. 1675, July 18, 1960, p. 4.
9. *Al-Ahram*, July 20, 1960, p. 4.
10. *Al-Ahram*, July 21, 1960, p. 1.
11. *Rose El-Youssief*, no. 1667, August 1, 1960, p. 4.
12. *Al-Ahram*, July 29, 1960, p. 1.
13. *Rose El-Youssief*, no. 1676, July 25, 1960, p. 3.

people who are fighting for their freedom that the U.A.R. is with you. . . . We have declared it loudly since the early days of our revolution. We support all freedom matters and the independence question.[14]

The U.A.R. felt that the Congo crisis confirmed its belief that the Western nations were attempting to maintain control in Africa, and, as a result, the U.A.R. asserted that the struggle for freedom could not end with independence. In an editorial in *Al-Jumhuriya,* Nasser al-Nashashibi stated:

> What happened in the Congo may happen tomorrow or the day after . . . in other African countries due to attain their independence. . . . All of these colonies will face the same conspiracies and intrigues faced by the Congo. That is why we must heed the lesson of the Congo.[15]

In explaining the U.A.R.'s position on the Congo problem to the Belgian ambassador to Cairo, Murad Ghaleb, then under-secretary of foreign affairs, stated that the U.A.R.'s most important view of the issue was that "interest requires the cooperation of all for the unity of the Congo and keeping it aloof from the Cold War." Justifying the African demonstrations in front of the Belgian Embassy in Cairo, Ghaleb stated that "The U.A.R. as an African state shares the same feelings. At the same time, we are careful not to allow any harm to come to the embassy or its employees."[16]

In early August, 1960, the U.A.R. began sending technical and medical missions to the Congo: two experts in airport maintenance and operations and a medical mission were among those who were dispatched. The government declared its willingness to ship all medical supplies on Egyptian planes if it were requested to do so.[17] Three experts in telephone communications and operations were also sent to the Congo. In this respect, Nasser was extending

14. *Al-Ahram,* July 27, 1960, p. 3.
15. September 20, 1960, p. 4.
16. *Al-Ahram,* August 4, 1960, p. 1.
17. *Al-Ahram,* August 9, 1960, p. 1.

the same type of aid that he had previously given to liberation movements and various newly independent African states. He may have hoped that the U.A.R.'s involvement would not extend any further. This is indicated by his hesitation in responding to Nkrumah's telegram of August 14, which asked for the creation of an African force to participate in the Congo if the U.N. did not succeed in solving the problem. It was reported that the U.A.R.'s decision to send a military mission to Ghana was made only after five letters were exchanged between Cairo, Accra, Conakry, and Leopoldville. The mission was eventually sent for the purpose of "coordinating military cooperation to face the Congolese crisis,"[18] and was placed at the disposal of the Ghanaian Government.

Nkrumah's telegram to Nasser reflects an attempt to push Nasser into an African issue and test his interest in African as well as Arab affairs. Nkrumah wrote that the All African Peoples' Conference, held at Tunis in January, 1960, called for the creation of a military unit to aid Algeria in its struggle for independence. The telegram stated:

> This recommendation was tied with the Algerian war because that was the only African issue then. The same resolution is true in all liberation movements in Africa. . . . This force should be permanent in order to be ready to intervene any time it is required.[19]

Following the arrival of Nkrumah's telegram, the U.A.R. government issued a statement declaring that the Security Council should intervene in the Congo and force the withdrawal of Belgium. The statement declared the U.A.R.'s willingness to send military assistance to the Congo, whose situation was described as "a turning point in the future of Africa."[20] Nasser's commitment to the cause of Congolese nationalism was not affected by the rift which was widening between Nkrumah's position and his own.

18. *Al-Ahram,* August 11, 1960, p. 1.
19. *Rose El-Youssief,* no. 1679, August 15, 1960, p. 5.
20. *Al-Ahram,* August 13, 1960, p. 1.

The opening of the U.A.R. Embassy in the Congo was also announced at this time.

Not until August 12 did the U.A.R. agree to contribute a unit to the U.N. military force in the Congo.[21] The background of the commander of these troops, Col. Sayid al-Shathili, indicates the nature of his assignment. He holds a masters degree in political science and has had two years of special training, one in the U.S.S.R. and one in the U.S. The political aspect of his commission was indicated a year later by Muhammad Heikal when he suggested that the African states should have regarded their assignment to the U.N. forces as a political mission. Heikal asserted that their purely military role and complete obedience to U.N. orders contributed to Lumumba's failure.[22]

On August 23 Nasser sent to the Congo a special mission composed of Abdul Majid Farid, secretary of the presidential office; Muhammad Fayek, the presidential advisor on African affairs; and Nabiah Abdul-Hamid, the U.A.R. ambassador to Ghana. The delegation was reported to have carried a personal message from Nasser to Lumumba. Lumumba met with the delegation for two hours in his private home. Immediately following this meeting the delegations returned to Cairo and then flew directly to Alexandria to report to Nasser personally on the results of their urgent mission.[23]

Nasser maintained close contact with Lumumba and other African leaders, exchanging letters with Haile Selassie of Ethiopia, Abboud of the Sudan, and Muhammad V of Morocco. On August 25 Husain Zulficar Sabri, the vice-minister of foreign affairs, flew to Leopoldville to attend an Independent African States foreign ministers conference. He carried a special dispatch from Nasser to Lumumba. Sabri and Lumumba met and "exchanged opinions on President Nasser's message. The latest of President Nasser's messages to the Prime Minister of the Congo . . . [dealt with] U.A.R. assistance to the Congo."[24] In a subsequent interview with

21. *Al-Ahram,* August 13, 1960, p. 1.
22. "Bisaraha" [With frankness], *Mulhaq Al-Ahram,* February 17, 1961, p. 1.
23. *Al-Ahram,* August 24, 1960, p. 1.

Al-Ahram, Lumumba announced that Nasser would be visiting the Congo. When asked about the content of the message sent to him by Nasser, he replied, "You know President Nasser offered us all kinds of help. We declared our pleasure in accepting this assistance. We want to build friendly relations with your country and all African states."[25]

In early September, Dr. Murad Ghaleb, a close friend of Nasser and undersecretary of foreign affairs, was appointed ambassador to the Congo. The *New York Times* stated that this appointment "illustrates the importance . . . Nasser attached to the Congo."[26] *Rose El-Youssief* also stated that Ghaleb's appointment "proves the special importance the U.A.R. gives to the liberation movements . . . in Africa."[27] At the same time, Muhammad Abdul-Aziz Ishaq, chief editor of *Nahdhat Ifriqiya* and organizer of the African Association, was appointed cultural attaché to the Congo.

In an interview with *Rose El-Youssief* after his appointment, Ghaleb attempted to draw a comparison between the secession of Katanga and the creation of Israel. He hoped that the Congo situation would make the Africans more sympathetic toward the U.A.R.'s fight against Israel. Ghaleb stated that the U.A.R.'s role in the Congo was proof of its struggle for African and Asian freedom. Commenting on the cause of the crisis, he stated:

> We learned from imperialism that when it leaves a place it will try to carve out a strategic position in order to establish a base in it and leave its agents to become the guardians of its interests and executors of its destructive policies.[28]

Ghaleb's departure for the Congo was delayed until the return of Husain Zulficar Sabri with the results of his meetings with Lumumba and the other African foreign ministers. Meanwhile, the Congo crisis further deteriorated when, on September 5, Pres-

---

24. *Al-Ahram,* August 26, 1960, p. 1.
25. August 27, 1960, p. 1.
26. September 1, 1960, p. 3.
27. No. 1683, September 12, 1960, p. 6.
28. *Rose El-Youssief,* no. 1683, September 12, 1960, p. 6.

ident Kasavubu and Premier Lumumba each proclaimed the revocation of the other's authority. *Al-Ahram* reported that upon his return on September 9, Sabri went directly to Nasser with "the truth of the situation in the Congo." The meeting was also attended by Mahmud Riad, Nasser's adviser on political affairs. On the same day Riad attended a "very important meeting" in the Ministry of Foreign Affairs with Mahmud Fawzi and Ali Sabri.[29] Shortly after Husain Zulficar Sabri's return it was reported that one of Lumumba's top aides would visit Cairo at the end of September.[30] (On September 4, it had been announced that Lumumba himself would visit Cairo.)[31]

It is apparent that the U.A.R. threw all its support behind Lumumba and that he depended heavily upon it. As the relations between Lumumba and Kasavubu deteriorated, Lumumba met with the U.A.R., Moroccan, Tunisian, Yugoslavian, Russian, and Czechoslovakian ambassadors and reportedly "complained about the stand of the U.N. Command in the Congo."[32] The U.A.R. chargé d'affaires sent to the Ministry of Foreign Affairs a detailed report about the meeting and the latest developments of the situation. Later that month, the U.A.R., Morocco, and Ghana attempted to mediate between Lumumba and Kasavubu.

The U.A.R.'s support for Lumumba was based on the firm belief that he would be successful. Murad Ghaleb expressed this when he emphasized that the "nationalist elements must win" and eventually would win. In mid-September, 1960, Ghaleb departed for the Congo, reportedly as a result of an "important message received from the Congo."[33]

THE U.A.R.-U.N. DISPUTE

On September 12, 1960, the U.A.R. decided to withdraw its troops from the U.N. Command in the Congo, although the official re-

---

29. September 10, 1960, p. 4.
30. *Rose El-Youssief,* no. 1683, September 12, 1960, p. 9.
31. *Al-Ahram,* September 4, 1960, p. 1.
32. *Al-Ahram,* September 8, 1960, p. 1.

quest was not made until late January, 1961. Abdul Qader Hatim, the vice-minister of presidential affairs, announced that the decision was taken because "the development of the situation in the Congo showed that the U.N. was deviating from its trusted mission." Commenting on the neutralization of the broadcasting station and the occupation of the principal airports by the U.N. forces, Hatim stated:

> The U.A.R. government considers this action an outrageous violation of the sovereignty of the Congo . . . and since the U.A.R. considers the Congo government as the only authority which has the right to control its territory, broadcasting stations, and airports, accordingly the U.A.R. government decided to withdraw its battalion.[34]

Rose El-Youssief reported that the U.A.R. troops under the U.N. Command had been ordered to move from the northern borders of the Congo into Leopoldville airport and fire at anyone who attempted to gain access to it. The U.A.R. considered that the U.N. made this move to discredit the U.A.R. among the Congolese people.[35] Thus, the U.A.R. instructed its troops "not to move anywhere except to board aircraft taking them back to Cairo."[36] Hammarskjold, reportedly disturbed by the withdrawal of many African troops, attempted to dissuade Nasser from this move.[37]

In a discussion of the situation in the National Assembly, Husain Zulficar Sabri accused the U.S. of attempting to penetrate the Congo, asserting that another "imperialist state has started to become active in order to control some parts of the Congo in case of Belgium's failure to regain it. . . . The business companies of these states have started attempting to penetrate into the Congolese regions."[38] Cairo newspapers also described the U.N. as "a toy

---

33. *Rose El-Youssief,* no. 1684, September 19, 1960, p. 11. The nature or transmitter of the message was not disclosed.

34. *Al-Ahram,* September 13, 1960, p. 17.

35. No. 1686, October 3, 1960, p. 10.

36. *Times* (London), January 27, 1961, p. 12.

37. *New York Times,* January 27, 1961, p. 1; January 29, 1961, p. 2.

38. *Al-Ahram,* October 5, 1960, p. 4.

in the hands of imperialism and directed by it toward one aim, and this is the destruction of Congolese national unity and the loss of Congolese independence."[39]

In November, 1960, it was reported that the U.A.R. was "in high political consultation with a number of Afro-Asian states which are concerned with the events in the Congo, especially those states that have military forces under the U.N. Command."[40] The U.N. action in seating Kasavubu's delegation and rejecting Lumumba's strengthened the former's position. On December 1, Kasavubu notified Cairo that it should withdraw its Embassy from the Congo. He declared that the Embassy was conspiring against the existing authority and asked the U.A.R. "not to send others at the present time."[41] On December 1, Lumumba was arrested by Congolese troops. This action led Gizenga to declare the seat of the Congolese government to be Stanleyville.

The U.A.R. established close contact with the Stanleyville administration. Bernard Salamu, a former aide to Lumumba and a member of the Stanleyville regime, arrived in Cairo in mid-December seeking aid.[42]

As the situation deteriorated, the U.A.R. realized it was very difficult to deal with a country torn by personal feuds among the political leaders. On his return to Cairo after the suspension of U.A.R.–Congolese relations, Murad Ghaleb commented on this, stating, "We still believe that the only way [to solve the Congo problem] is the coalition of all political leaders in the Congo. The U.A.R. will continue to work for the sake of the Congo."[43]

As has been pointed out, a very prominent characteristic of the U.A.R.'s Congo policy from the beginning of the crisis was the emphasis on anti-imperialism and the attempt to identify the Congo issue with the anti-imperialist movement. Now, at the end of 1960, *Al-Ahram* declared:

39. *Al-Ahram,* November 29, 1960, p. 1.
40. *Al-Ahram,* November 29, 1960, p. 1.
41. *Al-Ahram,* December 2, 1960, p. 1.
42. *Al-Ahram,* December 19, 1960, p. 1.
43. *Rose El-Youssief,* no. 1697, December 19, 1960, p. 8.

The opinion of the official circles in Cairo is that the Congo situation is very dangerous. The greatest danger is not what is happening within the borders of the Congo . . . but the reflection of these events on two important issues. The first is the stand of imperialism in Africa in general and its hopes to revive . . . after the Congo; the second is the great blow for the U.N. because of its policy in the Congo.[44]

Nasser declared that his reason for supporting the Stanleyville regime was "that we have no choice in Algeria and the Congo but to be faithful to our role—the role of our people as the vanguard and the role of our nation as a base [of freedom]."[45] In January, 1961, he emphasized the same concept in a speech on the results of the Casablanca Conference to the U.A.R. General Assembly. He declared:

It was our opinion that although the problems of imperialism in the Congo and Algeria were the most outstanding subjects for discussion in the conference, it should not be forgotten that the struggle against imperialism in the Congo and Algeria is part of the struggle against imperialism in the whole African continent.[46]

The 1961 Casablanca Conference indicated the dissension among the African leaders over the Congo issue. The first blow to the conference was the refusal of Nigeria, Liberia, Ethiopia, and the Sudan to participate. Most of the Afro-Asian countries had been invited, but they did not attend, and even within the participating group there was conflict. Nkrumah felt that the withdrawal of the African forces from the U.N. Command would create a vacuum in the Congo. He called for the creation of an African Command to coordinate these African forces. He felt that after establishing this command, they could ask the U.N. to recognize it and accept

44. *Al-Ahram*, December 15, 1960, p. 1.
45. *Majmu'at khutab wa tasrihat wa bayanat al-Rais Gamal Abdel Nasser* [Collection of speeches, statements, and remarks of President Gamal Abdel Nasser], *Part III, February, 1960–January, 1962*, comp. U.A.R. Information Department (Cairo, n.d.), p. 323; hereafter referred to as *Nasser's Speeches, February, 1960–January, 1962*.
46. *President Gamal Abdel Nasser on Africa*, p. 27.

it as the replacement of the U.N. Command in the Congo. Nasser, Keïta, and Mohammed V took an opposing view. They felt that the African forces could not, at their current strength, help the nationalist movement. As for the African command, they felt it would be very difficult for the U.N. to recognize it. All in all, they considered it an unrealistic approach to the problem. The conference participants considered the Stanleyville regime to be the legal government and gave their full support to it.[47] It was reported that a member of Lumumba's Cabinet represented the Stanleyville regime at the conference.[48]

The U.A.R. took the initiative in the establishment of a thirteen-nation international committee to coordinate material aid, including volunteers, for the Congo. Members included the U.A.R., the U.S.S.R., Communist China, Congo, Morocco, Guinea, Algeria, Ghana, Sudan, Mali, Indonesia, and Japan. The Congo's diplomatic mission in Cairo, which had been appointed by Lumumba and remained loyal to the Stanleyville regime, kept in close contact with the U.A.R. and other members of the committee. It presented the committee with a detailed report on the needs of the Congolese people and government.[49] In January, 1961, the committee sent a mission to Stanleyville to investigate means of aiding the Congo technically and materially. Muhammad Fuad Jala headed the mission, whose members represented Morocco, Guinea, Communist China, Algeria, Ghana, Sudan, and Mali. The mission was also supposed to tour African countries to rally support for Stanleyville.[50]

At the end of January, Kasavubu asked the Security Council to intervene and stop the U.A.R.'s interference in the Congo's internal affairs. The Katanga government expelled the Greek Orthodox archbishop on charges that he had plotted with Nasser to return Lumumba to power. In February, General Mobutu and Justin Bomboks, the civilian head of the army-appointed governing commission, displayed Czech-made arms and asserted that "the arms

47. *Rose El-Youssief,* no. 1702, January 23, 1961, p. 3.
48. *Al-Ahram,* January 4, 1961, p. 1.
49. *Al-Ahram,* January 26, 1961, p. 7.
50. *Al-Ahram,* January 24, 1961, p. 4.

214

constitute a proof of United Arab Republic meddling in Congolese affairs aimed at creating another Korea." They also claimed that an Egyptian officer, whom they identified as Major Hamid Murad, and three Czechs were military advisers to the Stanleyville regime.[51]

With the assassination of Lumumba, announced on February 13, 1961, U.A.R. news media intensified their attack on the U.N. and Hammarskjold. They accused the secretary-general of responsibility for Lumumba's death and repeated the charges made by Moscow Radio. A government statement declared:

> The responsibility for the blood of Patrice Lumumba falls on the authorities of imperialism whose agents in the Congo, like Moise Tshombe, are nothing but tools in their hands. This is shared by the U.N. which betrayed from the beginning its message and made a truce with imperialism and its tool until it became nothing but a toy.[52]

After Lumumba's assassination, Nasser immediately recognized Antoine Gizenga as the head of the only legitimate government in the Congo and urged Yugoslavia, India, Indonesia, Morocco, Libya, Algeria, Guinea, Ghana, Mali, and Ceylon to do the same. The U.A.R. opened a diplomatic mission in Stanleyville, and the Gizenga regime opened a mission in Cairo.[53] This mission was reported to be the coordinator of Gizenga's diplomacy, distributing messages from Stanleyville to various diplomatic missions in Cairo.[54]

Al-Ahram reported that the U.S.S.R. "in cooperation with other friendly states . . . will offer all aid and support possible for the Congolese people and their legitimate government."[55] The appoint-

---

51. *New York Times,* February 2, 1961, p. 3.

52. *Al-Ahram,* February 14, 1961, p. 1.

53. *Al-Ahram,* February 15, 1961, p. 1.

54. It should be noted that at this point there were four contending factions in the Congo: the Lumumbaist regime of Gizenga in Stanleyville and the Mobutu-Kasavubu-Ileo government in Leopoldville, each of which claimed to govern the entire Congo; the Tshombe regime in Katanga; and the Albert Kalonji regime in southern Kasai.

55. February 15, 1961, p. 1.

ment of Dr. Murad Ghaleb as U.A.R. ambassador to the U.S.S.R. reflects the importance of the Congo to U.A.R.–U.S.S.R. relations at this time.

The U.N. force in the Congo, originally supported by the radical or Pan-Africanist group of African states (the U.A.R., Ghana, Guinea, Morocco), was opposed by these states after the November 22, 1960, vote in the General Assembly which approved the credentials of President Kasavubu's delegation to the U.N. After this event the U.N. derived its support from the more moderate Afro-Asian states (including the Sudan and India), as well as from the Western bloc. The U.N. actions prevented the U.A.R. and its associates from playing the role they attempted to assume in the Congo. After April 17, 1961, when Kasavubu and Hammarskjold reached a major agreement as to removing foreign advisers not attached to the U.N. Command, the Congo government under Kasavubu, Ileo, and Mobutu had the upper hand. From then until the withdrawal of U.N. forces in June, 1964, there was little doubt of the failure of the rebellions Nasser supported.[56] Thus the U.N. action in the Congo, which Nasser initially supported, became a factor in frustrating U.A.R. policy.

U.A.R.-U.S. RELATIONS AND THE CONGO

Shortly after Lumumba's death, U.A.R.–U.S. relations became very tense. President Kennedy warned that the U.S. would back the U.N. and would oppose any nation's attempt at unilateral intervention. The *New York Times* claimed that this statement was aimed at Cairo.[57] Secretary Rusk affirmed that Kennedy's warnings applied to the U.A.R. as well as the U.S.S.R. and warned the U.A.R. against playing "this dangerous game."[58] He observed a

56. For the role of the U.N. in the Congo, see Ernest W. Lefever, *Crisis in the Congo: A U.N. Force in Action* (Washington, D.C.: The Brookings Institution, 1965); King Gordon, *The United Nations in the Congo: A Quest for Peace* (Carnegie Endowment for International Peace, 1962); and A. L. Burns and Nina Heathcote, *Peace-Keeping by U.N. Forces: From Suez Through the Congo* (New York: Praeger, 1963).

57. February 16, 1961, p. 1.

58. *New York Times*, February 17, 1961, p. 3.

parallel between U.A.R. and U.S.S.R. aspirations in Africa and declared: "The U.A.R. seeks to extend its influence by supporting sub-Saharan African regimes that think as it does while the Soviet Union seeks to use the U.A.R. as a channel for penetrating the continent."[59]

Husain Zulficar Sabri called on the American ambassador to Cairo and asked him for an explanation of Dean Rusk's statements regarding U.A.R. intervention in the Congo. Foreign Minister Fawzi stated: "We don't answer everything said but our reply will be positive action."[60] The U.A.R. government Middle East News Agency editor declared, with regard to Kennedy's statement, "We feel it is our task to resist colonialism and colonial diplomacy and no maneuvers shall stop us from doing so."[61] After Kennedy's statement, it was also reported that Nasser wrote three letters concerning the U.A.R. stand in the Congo to the three major permanent members of the Security Council—Britain, the U.S., and Russia.[62] The next day Nasser affirmed his support for the rebels, declaring that "the U.A.R. will aid the Congolese rebels and will continue to until they win their freedom."[63]

In mid-February, 1961, Cairo declared that it had documents to prove America's involvement in the killing of Lumumba.[64] On February 21, Nasser personally attacked America and declared that its support for Kasavubu indicated its participation in Lumumba's assassination. He stated:

> If America supports Kasavubu after the killing of Lumumba, America then must be a partner to Kasavubu and his crime. . . . This is our understanding; otherwise why is America supporting Kasavubu if she wants peace based on justice.[65]

Nasser continued to maintain close contact with various Afro-

59. *New York Times,* February 17, 1961, p. 3.
60. *Al-Ahram,* February 18, 1961, p. 1.
61. *New York Times,* February 18, 1961, p. 3.
62. *Al-Ahram,* February 21, 1961, p. 1.
63. *New York Times,* February 22, 1961, p. 3.
64. *Al-Raiy al-'Aam* (Khartoum), February 18, 1961, p. 8.
65. *Nasser's Speeches, February, 1960–January, 1962,* p. 385.

Asian leaders, especially after the arrest of Lumumba. Seven messages on the Congo issue were exchanged between Nasser and Nkrumah, Nehru, Touré, Haile Selassie, Mohammed V, Sukarno, and Abboud. In late February, 1961, the foreign ministers of the U.A.R., Mali, Morocco, and Ghana urged all diplomats to leave the Congo temporarily and to affirm their support of Gizenga as the only legitimate government.[66]

In February, 1961, Muhammad Heikal, in an article published in *Mulhaq Al-Ahram*, attempted to pinpoint the causes of the Congo situation as it had developed to that time.[67] He charged imperialism first, and the U.N. second, because "the U.N. was reluctant to carry out its responsibility toward the Congo." He considered the friction between Lumumba and Hammarskjold to be the reason for the secretary-general's "biased" stand. He leveled a third charge at the U.S., stating "Washington was the main pressure instrument on the U.N. headquarters in New York."

Concerning America's role in the Congo, Heikal disclosed that the U.A.R. attempted to assure the U.S. that Lumumba was not a Communist. He asserted that during the crisis Kasavubu and Lumumba met in the presence of the ambassadors of the U.A.R.. Ghana, and Guinea. Heikal claimed that Lumumba guaranteed in writing to Kasavubu that he would not accept any kind of aid or assistance unless it came through the U.N. Kasavubu reportedly took the note and told those present that he would give them his answer in the afternoon after he had studied the matter. At the time they returned to Kasavubu's office, Heikal stated, they were prevented from entering and were told that Kasavubu was too busy to see them. On their way out they saw the American military attaché's diplomatic car parked outside. Heikal was under the impression that the American CIA pressured Kasavubu. He also averred that Mobutu's coup the next day was designed by the U.S.

In this article Heikal also considered the reasons why the Casablanca Group could not participate effectively in defending the Congo. He gave two explanations for this: (1) if they did act,

66. *New York Times,* February 23, 1961, p. 3.
67. "Bisaraha" [With frankness], *Mulhaq Al-Ahram,* February 17, 1961, p. 1.

then imperialism would use its African allies to stop the Casablanca troops, and this would result in Africans killing Africans; and (2) reinforcing fighting troops and sending supplies to them would have been difficult because of the distance to the Congo. He alluded to the Sudan's refusal to allow such troops to cross its territory en route to Stanleyville.

POLICY MODIFICATION

At the end of February, 1961, a change occurred in the U.S.S.R.'s position on the Congo issue. The U.S.S.R. shifted all responsibility for action onto the African states. Khrushchev urged the formation of a common African force with troops in the Congo to restore peace and end foreign intervention. He also affirmed his support for Gizenga and called for the trial of Mobutu and Tshombe for the assassination of Lumumba.[68]

On August 1, 1961, a new phase in U.A.R.-Congolese relations was initiated when Cyrille Adoula, minister of the interior in the Ileo government, was asked to form a new government. Mr. Adoula's government was approved by the Chamber and Senate of the Congo and was thus the first government of unquestionably constitutional status since the constitutional crisis began in September of 1960. Adoula attempted to win the confidence of Gizenga by offering him the first vice-premiership. Gizenga's acceptance of this post and public recognition of the legitimacy of Adoula's government gave the U.A.R. an opportunity to withdraw from an increasingly difficult situation, a situation which it could ill afford in light of its other commitments.[69] In a gesture of solidarity, Mr. Gizenga told diplomats in Stanleyville that they must move their missions to Leopoldville, and Adoula referred to Gizenga as his right hand.[70]

68. *New York Times,* February 26, 1961, p. 1.
69. Relations with the Syrian region of the U.A.R. were deteriorating markedly during this period, ending in the dissolution of the Syrio-Egyptian Union on September 28, 1961. The summer of 1961 was also the beginning of socialism in Egypt, with major nationalizations beginning in July.
70. *New York Times,* August 19, 1961, p. 1.

Adoula and Gizenga were invited to attend the Belgrade Conference of Nonaligned Nations. The conference was organized by the U.A.R. and Yugoslavia, and thus the attitude of the U.A.R. toward the Congo was clearly reflected in the invitation. In an apparent effort to demonstrate their unity, Mobutu accompanied Gizenga and Adoula to the airport on their way to Belgrade.[71] The conference held a special session to hear Adoula and Gizenga. Both pledged the Congo to a policy of nonalignment as a Lumumba heritage.

With the Adoula government in power, the U.A.R. modified its Congo involvement, and there was a temporary normalization of relations between Leopoldville and Cairo. In January, 1962, a crisis between Adoula and Gizenga arose. On January 8, the Central Chamber of Representatives ordered Gizenga, who had returned to Stanleyville after only a brief stay in the capital, to return to Leopoldville to face charges of secessionist activities. On January 15, Gizenga was censured, removed from the vice-premiership, and arrested. The U.A.R. expressed concern and discomfort over this. Cairo news media stated that the split between Adoula and Gizenga "plunges the Congo back into its dilemma."[72]

Adoula attempted to keep his relationship with other African states as cordial as possible. At the O.A.U. meeting of May, 1963, he pledged his support to the liberation of the rest of Africa in an attempt to mollify the other African states.

In November, 1963, Adoula ordered the immediate expulsion of two Soviet diplomats from the Congo and declared the Leopoldville Soviet Embassy staff *persona non grata*. The Congo government announced that it had found some documents to prove U.S.S.R. involvement in the provocation of disturbances. However, Adoula stressed that the expulsion of the diplomats did not mean a break of diplomatic relations between the two countries. This decision was relayed to the U.N. secretary-general. The reason for this action was the alleged relationship of the U.S.S.R. with the Committee of Liberation (Conseil Nationale de Liberation)

71. *New York Times,* September 4, 1961, p. 2.
72. *Arab Observer,* January 22, 1961, p. 23.

headed by Christofe Gbenye, which had established a shadow government-in-exile in Congo (Brazzaville). The CNL reportedly was helping the Russians distribute literature calling for the restoration of Gizenga and attacking Adoula's regime as the instrument of capitalism and American influence. The Soviet attitude toward the U.N. operation in the Congo and the Adoula regime was made apparent by its refusal to pay the share assessed it for the operation.[73]

RESUMPTION OF U.A.R. INVOLVEMENT

Tshombe's appointment as prime minister in July, 1964, precipitated the resumption of the U.A.R's involvement in the Congo.[74] The U.A.R. considered Tshombe an instrument of imperialism and American capitalists. However, the peak of the crisis between the U.A.R. and Tshombe's government was not reached until the latter began to use mercenaries. Nasser, without referring to the Congo directly, called the use of mercenaries a bar to world peace.[75] The rupture of relations came when Tshombe attempted to attend the Second Nonaligned Nations Conference at Cairo in October, 1964. He was placed under house arrest, and it was reported that the U.A.R. ordered its Embassy to move to Brazzaville.[76]

The Congo army sealed off the U.A.R. and Algerian Embassies in Leopoldville in apparent retaliation for the detention of Tshombe. The U.A.R. held Tshombe as a diplomatic hostage and announced he would not be released until the police withdrew from the Embassy in Leopoldville. Foreign Minister Fawzi declared that U.A.R. diplomatic relations with the Congo had been suspended. The U.A.R. was able to obtain the support of twenty-

73. *New York Times,* October 19, 1963, p. 5.

74. The last contingent of United Nations forces (five hundred Nigerians) left the Congo on June 30, 1964, the fourth anniversary of Congolese independence.

75. *New York Times,* October 6, 1964, p. 3.

76. *New York Times,* October 7, 1964, p. 1.

eight African states in the Nonaligned Nations Conference in protest against Tshombe's move against the U.A.R. and Algerian Embassies.[77] However, the closing of the two embassies did not mean a severance of diplomatic ties. In a news conference held in Brazzaville, the Algerian and U.A.R. ambassadors to the Congo announced suspension of their diplomatic missions, but again emphasized the fact that relations with Leopoldville were not broken.[78]

On his arrival in Paris, Tshombe charged that Nasser was attempting to weaken and dominate the Congo. He stated that Nasser wanted the Congo to break ties with the U.A.R. so the U.A.R. would have an excuse to recognize the rebel government in Stanleyville. He declared that he would not give Nasser this opportunity, stating: "The U.A.R. wants a weak and chaotic Congo. . . . It does not want a strong Congo which might diminish Nasser's chance for leadership." President Nasser, he stated, is "motivated only by a feeling of domination vis-à-vis the Congo and Black Africa." [79]

On October 18, 1964, the *New York Times* reported that Tshombe had charged Nasser, Ben Bella, and Keïta with plotting to kill the Congo government's leaders. He ordered all Egyptians and Algerians out of the country. Up to this time the U.A.R. had not participated actively in supporting the rebels. A radio message by rebel leader Gbenye to the presidents of the U.A.R., Algeria, Guinea, Mali, and Ghana on November 1, 1964, reflects this. He stated:

> I inform your excellencies that the responsibility for the loss of Africa is shared between you and me. . . . I have done that which I could to safeguard the honor of Africa and you have left me alone under the American and Belgian bombardments. I ask you in a final appeal, in the name of Lumumba, if you don't intervene I will adopt a scorched earth policy and the Americans and Belgians will find only a desert.[80]

77. *New York Times,* October 8, 1964, p. 1.
78. *New York Times,* October 11, 1964, p. 20.

As the conflict intensified and the government troops, led by mercenaries, opened a drive on Stanleyville, the rebel foreign minister, Thomas Kanza, sent letters to the U.A.R., Ceylon, Yugoslavia, and Algeria.[81] On November 24, 1964, a U.A.R. government statement called for a meeting of the foreign ministers of the African states in order to "have urgent consultation to discuss this dangerous situation."[82]

In December, 1964, Musa Sabri, the editor-in-chief of *Al-Akhbar,* interviewed the Congolese rebel leader Soumialot. Soumialot declared that the revolution would eventually succeed. He claimed that Israelis and South Africans were fighting with Tshombe.[83]

Al-Akhbar disclosed that Soumialot visited Cairo twice in one week: on December 1, when he stayed for thirty-six hours on his way to Algeria, and on December 2 on his return from Algeria. He conferred with the leaders in Cairo on the situation in the Congo.[84] He also conferred with the U.S.S.R. ambassador and Nasser. He saw Ben Bella in Algeria and received the Sudan's permission to use Khartoum and Juba airfields. Communist sources announced that the U.S.S.R. would provide arms and help pay for an airlift of arms to the rebels by the U.A.R. and Algeria.[85]

A publication by the Leopoldville government charged that U.A.R. and Algerian support to the rebels started in September, 1964. It claimed that on September 4, Gbenye made this statement over the radio in Stanleyville:

> Several of our officers have returned from Moscow, Cairo, Algiers, Ghana, Guinea and Czechoslovakia. For those who are here we will do the same, that is to say, we will send

---

79. *New York Times,* October 10, 1964, p. 1.
80. *New York Times,* November 1, 1964, p. 12.
81. *Al-Akhbar,* November 26, 1964, p. 3.
82. *Al-Akhbar,* November 25, 1964, p. 1.
83. *Al-Akhbar,* December 9, 1964, pp. 1–3.
84. *Al-Akhbar,* December 6, 1964, p. 1.
85. *New York Times,* December 7, 1964, p. 1.

them to be trained so they become officers worthy of the name.[86]

The same publication stated: "The U.A.R., Algeria, Mali and Guinea have never hidden their hostility toward the Leopoldville government or their support for the rebellion."[87]

On December 8, 1964, Tshombe charged that Algeria, Sudan, and the U.A.R. were aiding the rebels and complained to the U.N. Algeria confirmed its support for the rebels and announced its aid. The *Times* (London) Middle East correspondent subsequently reported that Soviet aircraft with Russian crews (but with Algerian markings) had arrived at Khartoum and had flown southward to Juba. He stated that the Russian red star could be seen half erased under the Algerian markings.[88]

In late December, 1964, Tshombe, in a letter to the U.N. Security Council, complained that officers from Algeria and the U.A.R. were leading the rebels on the northern border. The Congo considered this a "veritable act of war." However, the *Times* (London) reported that Western intelligence agencies and diplomatic observers found no evidence that Algerians or Egyptians were serving with the Congo rebels.[89]

In a speech delivered in December, 1964, Nasser confirmed the U.A.R.'s aid to the Congo rebels. He declared:

> We say that Tshombe is merely an imperialist stooge working for the interests of the U.S.A. and Belgium in the Congo. Under no circumstances should we permit such an example to exist in Africa. Rather, it should fail in Africa, allowing the nationalist powers to succeed. They said that we extended help to the people of the Congo. I hereby confirm that we helped the Congolese people and sent them arms, and that we will send them more arms. There is no need to deny recognition to Tshombe, the imperialist stooge. We consider

86. The Press Service of the Democratic Republic of the Congo, *The Congo Rebellion* (Leopoldville: Imprimerie Concordia, December, 1964), p. 16.

87. *Ibid.*

88. December 16, 1964, p. 9.

89. December 28, 1964, p. 8.

that the nationalist powers in the Congo need the help of all nationalist and honest powers of the world.[90]

At the end of January, 1965, Gbenye arrived in Cairo with his foreign minister, Thomas Kanza, and met with Nasser. The same evening he met with Ali Sabri, the prime minister. In both cases, Muhammad Fayek, Nasser's adviser on African affairs, was present. Gbenye expressed his appreciation to the U.A.R. government and President Nasser and declared: "When the Arab president promises anything, he always keeps his promise. We all know that President Nasser and the people of the U.A.R. support the Congolese revolution." [91]

Meanwhile, the U.A.R. apparently was supervising and aiding the reorganization of the rebel movement. This is evidenced by the *New York Times* report that 3,000 Congolese rebels, led by Algerian officers, were receiving military training in the U.A.R.[92] Further indication of U.A.R. involvement was the February, 1965, general meeting of the Congolese rebels held in Cairo.[93] However, in April, 1965, the U.A.R. discontinued arms shipments to the Congolese rebels, although Algeria continued its shipments.[94] This was caused by the U.A.R.'s heavy commitment in Yemen and the inability of the Congo rebellion to change the situation in the Congo. Nasser apparently felt that the U.A.R. had become overcommitted in the Congo, and this overcommitment, with the coincident political isolation, led to a re-examination of U.A.R. foreign policy. It had become apparent that the U.A.R. was unable to augment its position in Africa by involvement with the Congo rebellion. Furthermore, domestic and Middle Eastern problems were straining the U.A.R.'s resources, precluding massive aid to any faction in the Congo.

90. *Arab Observer,* December 28, 1964, p. 13.
91. *Al-Jumhuriya,* January 28, 1965, p. 1.
92. *New York Times,* January 9, 1965, p. 11.
93. *Remarques Africaines* (Brussels), November 3, 1965, p. 19.
94. *New York Times,* April 23, 1965, p. 12; also, April 24, 1965, p. 5.

Chapter Nine

The U.A.R. in Africa: Retrospect and Prospect

Egypt's role in African affairs has been greatly influenced by its geographic location. Its expansion along the Nile River in the Pharaonic period was a natural process because of the geographic unity of the area. Commercial activity carried the ancient Egyptians deep into central Africa and resulted in cultural, racial, and social interchange.

In the modern era, Egypt's activities in Africa have been motivated by geopolitical, political, and economic considerations. Protection of the Nile-water resources has been the primary African goal of Egyptian policy makers. Safeguarding the position, extending the influence, and improving the economy of the U.A.R. constitute other incentives.

Egypt's policy toward Africa has also been greatly influenced by external factors. Nasser's commitment to nonalignment, the vicissitudes of Egypt's Arab world involvement, the Arab-Israeli conflict, and Egypt's East-West relations have all affected the direction of Egypt's policy on the African continent. Thus, the policy has evolved from the process of a constant reassessment of

Egypt's interests and from fluid external factors. Certain concepts, however, have been prevalent throughout the evolutionary process. The principle of anti-imperialism, which plays a prominent role in Egypt's foreign policy, has been a consistent and dominant factor in its African policy. Egypt's identification with the African continent, however, did not emerge until 1955. Thereafter the concept of Africanism was manifiested in Egypt's attempts to be accepted as a member of the African community and to create an African consciousness in the Egyptian public. The new and dynamic nature of this attitude and the Egyptian awareness of the growing influence of the African states in the U.N. led the U.A.R., the least African of the African Arab states, to become one of the most strongly Pan-Africanist.[1] The assumption of an ideological leadership over African independence movements has had a marked impact on Egyptian-African relation. Not only has Egypt gained prestige as a pioneer of anti-imperialism and a base for nationalists, but it has also firmly established its place in African affairs.

After the 1952 Egyptian revolution, the new military regime concentrated its efforts on removing the British presence from the Sudan and Egypt. The Unity of the Nile Valley, which had been a dominant theme since World War II, remained an important aspiration of Egyptian nationalism. Although the new regime agreed to the principle of self-determination for the Sudan, they concentrated their efforts on fostering and consolidating pro-Egyptian sentiment in the Sudan. Protection of its interests in the Sudan, of which the Nile-water resources are by far the most important, was Egypt's primary concern. Thus, until the Sudan's independence in 1955, the twentieth-century Egyptian activity in Africa was confined to the Sudan.

The Sudan's independence signaled the expansion of Egypt's activities in Africa. This was the result of a re-evaluation of Egyptian-Sudanese relations within an Afro-Arab framework. With the increasing deterioration of Egyptian-Western relations, initially caused by the Baghdad Pact and the Arab-Israeli conflict,

---

1. Ali A. Mazrui, *Towards a Pax Africana: A Study of Ideology and Ambition* (London: Weidenfeld & Nicolson, 1965), pp. 46–47.

Egypt regarded the nationalist movements in the neighboring countries as potential bases of influence that could exert pressure on the Western colonizers. The primary objective of the policy of support for the nationalist movements was to protect the Nile-water resources, but there was also the longer-range goal of establishing friendly relations with the Africans who would eventually emerge as leaders of the independent African states. By fostering an anti-imperialist orientation among the nationalist movements, Egypt hoped to undermine the West's dominant position on the continent.

The Bandung Conference had indicated the effect that a united Afro-Asian bloc could have on world politics. Nasser attempted to mobilize an Afro-Asian movement at the nongovernmental level as an ideological bloc based on anti-imperialism, nonalignment, and positive neutralty. Thus, during the period 1955 to 1960, there was a great expansion of Egypt's activities in Africa. This expansion was reflected in the number of Afro-Asian conferences sponsored by Cairo from 1957 to 1960, the amount of aid Egypt provided to the African nationalists, and the tremendous increase of Egyptian propaganda on the continent.

A result of Egypt's activities in Africa was the further deterioration of Egyptian-Western relations. In order to secure its position against the West, Egypt sought friendship with the Soviet Union. The Communist bloc also provided tools for countering Western cultural and economic influence in Africa. For its part, the Soviet Union viewed Egypt as a springboard into Africa. After the Suez crisis, Soviet-Egyptian cooperation dramatically increased as the Soviet Union poured aid and technical assistance into Egypt. This assistance, in turn, encouraged the African nationalist elements to turn to the Communist bloc for aid. Through the African Association, the Afro-Asian conferences, and the Afro-Asian Solidarity Council, Egypt provided the opportunity and the means for the Soviet Union to establish contacts with the nationalist movements and to funnel aid and propaganda to them. By 1958 there was a clear *de facto* foreign-policy alliance between Egypt and the Soviet Union. In consequence of this alliance and Egypt's activities in Africa, as well as in the Middle East, the West became Egypt's main adversary.

By 1958 Egypt's attempts to safeguard its interests in Africa and to protect the vital Nile-water resources were concentrated on the effort to reduce Western influence and to establish in its place a policy of an African "Monroe Doctrine"—Africa for the Africans. But geopolitical motives, although the primary objective of this policy, were not the sole consideration. Economic incentives were also important. Egypt's overpopulation was creating an internal crisis, and Egyptian leaders viewed emigration to Africa as a potential method for the relief of this problem. The Sudan has always figured prominently in Egyptian thinking in this respect. Industrialization has also encouraged Egypt to look to Africa as a market for its products and a source of raw material. However, prospects for any significant expansion have been limited by foreign competition.

By 1961 Egypt's policy in Africa was suffering severe setbacks. First of all, Egyptian intervention in the Congo—actually an attempt to implement an African "Monroe Doctrine"—failed, as Egypt was unable to influence the course of events except in very transitory fashion. Indeed, the Congo crisis brought the Cold War directly into Africa. The turn of events in the Congo not only indicated Egypt's inability to influence African politics, but also reflected the failure of its bid for leadership of the African states, as it was unable to rally the majority of African states behind its policy. In the Congo situation, Egypt found itself overcommitted and was forced to withdraw.

The Congo issue also polarized Pan-Africanist differences among the independent African states, stimulating the appearance of the Casablanca and Monrovia Groups. The Casablanca Group clearly reflected the U.A.R.'s attempt to utilize bloc politics to achieve its goal of creating an "Africa for the Africans" through economic cooperation and the establishment of an organizational framework for political cooperation. The subsequent development of the rival Monrovia Group resulted in the isolation of the Casablanca members from the mainstream of African initiative in

229

achieving cooperation. As Mazrui, one of Africa's foremost political thinkers, has suggested, the principle of nonalignment, originally oriented toward the Cold War, was extended by the Monrovia Group to mean the rejection of the formation of blocs within Africa.[2]

The development of the Monrovia Group indicated not only the rejection of Egyptian leadership in Africa but also the falure of Egypt's African policy. The members of this group repudiated the concept of Afro-Asianism through which Egypt had attempted to justify its involvement in both Africa and the Middle East, as well as its extreme anti-Westernism and Congo policy. Egypt also had failed consistently to obstruct Israel's penetration into Africa. All of the African conferences held outside of Egypt, except that at Casablanca in January, 1961, had rejected the Egyptian-sponsored resolutions on Israel. And, although Egypt was able to win a condemnation of Israel at Casablanca, it was ineffective. Ghana, Guinea, and Mali maintained friendly relations with Israel even after the conference. Disputes, especially between Nasser and Nkrumah, hampered the development of a positive approach even within the Casablanca Group.

Other problems in Egypt's African policy existed. The competition with Nkrumah, the constant injection of Arab issues into African politics, Egyptian involvement in both the Middle East and Africa, Egypt's radical anti-imperialism and its close cooperation with the Soviet Union, and, finally, black racism in African politics, together resulted in Egypt's isolation. This isolation was aggravated by the growing tendency for African states to concern themselves with internal problems rather than external adventures, a tendency reinforced by the succession of military coups occurring in Africa.

In addition to her problems in Africa, Egypt was experiencing difficulties in the Middle East and, indeed, internally as well. Consequently, in late 1961, the U.A.R. undertook a careful reevaluation of its policies. This resulted in the National Charter, which undertook to clarify all aspects of U.A.R. national policy.

2. *Ibid.,* p. 175.

The Charter attempted to rationalize Egypt's involvement in both the Middle East and Africa by identifying the Arab world as an internal-policy matter and Africa as a foreign-policy matter. It affirmed Egypt's support for Arab unity, Pan-Africanism and Afro-Asianism, but identified Egypt only with Arab unity.

Although the Charter did not indicate any major change in Egypt's African policy, it did mark a new phase in Egyptian-African relations. Egypt subsequently followed a relatively more moderate policy that aimed at establishing good relations with the largest number of African states possible and emphasized the creation of economic cooperation. This was exemplified by Egypt's encouragement of the establishment of the Organization of African Unity, which incorporated both the Monrovia and Casablanca Groups. Egypt separated its African and Middle Eastern policies and attempted to link them only loosely through the Afro-Asian and nonaligned movements. It also foreswore the injection of Arab issues into African politics, particularly the Israeli question. It was at this time that Egypt began a great expansion in the utilization of an asset in Africa unique to the Arab-Muslim countries— the influence of Islam, based upon the position of Al-Azhar University as a great center of Muslim learning.

The U.A.R.'s policy is greatly influenced by the political climate in Africa as well as the Middle East. As long as Egypt is so deeply involved in the Middle East in such affairs as the Yemen venture and the Arab-Israeli crisis, it is unlikely that the U.A.R. will become heavily entangled in African problems. This was made evident by the U.A.R.'s withdrawal of aid to the Congo rebels in April, 1965, although only after substantial efforts to help the rebels had brought little result. Also, because most of the African leaders are not sympathetic to the U.A.R.'s political doctrines, commitment on the continent to an extent similar to that in the Congo would result only in the U.A.R.'s isolation. However, if a more radical brand of nationalist element should come to power in Africa, it is likely that new alignments will be made.

At the same time, it is likely U.A.R. policy in Africa will continue to be active in pursuit of its vital interests and solutions to internal economic problems. There seems, however, to be a tendency toward increasing emphasis on the use of political instruments rather than ideology. Throughout the evolution of the U.A.R.'s policy, the diplomatic, cultural, religious, propaganda, and aid and technical-assistance instruments were expanded. The U.A.R. seems to be utilizing these instruments to a greater extent, especially since the policy adjustment. As René Vermont has said, "we appear to have entered into a phase of consolidation of interests with the era of expansion consigned to the past." [3]

The economic aspect of Egypt's penetration into Africa has only begun, and Egyptian exports to Africa are expanding rapidly. As Egypt's industry expands, the chief obstacles to this growth of trade—lack of demand in Egypt for goods the African states produce and competition with the major industrial powers—may be overcome. Egypt's anti-imperialist credentials are good, and she may be able to improve her economic position in Africa without arousing fear of neocolonialism. Egypt's best hope is to become the "Japan of Africa"; that is, to promote substantial economic relations without political involvement.

There is another point worth noting: the personal quality of Nasser's policy. While it is true that the U.A.R. may experience radical changes in political doctrine with the passing of Nasser, it does not follow that Egyptian policy in Africa will radically change. Indeed, the instruments of policy may change, and the orientation may shift; yet, Egypt's policy in Africa is motivated by basic interests that will remain, whatever the politics of the country. And with the peaceful transfer of power to his protégés that followed Nasser's untimely death, it appears that the main principles laid down by Nasser will continue as the basis of Egyptian policy.

Since the June, 1967, war with Israel, it is obvious that the African policy has been subordinated to the U.A.R.'s involvement in Middle Eastern issues. The U.A.R.'s African policy has borne some fruit since the war, but limited resources have inhibited a further expansion of involvement. In the main, however, the

3. René Vermont, "The Middle East and Africa: Arab-Israeli Rivalry, the Expansion of Islam," *Revue de Défense Nationale,* XXII (January, 1966), 92.

trends noted for the period before 1967 seem likely to continue; they express at least the goals of the U.A.R. when resources permit the free pursuit of her aims.

Appendixes

Appendix I

An African Policy for Egypt

Egypt, in its capacity as the leading African state, can contribute to the liberation of the peoples of Africa, for it is the largest and richest African state and occupies an eminent position in the Islamic and Arab worlds. It is a powerfully radiating center of influence for this continent and is the hope of Africa's peoples by virtue of its inherited humanitarianism, its tradition, its mental and moral heritage, its history, its faith in freedom and human dignity, and the geographical, physical, and historical factors which have linked it with the peoples of Africa.

For all these reasons, Egypt finds itself called upon to shoulder the great burdens thrown on it, to endeavor strongly and resolutely to liberate these peoples, to raise them from the deep abyss into which they have been driven by the power of foreign colonialism,

A suggested program by a "special correspondent" to the *Egyptian Economic and Political Review,* II (August, 1956), 21–24. It can be assumed that this program in fact comprises the recommendations of the Supreme Committee to Supervise African Affairs which was established by Nasser in January, 1956. This text, originally published in English, has been adopted here with minor editorial modifications.

and to help them by all possible means in all political, economic, and social fields, so that the peoples may regain their freedom and become strong and united. Africa will then be for the Africans.

Egypt, having now been liberated from the last bond of domination and proud of its freedom and its honorable past, has taken up a position in accordance with its principles and its attitude of neutrality between the two camps. It has no imperialistic ambitions or self-interest in view, but all its efforts are devoted to supporting the weak and enslaved peoples so that they may be strengthened and gain the right of self-determination. Egypt has the right now to occupy its just place in the international family.

Egypt has therefore to plan its African policy on the basis of "Africa for the Africans" and to direct this policy toward its liberation from foreign influence, politically, economically, socially, culturally, and militarily. It must also defend the Rights of Man which claim liberty for all and an equality in rights without distinction of race, religion, or language. It must endeavor to unify the peoples of the continent and discover a tie to join them so that they may form a united bloc in economy, defense and politics vis-à-vis the big blocs now existing in the world. It must also ensure that Africa with its peoples and resources shall be on the side of peace and not be an implement employed for war mongering, and that those peoples will stand together in international cooperation on the basis of liberty and equality and not as victims of exploitation.

In order that Egypt may realize these high aims and be able to carry out this new African policy, it must take those steps necessary in the various fields of politics, economy, and culture.

POLITICS

1. CONSULAR SERVICES. The government must start at once to establish a net of consular services in Africa. When positions in Africa are changed and the system of government is altered, the government of Egypt must be quite ready to establish diplomatic representation. The Egyptian diplomatic envoys must have received

the necessary preliminary studies made by those consuls or those acting for them, so that it may be possible to start at once calmly to execute the new African policy referred to above.

2. PROPAGANDA. Attention must be given to propaganda as an effective weapon calling for support for Egypt and its policy. Forms of propaganda are many:

    a. Egyptian broadcasting: Great attention must be paid to strengthening it so that it shall reach all parts of the continent, directed to the natives of the various zones, and to broadcasting in the African languages and dialects.

    b. The cinema: Documentaries, cultural films, and others with useful subjects must be allocated and distributed regularly. Such films open the mind and enable people to grasp the extent of Egypt's civilization. They would induce African peoples not to delay joining the caravan that marches on the path of civilization that Egypt has prepared for them.

    c. Press, printed matter, and publications: The press must adopt the policy of supporting Africa and the Africans and follow the instructions of all organizations concerning their importance. As for printed matter and publications, they must be written in Arabic, English, and French, possess simplicity of style and good printing, and call for support of Egypt and its African policy. All this printed matter should bear the impression of realism and be remote from exaggeration and artificiality.

3. MISSIONS.

    a. Egypt must send selected missions of experts in science, religion, politics, economics, commerce, and social services to aid the African peoples, to support them, to collaborate with them, and to light the path before them.

    b. Egypt must accept the largest possible number of natives from African countries to be educated in Egypt, and must care for their social and financial problems and help to

settle them. It should also invite the leaders of the peoples
of Africa from time to time to visit Egypt, discuss with
them the renaissance of Egypt in all its aspects, and come
to an understanding as to what can be done in their own
mutual interest.

4. AN ANNUAL AFRICAN CONFERENCE. An invitation should be
sent annually to hold an African conference where the affairs and
problems of the continent can be studied, together with the people's requirements and the organization of their efforts. This conference should be held in Cairo once each year. No doubt the pilgrimage season would provide a good opportunity and a time when
the best means are available for spreading Egypt's principles
among the peoples of this continent. If propaganda is well organized during that season, it would yield a great benefit.

5. THE CONSTRUCTION OF A NET OF EGYPTIAN COMMUNICATIONS
TO CONNECT EGYPT WITH THE DIFFERENT PARTS OF THE CONTI-
NENT.

    a. The establishment of an airline crossing the continent from
       north to south and subsidiary lines to the other parts situ-
       ated east and west of this line, using Egyptian airplanes.

    b. The establishment of ocean and coast lines around Africa
       in order to develop commercial exchanges and facilitate
       the connection of the African peoples with Egypt.

6. INSTITUTE FOR AFRICAN STUDIES. Our African policy and its
execution should be planned and directed in the light of knowledge
of, and an accurate study of the conditions in, African countries.
It is therefore desirable to establish as soon as possible an Institute
for African studies managed by a group of scientists and professors specializing in African affairs. The function of this Institute
will be the study of and regular researches in:

    a. Every country and every people of the continent, provided
       that this study includes:

(1) The formation of African peoples as regards their race relationships. These are of fundamental importance in their life.

(2) The habits, languages, and traditions of each people.

(3) Their needs and economic and social problems.

(4) The geography of each region and its most important sources of wealth.

b. The general imperialistic methods used in the African countries; the extent of the competition between states in Africa; and the analysis of the benefits derived from that competition.

c. The extent of ties binding each country with Egypt from the point of view of nationality, language, religion, society, economics, national aspirations, and political objectives, and also the extent of the ties binding Egypt's interest to each country.

d. The objectives of the Institute are to prepare groups of experts specialized in African affairs, and in particular in the study of the imperialistic methods which have enabled some European states to maintain their hold on those regions. These experts may be given appointments in the Ministry of Foreign Affairs which will later send them into Africa for service.

e. A section of this Institute is to be allocated for special studies by those who will be sent on missions from Al-Azhar and the Ministry of Education and Instruction. They will go to Africa for teaching, preaching, and giving lessons in the fundamentals of religion, so that they may by this means be able to preach Egyptian politics there.

7. AFRICA FOR THE AFRICANS. Egypt's declaration of this principle at a suitable time, its endeavors to stabilize this principle and not to deviate from it or go against it, resembles the Monroe Doctrine (America for the Americans). The reaffirmation by Egypt of this principle, keeping staunchly to it and defending it, will enable her to win a high position in the hearts of the peoples of Africa. This

will make all these countries direct their gaze toward Egypt and gather around her.

8. EGYPT'S ACTIVITY IN THE EUROPEAN FIELD. The United Nations is considered a fertile field where Egypt can carry out her African policy. It can utilize the pulpit of this organization for defending her policy which has for its aim the welfare of the Africans. Another reason for the importance of this field is the participation of Egypt in the Afro-Asian group. This is a great help in the organization of cooperation in international fields for the realization of this policy. It will help to refer here, for example, to the aspects that the activity of Egypt has assumed in the United Nations in the African field, and Egypt's defense of Tunis, Morocco, and Algeria, as well as her stand on problems of race distinction in the Republic of South Africa, or the interests of peoples not enjoying home rule and of those under the system of international tutorship, as well as Egypt's participation on the U.N. Advisory Council for Somaliland.

It is therefore the duty of the Arab nations to secure permanent seats for themselves on the Security Council. This does not contain one single African nation. Egypt must endeavor to replace Iraq on the committee for countries not enjoying home rule at the expiration of Iraq's term.

ECONOMIC OBJECTIVES

1. COMMERCIAL RELATIONS. The enlargement of the net of consular representation on the continent, the establishment of commercial bureaus, propaganda for Egyptian products, and the conclusion of commercial agreements with African countries.

2. ECONOMIC MISSIONS. The study of African markets to discover the desires of the various peoples and the extent of their approval of, and demand for, various Egyptian products. Demand for a certain article is subject to taste, which differs from one coun-

try to another. The study of the different tastes, therefore, and meeting the requirements of the inhabitants is an important factor in the disposal of products. This can be realized by only two means: First, sending economic missions to the different regions and charging those missions to make accurate reports on the different demands of the people for Egyptian articles. Second, the establishment of exhibitions and commercial markets in every region in Africa in order to discover the information and statistics necessary for traders and to make propaganda for Egyptian products.

3. TECHNICAL ASSISTANCE. The peoples of Africa are weak and cannot come to Egypt. Egypt must therefore go to them in the following ways:

   a. The frequent sending of exports and Egyptian technical missions, such as engineers and physicians, to take part in their turn in the development and raising of the standards of the countries to which they are sent.
   b. The establishment of joint-stock companies, agricultural, industrial, and commercial, in collaboration with the local inhabitants for the utilization of resources of their country, taking into consideration that they must be treated very well and justly. Egypt must be liberal with them so that they may know that the objectives of Egypt are sound and that our aim is the welfare of the country and its peoples, and not to exploit them as the foreign imperialist does.
   c. The encouragement of the emigration of Egyptians to many African countries such as the Sudan and the states of Africa and to facilitate their journeys and grant them subsidies.

CULTURAL DIRECTIVES

1. CULTURAL MISSIONS. Expansion in sending cultural and preaching missions, particularly from Al-Azhar, calling for the spread of Islam in Africa.

Appendixes

2. EDUCATIONAL INSTITUTES. The establishment of educational in-
stiutes, mosques, and hospitals all over the African countries, and
the acceptance of African students in Egyptian educational institutions on a large scale.

3. BROADCASTING. The utilization of the Egyptian broadcasting
station for broadcasting scientific and cultural lectures specially
designed for these regions and the allocation of special cultural
and educational programs to enlighten the Africans on their affairs
and to direct African public opinion. This can be done by a specialized broadcast under the name of "The Voice of Africa" similar
to "The Voice of the Arabs."

4. TOURISM. The organization of tourism affairs pertaining to
travel expenses, cost of residence, and entry facilities, particularly
for African students, so that African students may be helped to
visit Egypt and its monuments. This will help to increase the contacts of the peoples of Africa with Egypt and the Egyptians, thus
increasing the spiritual and mental connections between them and
strengthening the ties of cooperation and similarity among them all.

5. ATHLETICS. The organization of athletic tours for African countries and increasing the number of Egyptian athletic teams sent to
those countries. It is quite obvious that Egyptian athletic teams
would make great and vast propaganda for Egypt.

No doubt the success of our policy in Africa necessitates care
for the organization of this policy through:
1. Our general Arab policy, because of the existence of Arab
   peoples in Africa.
2. Our Islamic policy, because of the existence of Islamic peoples
   and races who can rely on Egypt to safeguard their Islamic
   personality.
3. Our European policy, because of the existence of European
   imperialistic states in Africa.

Moreover, the success of Egypt's African policy necessitates drawing the attention of all Egypt's people to Africa and the collaboration in all efforts and powers of all Egyptian ministries in order to carry out this policy with accuracy and enthusiasm. Each ministry will act within its own competence and have the possibilities of this policy completely and abundantly in mind before beginning to carry it out.

Appendix II

Administration of the Policy

The Provisional Constitution of the United Arab Republc invests in the president the sole responsibility for foreign-policy matters. Article 113 gives him the duty, in conjunction with the government (which consists of the prime minister, deputy prime ministers, and the ministers [Article 131], and which he appoints and relieves of duty [Article 114]) to "lay down the general policy of the State in all political, economic, social and administrative domains and supervise its implementation."[1] The president is also given the duty to conclude treaties (Article 125) and declare war (Article 133).[2] So it is evident that constitutionally, as well as in fact, Nasser is the supreme foreign-policy formulator for the U.A.R., as he has been since late 1954.

Formulation of foreign policy, even today, is strictly the prerogative and sole responsibility of the chief executive. The

1. United Arab Republic, *The Constitution, March 25, 1964,* trans. U.A.R. Information Department (Cairo, n.d.), pp. 31–36.
2. *Ibid.,* pp. 34, 36.

246

extent to which the executive is guided by the counsel of his principal associates, including the minister of foreign affairs, is a matter of his personal choice, made in the light of the interests of the state.[3]

Nasser's speeches constitute the most important body of statements on Egypt's foreign policy. Government statements are always consistent with Nasser's, and the controlled mass media—press, radio, and television—directly reflect his attitudes and positions.

African policy formulation begins in the African Bureau of the Presidential Office, which was headed by Muhammad Fayek until his appointment as minister of national guidance in 1966. The Bureau conducts research and presents policy alternatives to Nasser. With the aid of political advisers and special committees that he personally appoints, Nasser makes the final policy decisions. The policy is then transmitted to the Ministry of Foreign Affairs, which channels it to the necessary departments for execution. There are many agencies concerned with African matters, and they may be categorized as falling into four major groups.

The first is the African Bureau of the Ministry of Foreign Affairs, whose duty it is to coordinate actions at the various levels and among the various agencies. Cooperating with the African Bureau are the Research Bureau, Conferences Bureau, Economic Bureau, and Cultural Bureau of the Ministry of Foreign Affairs. The African Bureau itself supervises the Egyptian Embassies in Africa. The typical Egyptian Embassy staff consists of an ambassador, a counsellor, a cultural attaché, a military attaché, a religious attaché, a labor attaché, and an economic or commercial attaché.

The second group of agencies dealing with African affairs are the African sections within various ministries other than that of Foreign Affairs. These include the African Section of the Supreme Committee on Cultural Relations in the Ministry of Higher Education. This African Section channels the policy directly to the cul-

3. Butrus Butrus Ghali, "The Foreign Policy of Egypt," *Foreign Policies in a World of Change*, ed. Joseph E. Black and Kenneth W. Thompson (New York: Harper and Row [1963]), p. 320.

tural attachés in the Egyptian African Embassies and to the cultural bureaus that Egypt has established in some African countries. Under this section are the Section for Foreign Students and the Club for Foreign Students, which includes many African students, and the Higher Technical Institute for Afro-Asian Students. Policy concerning riparian issues is channeled to the Agency for Common Water Services and the Agency for the Nile Water Problems in the Ministry of Works. The Information Department of the Ministry of Culture and Guidance also has an African Affairs Bureau which coordinates policy with the East African Section, West African Section, and Sudanese Section of the Radio Programs Department and with the Office of Press Attachés, which supervises the Egyptian African press attachés. There is also a special African Journal Section in this ministry which publishes in English and Arabic. In this same category, there is the African Economic Cooperation Administration of the Ministry of Economics, including the International Economics Section and the International Economic Conferences Section, the Anti-Israel Administration, and the Office of Commercial and Economic Attachés. The African Economic Cooperation Administration also coordinates policy with the Economic Organization. Under this organization are the companies dealing in import, export, and international trade. The Bureau for Boycotting Israel of the Arab League cooperates with the Anti-Israel Administration of the Ministry of Economics and with the Ministry of Foreign Affairs to coordinate policy with the Egyptian Embassies, especially those in Africa.

The third group of agencies concerned in policy execution are the ministries having general administrations which are active in African affairs but do not have a specifically African section. The Office of Military Attachés of the Ministry of Defense channels policy to the Egyptian African military attachés. The Ministry of Labor functions similarly with regard to the labor attachés. Within the Ministry of Labor there are also the Organization for Labor Education and the Organization of Regional and Arab Labor Unions, whose activities extend into Africa and which cooperate with the Bureau for Boycotting Israel of the Arab League. The

Ministry of Agriculture supervises agricultural attachés. The Conference Administration within this ministry participates in African conferences, as does the Ministry of Supplies. The Ministry of Endowments and Al-Azhar Affairs has an administration specializing in Islamic Missions from Africa which cooperates with the Islamic Missions City and Missions Institute of the Cultural Administration of Al-Azhar University.

The fourth group of agencies executing African policy are the nongovernmental organizations. These organizations are supervised and subsidized by the government but are not official organs of policy execution. They include the African Association, which was started by Muhammad Ishaq;[4] The Afro-Asian Solidarity Council, headed by Youssief al-Sabal; and the Islamic Congress and the Supreme Council for Islamic Affairs, which together award scholarships and participate in Islamic missions to Africa. Also in this category are the teachers, technicians, and doctors sent to Africa under the auspices of their respective ministries. Cairo University has an Institute of African Studies, and the Ministry of Scientific Research's Council for External Research includes a Center for African Studies.

This complicated framework of administrative organizations grew sporadically to meet the expansion of the U.A.R.'s African policy. The lack of planning, coordination, and clear lines of communication between the agencies resulted in the creation of a cumbersome bureaucracy. Abdul Malik Audah, an Egyptian specialist in African affairs, suggested a major reorganization.[5] He noted that African policy execution is centralized around the Ministry of Foreign Affairs, with the result that no initiative can be taken without the red tape involved in channeling it through that ministry. Audah asserted that one of the chief problems was the unnecessary delay between policy formulation and policy execution. Other problems that Audah observed included the overlapping

4. Muhammad Ishaq is now Director of the African Bureau of the Ministry of Foreign Affairs.

5. "Al-Ajhiza al-hukumiyya al-Misriyya al-'aamila fi al-maydan al-Ifriqi" [The Egyptian governmental agencies active in the African field], *Al-Ahram al-Iqtisadi,* February 15, 1964, pp. 18–20.

and lack of coordination of the activities of the various agencies and the heavy dependence of the agencies' effectiveness upon the initiative of the directors.[6] However, the administrative bureaucracy was unresponsive to the criticism against it and still functions in the same manner.

6. "Ajhizatuna al-Ifriqiya" [Our African agencies], *Al Ahram al-Iqtisadi,* September 1, 1963, pp. 14–15.

Appendix III

U.A.R. Aid to African Countries

TECHNICAL AND CULTURAL

SOMALIA

    a. Experts in agriculture, hygiene, justice, transportation, electricity and irrigation (19 experts), as well as teachers and other instructors (332).

    b. Scholarships for study and vocational training in agriculture, university teaching and the teaching of Arab and Islamic studies (330).

    c. The government of the U.A.R. also contributed a great deal to the construction of numerous university and Islamic institutions and a cultural center in Mogadiscio. The U.A.R. also donated the Harguissa library.

    Unsigned article entitled "U.A.R. Technical and Cultural Aid to African Countries," trans. JPRS from *Remarques Africaines* (Brussels), October 19, 1967, pp. 517–20.

Appendixes

TANZANIA

    a. Experts in agriculture, irrigation, transportation and electricity (31 experts), as well as teachers and other instructors in higher education (5).

    b. Scholarships for the study of agriculture and for training in the agricultural centers of the U.A.R., and also for the teaching of Arab and Islamic studies (190 scholarships).

GUINEA

    a. Experts in agriculture, hygiene and biology (7).

    b. Scholarships for study and vocational training, notably in agriculture and university studies (135).

KENYA

    a. Scholarships in agriculture and higher education (57 scholarships).

MAURITANIA

    a. Health and hygiene experts (9).

    b. Scholarships for university studies, Islamic studies and vocational training in agriculture (80). Contributions to the Nouakchott cultural center.

SIERRA LEONE

    a. Experts in agriculture, irrigation, civil aviation and meteorology (30 experts).

    b. Scholarships for university study in agriculture (203).

    c. Contribution to the Freetown cultural center.

NIGERIA

    a. Experts in agriculture, health, finances, irrigation, and also teachers of university and Islamic studies (31).

    b. Scholarships in agriculture, health, university studies and Islamic studies (192).

    c. Contribution to the Kano cultural center and to the Islamic center.

SENEGAL

    a. Scholarships for university and Islamic studies (156).

UGANDA

    a. Professors of university and Islamic studies (7).

    b. Scholarships in agriculture, university and Islamic studies (75).

ZAMBIA

    a. Experts in transportation and communications (15).

    b. Scholarships for university study, Islamic studies and vocational training (11).

ETHIOPIA

    a. Professors and instructors of university and Islamic studies (14), the same in Eritrea.

    b. Scholarships for university study, agriculture and Islamic studies (1,032). Idem in Eritrea.

CONGO (BRAZZAVILLE)

    a. Experts in higher education and health (16).

    b. Scholarships for agricultural training and university study (25).

GHANA

    a. Experts in health and higher education (8).

    b. Scholarships for training in agriculture and for university and Islamic studies (61).

TOGO

    a. Instructors of university subjects (6).

    b. Scholarships for agriculture and university studies (35).

CAMEROON

    a. Scholarships for health and university studies and training in agriculture (17).

Appendixes

BURUNDI

a. Scholarships for university studies and agricultural training (12).

LIBERIA

a. Scholarships for university studies and agricultural training (28).

NIGER

a. One health expert and five professors of Islamic studies.

b. Scholarships for Islamic studies and agricultural training (45).

GAMBIA

a. 39 scholarships for university studies and Islamic studies.

SOUTHERN RHODESIA

a. One scholarship for Islamic studies.

b. Two scholarships for university studies.

IVORY COAST

a. 15 scholarships for Islamic studies and 9 for university studies.

UPPER VOLTA

a. 20 scholarships for university and Islamic studies.

MAURITIUS

a. 17 scholarships for university and Islamic studies.

CHAD

a. 207 scholarships for university and Islamic studies.

MALAWI

a. Five scholarships for university and Islamic studies.

254

MALI

a. Experts in agriculture, health, teaching and scientific research (11).

b. Scholarships for university and Islamic studies and agricultural training (88).

ECONOMIC AND COMMERCIAL

NIGERIA

a. An agreement on general principles, signed 15 October 1962 concluding a commercial treaty between the two countries.

b. In answer to a request by the Nigerian government, the government of the United Arab Republic has granted a loan of 3,000,000 in £ sterling. The details of this loan remain to be discussed.

c. The Egyptian import-export company "EL NASR" opened a branch in Lagos and has inaugurated a permanent exhibition of Egyptian products.

MALI

a. A commercial and payment agreement was concluded on 5 March 1961.

b. The U.A.R. agreed 6 March 1961 to grant a long-term loan of 6,000,000 in £ sterling for the financing of hotels and housing (work now in progress) and also for the Sinio-Kwitala road construction project (work in progress).

c. The "EL NASR" company has a branch and a permanent exhibition hall in Bamako.

DAHOMEY

a. Agreement has been reached on a commercial and payment treaty.

b. The "EL NASR" company has a branch in Cotonou.

c. The Dahomey government had requested a loan for financing various economic and social projects. An economic mission went to Dahomey to study the possibility of carrying out these projects on 6 May 1965.

An agreement on general principles was signed, with a view to granting a long-term loan to Dahomey.

MAURITANIA

a. A commercial agreement was concluded 7 April 1964.

b. There is an office of the "EL NASR" company in Nouakchott.

SENEGAL

a. An agreement on fundamentals was reached on 1 February 1967.

b. A branch of the "EL NASR" company was established in 1962 in Dakar.

NIGER

a. The countries have had a commercial and payment agreement since 15 March 1962.

b. There has been a branch of the "EL NASR" company in Niger since August 1963.

GUINEA

a. On 16 May 1961 the government of the United Arab Republic granted Guinea a long-term loan of 6,000,000 in £ sterling for the financing of several economic projects (projects for the cultivation of corn, construction of housing and schools).

b. A commercial agreement reached 16 May 1961 granted to Guinea easy payment terms and credit for the sum of half a million in £ sterling. This agreement was renewed on 8 June 1966.

c. The "EL NASR" company has a branch in Conakry.

CONGO (BRAZZAVILLE)

a. On May 4, 1965, the United Arab Republic granted a loan of 1,500,000 in £ sterling for the construction of a hotel. Work is in progress.

b. The "EL NASR" company has a branch in Brazzaville.

TOGO

    a. A commercial agreement was reached 17 March 1964.

    b. The "EL NASR" company has had a branch since 1966.

CAMEROON

    a. A commercial agreement was reached 19 December 1961.

    b. A branch of the "EL NASR" company was established in Douala in October 1962.

GHANA

    a. A commercial and payment agreement was reached on 31 May 1961.

    b. There is a branch of "EL NASR" company in Accra.

SIERRA LEONE

    a. The two countries have a commercial agreement, concluded on 8 July 1965.

    b. The two countries have discussed an agreement by which the United Arab Republic would grant a loan of 2,464,000 in £ sterling.

    c. "EL NASR" company branch in Freetown.

IVORY COAST

    a. Several import-export transactions have been carried out by the branch of the "EL NASR" company that has been in Abidjan since 1964.

UGANDA

    a. A commercial agreement was concluded 27 October 1964.

    b. "EL NASR" company branch in Kampala.

KENYA

    a. Commercial agreement concluded 24 December 1963.

    b. "EL NASR" company branch in Nairobi.

Appendixes

   a. Commercial agreement reached in September 1964.

   b. "EL NASR" company branch in Dar es Salaam.

ETHIOPIA

   a. Commercial agreement concluded on 20 October 1959 and renewed in July 1965.

   b. Branch of Economic and Commercial Society permanent exhibition hall in Addis Ababa.

ZAMBIA

   a. Commercial agreement reached in February 1965.

   b. "EL NASR" company branch in Lusaka.

SOMALIA

   a. Commercial and payment agreement concluded on 10 December 1960.

   b. Agreement reached 15 December 1961 for the grant of a loan of 4,000,000 in £ sterling for establishing several industries, such as cement, textiles, meat processing, sugar, and building.

BURUNDI

   a. Commercial agreement reached on 6 March 1967.